The Manager's Good Study Guide

Sheila Tyler

Academic Editor: Sheila Tyler

Contributors to this book:

Julian Batsleer, Don Cooper, Charles Edwards, Noel Entwistle, Mark Fenton-O'Creevy, Martin Friel, Funmi Folami, Ken Giles, Mike Green, Nicki Hedge, Alison Macmillan, Kevin McConway, Judith Margolis, Jill Mordaunt, Hilary Morris, Terry O'Sullivan, Alan Parkinson, Jennifer Powell, Philip Woolford.

Project Manager: Marie Stanley

Production Team:

Media Project Manager: Julie Fletcher

Compositor: Diane Hopwood

Editor: Simon Ashby

Graphic Designer: Jonathan Davies

Media assistant, picture research and rights: Holly Clements

Materials procurement: Nikki Smith

The idea for this book came from Andrew Northedge's highly successful *The Good Study Guide*, published by The Open University since 1990. We are indebted to him for his inspiration.

The Open University
Walton Hall, Milton Keynes
MK7 6AA

First published 1994. Second edition 2004. Third edition 2007.

Edited and designed by The Open University

Typeset in India by Alden Prepress Services, Chennai

Printed in the United Kingdom by TJ International Ltd, Padstow

Cover photo: © Colin Anderson/Blend Images/Corbis

ISBN 978 0 7492 1387 9

A catalogue record for this book is available from the British Library

Details of Open University courses can be obtained from the Course Information and Advice Centre, PO Box 724, The Open University, Milton Keynes MK7 6ZS, United Kingdom: tel. +44 (0)1908 653231, email general-enquiries@open.ac.uk. For information on Open University Business School courses, see page 354 or visit oubs.open.ac.uk

Alternatively, you may visit The Open University website at http://www.open.ac.uk where you can learn more about the wide range of courses offered at all levels by The Open University.

To purchase a selection of Open University stand alone course materials and packs visit the webshop at www.ouw.co.uk, or contact Open University Worldwide, Michael Young Building, Walton Hall, Milton Keynes MK7 6AA, United Kingdom for a product catalogue.

Tel. +44 (0)1908 858785; fax +44 (0)1908 858787; e-mail ouwenq@open.ac.uk

3.1

CONTENTS

Introduction to *The Manager's Good Study Guide*

This book is designed to:

- help you improve your learning skills

- provide you with management concepts, tools and techniques.

Why do you need both? The text is based on the notion of adult vocational learning – the idea that managers apply their knowledge in the workplace and learn from the results. The book is designed to help you understand this process and provide you with a wealth of management tools and techniques that you can use at work.

Who is this book for?

The book is aimed at managers who are following formal courses of study, and those who want to improve their skills informally without the aid of courses and tutors. Fortunately, almost all study skills are ones you need everyday in your professional life. For example, the writing skills you may need for a course assignment are just as relevant when you write reports at work. The inclusion of management concepts, tools and techniques in the book is self-explanatory: they constitute the basic 'kit' every manager should have. The book will be valuable as a handy reference text whether or not you are currently studying a management course.

How to use this book

The Manager's Good Study Guide is not designed to be read chapter by chapter, cover to cover. We know you are too busy for that! Instead, it is organised so that you can look up specific topics.

The only parts of the book which you would benefit from reading as complete texts are Chapter 1 on adult learning and Chapter 9 on career development. The reason for this is that there are no 'quick fixes' to learning or career development and these chapters contain a progression of ideas.

You need to understand what learning is and how to learn as an adult, using strategies and tactics that ensure you get the most from your time and effort. As a manager or someone who is aspiring to be one, you already know how valuable resources can be wasted when people have insufficient knowledge and, worse, are unaware of it. Are *you* sure you know how to learn the *adult* way? And are you *prepared*?

The remainder of the book can be used for reference. It is a book to which you can turn regularly for guidance both when you are studying and when you are dealing with everyday situations at work. You can explore and identify the kinds of techniques that every manager should know.

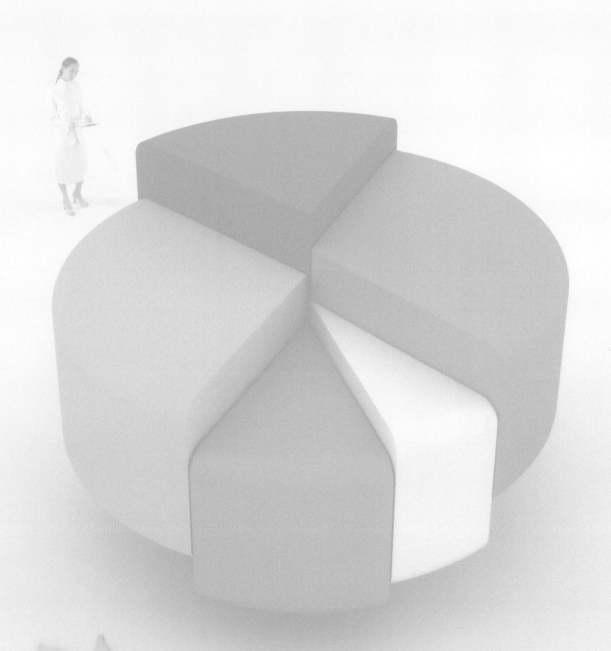

SECTION 1 LEARNING

This first section of *The Manager's Good Study Guide* is about laying foundations. As working managers, we all want to improve our management skills, and we want to improve them as easily and effectively as possible. This involves learning. To do this, you need to understand the nature of *adult* learning and to prepare and organise yourself to make the most of your learning effort. This section is designed to help you 'learn how to learn' – to become an independent and reflective adult learner. Almost all study skills are *learning* skills and are *transferable* – they are skills you need in your everyday life as a manager. Think of all the occasions when it is (or will be) vital to:

- think logically and critically

- communicate clearly, both face to face and electronically

- write effective reports that put your message across objectively but persuasively

- negotiate

- give and receive feedback

- present information to others

- use techniques for working in groups or teams

- work with others in a virtual environment.

You will find much of the material in this section useful even if you are not currently following a formal study course. For those of you who are on a course or are about to embark on one, you will also find ideas and advice: from organising your life to make room for study, to negotiating support and help in your workplace, and monitoring your own development.

Like the rest of *The Manager's Good Study Guide*, much of the text in Section 1 is organised as a series of short, self-contained items which can be referred to and read independently of one another. We suggest, however, that you approach Chapter 1 as one that should be read through completely. This is because the ideas build on one another. They culminate in a tried-and-tested method for identifying your strengths and weaknesses as a learner, and ways of improving your approach to learning.

CHAPTER 1 — WORKING WITH YOUR NATURAL RESOURCES

Learning comes naturally

Learning is our greatest survival mechanism. It comes naturally. So why do we need to know about learning and how to learn? As a manager, you know that if you want to achieve a goal effectively and efficiently, it is best to understand what the goal involves, set objectives, plan, implement the plan, and then monitor progress. Being organised and systematic is the key to making the most of your natural capability.

When we learn we do not always succeed in learning as much as we intend to. We may be clear about our learning goal but not so clear about the best strategy and tactics. If this is the case, we are not in the best position to get the most out of our study efforts, or to improve our learning. You might think of this as return on your investment – it makes sense to maximise it. In the past, you may have followed a set learning pattern that may not have been a very effective one, or it may have been suited to a particular type of learning task or situation. Either way, if you want to adjust your learning pattern to suit your new vocational learning goals and circumstances – those of professional development – you will need to know something about learning.

Chris Argyris, a Professor at the Harvard School of Business and Education in the USA, puts it like this:

> A thermostat can be programmed to turn the heating on when the room temperature drops below 20°C. But say the thermostat could ask 'Why am I set at 20°C? Is there some other temperature which might better achieve the goal of heating the room?'

> *(Source: Argyris, 1999)*

The thermostat's question illustrates the importance of understanding the 'how and why' in learning and not just the 'what'. In work situations, 'how and why' may be questions you are used to asking. So why not ask the same questions about learning?

What we learn

Ways of knowing

Imagine that you run a small chain of gourmet restaurants. Proud of your enterprise, you take your bright young nephew into one of the restaurant's kitchens to see the chefs at work. The head chef asks the boy what he likes to eat, and then devises a new dish based on several of the boy's favourite foods. The boy, whose busy parents buy only pre-prepared meals from the supermarket, has very limited experience of food preparation. He is used to seeing ready-meals move from shop to freezer to microwave. He is full of questions as the head chef produces the meal:

- How did the head chef know which foods would go together without anyone telling him or without referring to a recipe book?

- How did he know how much of the different ingredients to combine and for how long the dish should be cooked?

- How did he know what to do (and when) so that all the different parts of the dish were ready together?

- How did he learn to chop onions so fast?

- Was the head chef being kind in offering to cook for him or was he trying to impress you, the restaurant owner?

Fortunately, one of your regular diners is a professor of learning who offers to answer your nephew's questions. She explains that there are a number of types of knowledge and what can be thought of as 'ways of knowing'.

Tacit and explicit knowledge

While some knowledge can be explained in words (it is 'explicit') other knowledge is hard to communicate (it is 'implicit' or 'tacit'); you may not even know that you possess the knowledge. It may reveal itself as a hunch, intuition, a feeling or an emotion. It is a fascinating thought that we know far more than we think we do!

What, how, and knowing you know

Knowledge generally falls into four categories – *what* (or knowing *that*), knowing *why*, knowing *how* and *knowing you know*. The boy knows *that* the chef is chopping an onion but does not know *why* or *how*. The chef knows *why* he is chopping the onion and can explain. But he can describe only some aspects of *how* he chops onions so fast because it is not something that can be taught just by telling. Some things, such as riding a bicycle or kneading dough to make bread, cannot be learned this way. This knowledge is *procedural*. You can be told the theory, but then you need to put theory into practice (lots of times!). The head chef needed more than knowing *what*, *why* and *how* to produce the dish. To create a new dish he needed to be aware of what he knew. This is *metacognitive* knowledge. It involves knowing what one knows, one's thinking processes and some self-knowledge (for example, 'how/why I usually do this'). The head chef used this kind of knowledge to create the new dish.

Theories

A collection of *what, why, how* and *knowing you know*, does not quite add up to the knowledge the chef is using. The chef has a *theory* of food and cooking – an organised, integrated set of facts and ideas, together with the necessary procedural knowledge and well-practised motor skills to turn his theory into practice. He may well have started out by following a catering course to learn some *formal* theory and put it into practice. He would have started out as a novice cook, as most of us do (and perhaps still are!). Often our learning is less formal. We might begin by following instructions on how to boil an egg from a recipe book, or by asking someone, or by watching someone. Then, after a good deal of practice cooking a variety of dishes (and some salutary disasters) we develop an *informal* theory of cooking. At first this would be a rather naive theory but it becomes more comprehensive and complex as we become more expert. Along the way we will have gained a lot of procedural knowledge too – the *how* as well as the *what* and *why* – although a lot of this may be implicit or tacit.

The difference between formal and informal theories is that a formal theory will have been tested and found to offer a sound explanation of something as in, for example, the science of gluten in flour and the action of yeast. An informal theory will not have been tested in the same rigorous way and may explain something in a rather limited, or imprecise way – 'the bread did not rise because the yeast was old'. Informal theories have huge practical value in many areas of our lives, but they can be limiting when we are aiming to gain expertise. Informal theories are likely to be *personal theories* but even formal ones are likely to be *personalised*. We make knowledge our own: it shapes the way we see our world.

Knowledge types and processes

The various types of knowledge we use and the kinds of processes that are needed to use them can be summarised fairly simply.

Knowledge types

Types of knowledge are shown in Table 1.1.

Knowledge can also be of various sorts, practical, intellectual, social, cultural and emotional, as we shall see. And it can be tacit (implicit) or explicit. The head chef was using all of these types of knowledge. He has facts about food and cooking, theories and procedures. He knows what he knows and how he came to know it.

Table 1.1 Knowledge types		
Knowledge type	**Description**	**Specific knowledge needed**
Factual	The basic elements that people must know to be acquainted with a field or domain of knowledge or to solve problems in it	■ Terminology ■ Specific details and elements
Conceptual	The relationships between the basic elements within a larger structure so that the elements can function and be used together	■ Classifications and categories ■ Principles and generalisations ■ Theories, models and structures
Procedural	How to do something; criteria for using skills and techniques; methods	■ Specific skills, techniques and methods ■ Criteria for deciding when to use appropriate procedures
Metacognitive	Knowledge of cognition in general as well as awareness and knowledge of one's own cognition	■ Strategic knowledge ■ Knowledge about cognitive tasks, including appropriate contextual and conditional knowledge ■ Self-knowledge

(Source: based on Krathwohl, 2002)

Knowledge processes

In using different types of knowledge, the head chef also used the processes set out in Table 1.2.

What underpins these processes is *understanding*. A simple way of thinking about this is to consider the development of understanding as a series of steps. In the first step we can understand something when we are told. In the second step, we can understand something well enough to be able to use it or explain it to someone else. The third step is being able to understand it in such way as to be able to 'play' with the ideas.

Knowledge in action

Back in your restaurant, your nephew begins to see that the restaurant chefs are using many forms of knowledge and many processes. The head chef has a sophisticated personal theory of food, and the necessary procedural knowledge and motor skills to turn it into practice. As a result, he knows what flavours will work together, he can make an informed judgement about how to prepare a new dish and he can carry out all the tasks required with impressive speed. He can *create*.

Table 1.2	Cognitive processes	
Cognitive task	**Description**	**Specific activity**
Remember	Retrieve relevant knowledge from long-term memory	■ Recognise ■ Recall
Understand	Work out the meaning of instructional messages, including oral, written and graphic communication	■ Interpret ■ Exemplify ■ Classify ■ Summarise ■ Infer ■ Compare ■ Explain
Apply	Carry out or use a procedure	■ Execute ■ Implement
Analyse	Break material into its constituent parts and detect how the parts relate to one another and to an overall structure or purpose	■ Differentiate ■ Organise ■ Attribute
Evaluate	Make judgements based on criteria and standards	■ Check ■ Critique
Create	Put the elements together to form a novel, coherent whole or make an original product	■ Generate ■ Plan ■ Produce

(Source: based on Krathwohl, 2002)

Cultural and emotional knowledge

The head chef's personal theory of food and cooking will be culturally influenced, of course, and will involve many implicit assumptions about 'good' food and what people like to eat (insects and amphibians can be on or off the menu depending on your culture). But the head chef is also using cultural, social and emotional knowledge in other ways. For example, although he has no children of his own, he knows how to pay attention to the nephew in a way that is appropriate to the context and to the boy's age and likely experience. Moreover, the head chef knows that by paying attention to the nephew he is likely to impress 'the boss' with both his kindness and skill. Praise or acknowledgement from others – and doing his job well – increase his confidence and self-esteem, and his sense of job satisfaction.

The link between knowledge and action

Your nephew is struck by an important practical point: that a person's personal theories will guide their strategies, plans and actions. He thinks of some analogies from his history lessons. When people believed the world was flat, like some of the contemporaries of Christopher Columbus, they were worried about sailing off the edge. Their theory determined their travel strategy and plans. Your nephew realises that his own personal theory of food is like this. It is the 'naive' personal theory of an absolute novice whose ideas would lead him to the frozen ready-meals in the supermarket. 'Thank goodness we are only considering food,' your nephew thinks. 'Say I had to run this restaurant chain with a 'naive' theory of management!'

Virtuoso performance

Clearly, when we consider the head chef at work we are seeing an expert engaged in a 'virtuoso performance' – one that involves many types and levels of knowledge. As a manager, you will also be aspiring to virtuoso performance. As a student, you have the opportunity to increase your knowledge and develop more sophisticated and complex concepts, and more formal theories about aspects of management and organisations. If you are working while you study you will be able to put these ideas into practice; if you are not currently a professional manager, then do not worry. In our daily lives we have to manage many things – ourselves, a household perhaps, or contribute to the running of a social, environmental or political group. You can make good use of these contexts. But first you will need to have a strategy for effective learning – and what better way to start than with some theory!

How we learn

Knowing what you need to learn doesn't necessarily help with the actual task of learning. But if you understand something of what happens when you learn, you can consciously help your acquisition of knowledge, and become an effective and efficient learner.

What it means to learn

Each of us is likely to have a personal theory of learning. The following list shows the six most common conceptions:

1 Learning as an increase in *quantity* of knowledge.

2 Learning as memorising.

3 Learning as acquiring facts, procedures and so on, which can be memorised or used in practice.

4 Learning as the abstraction of meaning.

5 Learning as a process of interpretation aimed at understanding reality.

6 Learning as a process by which you change as a person.

(Source: Säljö, 1979 and Marton *et al.*, 1993)

Which is nearest to your current theory? If you hold one of the first three, you may be inhibiting your learning. All three are associated with *reproductive* approaches to learning based on remembering for the purpose of recall of knowledge in more or less its original form. All three embrace aspects of learning which are *necessary but not sufficient.* The other three represent a progression through increasingly sophisticated ideas about learning.

Gaining knowledge

So how do we learn? We first acquire simple knowledge by simple means – our actions in the world produce consequences. From these basic beginnings we begin to make sense of the world of objects, actions and people. We can think of this in terms of an ever-changing jigsaw. When the first pieces of a jigsaw are in place, some pieces cluster together to form an idea or concept about something: swans are birds and are white; only birds lay eggs. But when we find black swans at a zoo and discover that platypuses, tortoises, snakes and fish lay eggs too, the jigsaw pieces need to be rearranged to form a different picture. Sometimes new jigsaw pieces can just be added without changing the picture, at other times new pieces will rearrange the picture into quite a different one because they do not fit the original picture – there is a conflict which can be resolved only by change.

In building our jigsaw, we are doing more than storing away in our minds memories of particular events such as our visit to the zoo. We are *abstracting* some key information. Abstraction means 'to draw away' – to remove and retain key pieces of information from all the other details. The information we draw out is what is general or common to things, events or situations. A simple example is that we recognise a chair we have never seen before *as* a chair because, from our previous experiences of chairs, we have abstracted the common features – four legs, a seat, a back – and we can *generalise* this knowledge. In short, our abstraction has provided us with the *concept* of chairs. Concepts are *abstract* (our knowledge of the *particular* chair we are sitting on is more *concrete).* Abstraction allows us to remove our knowledge from the here and now so that we can think about ideas, examine them and play with them.

Developing thinking

As we acquire knowledge, our thinking processes also develop. There would not be much point in having something we did not know how to use. We need to be able to think about objects, situations and events that are not present or currently happening. We need to be able to think in the abstract, but we also need to be able to think *logically* and *hypothetically.* This last type of thinking is involved in considering 'what if' – the kind of thinking managers engage in when using scenarios to anticipate and plan in uncertain situations.

Learning as a social activity

Our own knowledge and thinking are in some sense, unique to each of us because we 'construct' them individually. But they are likely to have much in common with those of the people around us. This is because knowledge, meaning, understanding our experiences and ways of thinking have not been developed in isolation. They are everywhere embedded in social processes and practices. They are shaped during childhood, in education and in daily life. Learning is essentially a social activity – we learn from one another – which is shaped by culture since all our social activities are carried out in culturally-prescribed ways. To be sure, we 'construct' our knowledge, but not in a vacuum.

You might like to revisit the six statements about learning set out earlier. Have you changed your conception in any way? Can you think of ways in which learning might be life-changing or transformational?

How to learn better

We have covered some basic aspects of knowledge and thinking. But do we need something else to help us as *adult* learners?

Adult learning

Adult learners are not the same as younger learners. Here are some of the ways in which adults are different:

- They have independence and can direct their own learning.

- They have a wealth of experience which is a valuable learning resource.

- They have learning needs which are closely related to changing social or professional roles (for example, becoming a mother or a manager can act as triggers for learning).

- They are task- or problem-centred and interested in applying new knowledge immediately.

(Source: Knowles, 1978)

As an adult, then, you take responsibility for your learning, for what you learn and for how you learn it. You choose the topic of your learning and decide how much time and effort to invest. The pressure to learn is likely to come from yourself as a result of your current situation, not your educators. You have a reason to learn and an active interest in the utility of the outcomes. Adult learners need to work with these characteristics to their best advantage. The trouble is that old conceptions of classroom learning from school or college are often brought to the new, adult learning situation. In other words, adults often know how to be taught, but they do not know how to learn.

Experiential learning: a model for adult learning

Adult learning can be conceptualised as a cyclical process.

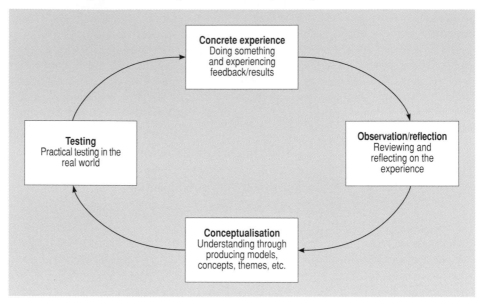

Figure 1.1 **The experiential learning cycle**

(Source: Kolb and Fry, 1975)

In this cyclical learning process, knowledge is created through the transformation of experience. The central idea is that we have basic, concrete experiences which first need to be *comprehended* to be of use to inform our actions. Comprehending a situation you have just experienced means you can create for yourself an explicit model from which you can make predictions about what will happen next time this situation occurs. But creating this model – *an abstract conceptualisation* – requires you to reflect on the impact and meaning of the concrete experience. It requires you to make sense of your experience. Once you have developed your conceptual model (it may take time and effort) you can transform it into action. Acting on the basis of your conceptualisation, of course, will test its soundness and will produce more concrete experience on which to reflect. So the cycle goes on.

As shown in Figure 1.1, the stages of the learning cycle are:

1 **Concrete experience** – being personally involved; giving conscious attention to and being interested in your experiences.

2 **Observation/reflection** – gathering information, thinking, sense-making.

3 **Conceptualisation** – using ideas, logic, systems thinking, analysis, building mental models.

4   **Testing (acting or experimenting)** – using opportunities, setting and committing to goals, taking risks, making decisions, being entrepreneurial.

Reflection does not mean passive thinking. It involves *critical* reflection and *critical* thinking to refine, elaborate and integrate conceptual knowledge. This requires a reflective, analytic, objective stance that distances you from the concrete here-and-now experience.

For managers who are engaged in formal learning while working, course materials will draw your attention to particular experiences. They will help you to reflect on these experiences and to conceptualise them by providing formal theories and models devised by others, usually on the basis of research. They may also set out strategies and plans for actions. These theories and models may not fit your own conceptualisations but conflicts can be beneficial to learning. You will find that *The Manager's Good Study Guide* is full of material which can help you at each phase of the learning cycle.

See Critical thinking, p.63.

Kolb and Fry's (1975) model provides a useful strategy that can be used in any situation to monitor learning. It can even be used by teams or groups as a way of monitoring and managing collective knowledge. But, remember, all the steps in the learning cycle are necessary. An action that is repeated without reflection is just a repetition. Capture your experience and learn from it.

The cultural dimension

The experiential learning cycle is not without its critics. It tends to focus on the individual, but as we know, the individual is not the sole source or shaper of experience and actions. Our experience, thinking, construction of meaning and actions are *mediated* by contexts and culture. Culture, of course, operates at many levels below ethnic culture. The organisation you work for, or groups to which you belong are likely to have a subculture in the sense of having common practices, shared meanings and values. (Think of your own organisation, a club, a group of nurses or a group of technicians.) Our knowledge of how our experiences, constructions and actions are mediated by our ethnic culture (and subculture) is likely to be *tacit*. To make it available for scrutiny we must bring it into conscious thought. In doing so we are more likely to see that our conceptions are constructed through our interactions with others. Knowledge is not absolute or non-negotiable. When we realise this we will also be able to bring to bear our imagination, ethics, feelings and values on our actions. As well as know-what, know-how and know-why, there is also *care-why*.

Using the learning cycle systematically

In reality, the learning process is not a neat series of separate steps. Busy managers are unlikely to have the time to collect all the evidence or think everything through before acting. We tend to act even before a problem is thoroughly identified. But action produces an experience and consequences which can be reflected on, along with the solution to the problem, the knowledge and processes we used. Be attentive to the cyclical learning process and use it systematically so that it becomes second nature.

One way of reflecting systematically on your experiences and so learning from them, is described below. After an event – such as a presentation, an interview, a project, or a particularly significant situation – work through the following process:

- Describe the event or situation, together with your intended outcomes.

- Describe what happened – be specific and exact. Was there a gap between what you intended and what actually happened?

- Analyse why there was a gap.

- Ask yourself what you learned about yourself and what you would do differently next time.

How do you go about your learning?

People have different conceptions about what learning is, as we saw earlier. It turns out that these kinds of conceptions – for example, learning as memorising or learning as life changing – influence the way people go about their learning. Find out what your own approach to learning is right now. Complete the 'Approaches to Learning and Studying Inventory: Self-score Version' which can be found in Appendix 1 of this book, then use the scoring system to work out your preferred or usual approach to learning. Do this before reading any further, so that your responses to the statements are not biased.

Approaches to learning

Noel Entwistle and his colleague (Entwistle, 2000 and Entwistle and McCune, 2004) have described approaches to learning and studying in terms of a number of main aspects or characteristics. These aspects typically combine in understandable ways or *approaches*. The most commonly found ones are set out below. These approaches parallel the way scores are interpreted in the 'Approaches to Learning and Studying Inventory: Self-score Version' (see Appendix 1).

Deep approaches

Active deep approach

Learners using this approach are characterised by their intention to understand what they study, although they may sometimes decide it's best to memorise some things. They are interested in ideas and in relating them to one another. They question and use evidence critically; they seek out the main points and aim to gain an overview; they draw conclusions. They see the purpose of a task or its use in a wider context than the study situation. Another strong characteristic of this approach is *monitoring*. Learners ensure that their work meets their own requirements as well as assessment demands. They monitor their understanding of what they are studying, check their own reasoning and pay attention to feedback. They also monitor their general skills such as communication and locating learning resources. One or more secondary characteristics complete the active deep approach: *organised studying* and *effort management*. Learners are systematic, prepare for study sessions, organise their time, prioritise, and work steadily through a course. They also channel their efforts and push themselves. They focus on their studies and keep going even when things are not going too well. They do not seem to find concentration a problem and can force themselves to stay focused even when they are bored by what they are studying.

Deep approach without much effort

Learners adopting this approach are similar to those with an active deep approach, except that *organised studying* and *effort management* are not much in evidence.

Surface approaches

Active surface approach

Learners who describe themselves in this way often study without much sense of purpose. They are primarily concerned with memorising information with a view to reproducing it when required, for example, in assignments and tests. Material may be memorised without understanding. Learning is unreflective; information is accepted unthinkingly and knowledge may be fragmented. Rarely do learners with this approach stray beyond the syllabus of a course. However, like those who adopt an active deep approach to learning, they also possess the characteristics of *organised studying* and *effort management*, but usually in more moderate levels. Learners with an active surface approach often study quite hard but may wonder why they do not do well.

Surface approach without much effort

In learners adopting this approach, the *organised studying* and *effort management* characteristics are absent or present only at low levels. The approach is characterised by unreflective learning and routine memorisation or following procedures without thinking about them just to complete the required work.

Organised and managed approach

In learners with this approach the *organised studying* and *effort management* characteristics are dominant. Other characteristics may be present but at more moderate levels. The learner takes neither a deep nor surface approach but organises their studies and manages their efforts to achieve good outcomes. The learner may be someone who is very keen to succeed in terms of course grades, but is less concerned with understanding than someone using a deep approach.

Combined approach

A few patterns may show fairly high levels of both deep and surface approaches, with moderate levels of monitoring, organised study and effort management. The presence of both deep and surface approaches is contradictory and seemingly implausible, but research indicates that learners describing themselves in this way may have a misunderstanding of what is involved in learning and a lack of awareness of how to use learning support.

Profile of a learner

Looking back to a previous learning situation, we can probably recognise some of these approaches: the person who was disorganised and concerned only with scraping through the assessment; the student who was motivated by academic success; the person who constantly interrupted with questions starting with 'if' and 'why'. What is important to understand, however, is that the learner characteristics which make up each of the recognisable approaches to learning are not mutually exclusive. We can show elements of a number of them. This is why your completed questionnaire provided a *profile* of your approach. An *ideal* profile would show a combination of strengths in four characteristics: the deep approach; monitoring; organised studying; and effort management. Few learners will have this profile, but it is one we should aspire to.

Our approach to learning is not fixed. Consider situations in which you are seriously pressed for time or very anxious, or when what you need to learn is uninteresting or irrelevant to you. Consider the difference between studying a management course that may be career enhancing, and learning about your new mobile phone. Your approach to learning will be influenced by your time, your interest and the value you place on particular knowledge. But your approach to learning does matter if you intend to make the most of your time and effort to improve your performance as a manager. A deep approach will produce a deeper understanding of what you are learning. Moreover, as we have found in our research at The Open University Business School, a deep approach among managers is associated with application of learning in the workplace *and* the important 'diffusion' that happens when new knowledge is used with others at work. Interestingly, perhaps, approaches to learning are not *consistently* associated with academic learning outcomes in terms of course grades, although learners using surface approaches often perform less well, those with an organised, managed approach are usually successful, while learners using deep approaches will be associated with success if the assessment demands understanding.

Developing deeper learning

Discovering your approach to learning is just the first step. If you identified a profile that was not predominantly deep and monitoring, or with too little organisation and effort management, you can improve your learning. You will need to explore and identify your beliefs and attitudes to learning and attend to those which are not helpful to you. You will need to think again about what learning is. You will also need to adopt learning methods that develop your understanding and the quality and depth of your thinking. You will find a number of ways of doing this in the next chapter of this book. You may find you need to organise your time better, to make way for experimenting with and developing better ways of learning. Disorganised study wastes time, and deep learning takes longer, at least in the short term. Learners who already possess a deep approach may need to adopt techniques to produce efficiencies to avoid overload, without damage to understanding. Conversely, those of you striving to adopt a deep approach may have to forego some of your shortcuts!

The key to changing your approach depends on both *attitude* and *intention*. If you think differently about learning, you will behave differently. Moreover, you have to *want* to behave differently. Learning how to learn, including the accompanying attitude change, is not 'comfortable' but you will come to accept a degree of discomfort when you associate this with effective learning – moving onward and upward.

The novice–expert shift in learning

People can be novices at learning. We may know how to be taught, but not how to learn. Novice learners may have some of the characteristics of surface learners. But using appropriate techniques, novices can turn themselves into more expert learners.

Learning, as we have seen, is not just the process of acquiring knowledge, but one by which people develop the way they think. Some types of education help more than others because of what they expect of learners. A study which followed the progress of university students over their undergraduate years found a pattern of development. This is shown in Figure 1.2.

At first students saw 'facts' in a rather black and white way, regarding them as offering separate, even opposing, but equal perspectives (*dualism*). They also saw education as the acquisition of facts. By the time they left university, the students had a more sophisticated understanding of knowledge as relative, that is, not absolute and not independent from the way the knowledge was derived. This meant they were able to examine different perspectives to see how soundly each was supported by evidence, and to decide between competing views. Students had shifted from *acquiring* 'facts' to *making sense* of what they now saw as provisional information that might be overturned by evidence at some time in the

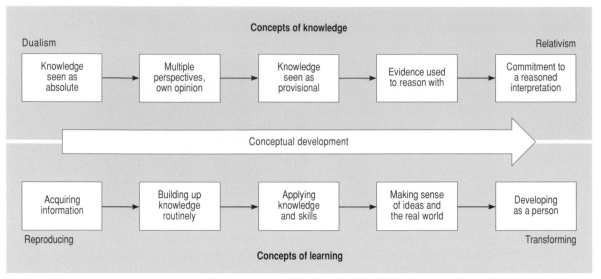

Figure 1.2 Concepts of learning and their development

(Source: Entwistle, 2000, based on Perry, 1970)

future, or on the basis of their own experience. In essence, this is the development from surface to deep learning, facilitated by appropriate teaching which aids understanding and encourages conceptual change. The result is a more expert learner and a more developed way of thinking: a more *independent* learner. If you are studying a formal course, you may wish to revisit the 'Approaches to Learning and Studying Inventory' in Appendix 1 and Figure 1.2 some time in the future to monitor your progress. See yourself develop!

CHAPTER 2 MANAGING YOUR LEARNING

Returning to study can be both exhilarating and daunting. You may be enthusiastic about studying a topic of particular relevance to you, and which can further your career. At the same time, you may have concerns about how you will handle learning while perhaps holding down a busy full-time job, participating in your family life, organising a household and having a social life. You may also have doubts about your ability to study effectively, especially if it has been some time since you last undertook a course of formal learning. If you are not following a formal course, you may be trying to improve your management competence by other means. Either way, you will need to face your concerns, and prepare. After all, when you invest your time and effort into a task you want to make sure that the return on your investment is as high as possible. Good preparation and organisation will help you to achieve your goal.

Dealing with concerns

Most of us enjoy learning, at least some of the time! You may feel quite confident about returning to study. However, if you are now embarking on a learning experience a long time after your last one, which was perhaps as a student in a school or college setting, then returning to study might arouse concerns. A common problem is that your previous experience of study may not have been a particularly good one. For example you may have:

■ 'failed' at some previous stage in your education

■ encountered a teacher who destroyed your confidence

■ had a more successful sibling who seemed to get all the praise

■ failed to meet your parents' high academic expectations.

Any one of these experiences may have damaged your confidence or reduced your inclination towards fresh studies. Such experiences may also lead to difficulties with studies later on, such as:

■ **Perfectionism** There may be a sense that 'My answer has to be perfect'. You may feel the need to cover all the ground before attempting an assignment and may write draft after draft in an attempt to achieve the perfect answer.

■ **Inadequacy** There may be a sense of personal inadequacy. You may feel 'I am incompetent'. As a result, you may avoid the risk of being put to the test.

■ **Avoidance of discomfort** This inclination is another way in which you may seek to minimise risk.

Overcoming fears

There are remedies that can help you overcome bad past learning experiences. Among them are:

■ **Develop new ways of thinking about yourself** Examine any negative self-conceptions and create positive ones. Develop a positive self-image.

■ **Design clear goals** Map out your main study tasks or learning goals and set realistic and achievable targets.

■ **Prioritise** Identify the urgent study tasks and do those first, for example, meeting an assignment deadline. Then turn your attention to the important tasks (that were not among the urgent ones). Lastly, if there is still time, tackle any remaining tasks.

- **Divide tasks into manageable parts** For instance, tackle a part of a learning task rather than all of it at once.

- **Organise yourself** Make a schedule before you start and check off the tasks as you complete them.

- **Commit yourself** Tell other people about your study plans. Write prompts and reminders for yourself and display them prominently.

- **Reward yourself** When you have achieved an objective, reward yourself. Do something that you enjoy.

Some of these remedies will require effort on your part, but it will be worth it. Sometimes the problems can seem intractable. If they do, then seek professional advice. With the aid of an adviser you may find new ways to study. If you are following a formal learning course, discuss your difficulties with your teacher or tutor in the first instance.

A common fear among adults about to return to study is not only that their minds are not as sharp as they were, but that they may have problems remembering material. This is a particularly common concern if a course of study involves assessment in the form of examinations. Here are some psychological research findings to reassure you:

- The best work of adults is done at the age of about 40 when productivity is highest.

- The quality of their work can remain high for decades beyond that.

- Creativity can be highest in late-in-life work.

- Short-term memory – the sort we use for remembering telephone numbers while we key them in – begins to decline around the age of 60.

- Long-term memory declines after the age of 60.

Thus, there is not much basis for concern about cognitive ability in adulthood. We retain our ability for high-level productive work and problem solving, and even the declines in short- and long-term memory are not inevitable. One change that does seem to occur in adulthood, however, is that we are less likely to focus on surface detail and more likely to remember meaning. This is hardly a problem!

Assessment

Imagine a world in which you could not see the results of the actions you took. You would never know whether to repeat the action, abandon it or modify it. Quite simply, in such a world no one would learn anything! Feedback is vital to learning. We monitor the consequences of what we do and learn from them. It's obvious when you think about it. Consider an archer who never saw where his arrows struck. He would never know how to improve his aim. Often, though, feedback comes in the form of assessment by *others*, ranging from annual appraisals of work performance to attending job interviews, from producing one's first report to chairing a meeting of a new group. Sometimes there are definite hurdles that one must clear; on other occasions assessment may be more subtle, for example when one feels 'on show'. There is often a sense (real or imagined) that one is being *judged*. Most programmes of formal study include assessment of some kind and the knowledge that 'I will be assessed' can be unsettling. The unease about being assessed, particularly on a first assignment or learning task, can be part of a general unease about 'my ability to keep up'. You will quickly find that you are not alone and that your feelings are shared by other managers on your course. However, good educators will ensure that the process of assessment is one of providing constructive feedback. Appropriate feedback will help you to learn. It will feel less like judgement and more like encouragement, support and coaching. And, like everything else, when you have completed an assignment or learning task for the first time, the second and subsequent times will be much, much easier.

Planning your studies

Treat your studies as you would any other management task. First, you need to plan your overall approach (your strategy), and second, you need to plan each individual study session (your tactics).

Planning your study strategy

You will find it helpful to list the things that are driving you towards success in your studies and the things that are holding you back. Consider how to strengthen the drivers and how to convert the restraining forces into drivers. Suppose you are concerned that your busy social life will impede your studies. Recognise that you will have to find the time to study. This may mean using social commitments as rewards for periods of effective study. You may need to alert other people to your commitments, so that they understand that you will be busy. Engage the support of your family, friends, employer and work colleagues:

- **Your family** Discuss your study plans and negotiate how you will deal with family obligations.

- **Your friends** Tell them about your new commitments as study will affect your free time, particularly when you have a deadline to meet.

- **Your employer** You may be sponsored by your employer who will have an interest in your progress. You may need to make special arrangements around the time of an examination.

- **Your work colleagues** Tell colleagues what you are planning to do and how you will be organising your study time. Colleagues can be supportive in a variety of ways.

A calendar is a key document. Display it in a prominent place and use it to keep up with your course work. Add in major personal commitments – peak times in your job, holidays and so on. Do not get caught out by a deadline. Be particularly aware of the likely demands on your time at crucial periods in your course, for example, before assignment submission dates. Add important dates and deadlines into your calendar as you are given them.

Include in your calendar or diary realistic and regular weekly periods for uninterrupted study. You need to think about when you will study, where you will study and for how long.

You are likely to benefit more from planned periods of study than from unplanned ones. You will need time to warm up and to achieve a meaningful study goal. (But you can use short, unexpected opportunities productively as part of your study tactics provided that you are clear about what you can achieve in such circumstances.)

Finally, remember that you will use your study time most efficiently and effectively when you apply good study skills to your course work. Regular reflection, including notes in your diary, on the way you tackle particular pieces of work will alert you to the need for a change of approach or to a need to sharpen an existing study skill.

Setting up your place of study

An important part of your study strategy is to identify a suitable place to study. You will also have to organise your chosen study area so that all the equipment you need is close at hand.

Where you study

- If you can, identify somewhere in your home as your dedicated study area. It may be a room or part of a room, for example a workstation.

- Protect yourself as best you can from *interruptions*. When you study you will want to give full attention to your work.

- Reduce the likely *distractions*, such as telephone, television and radio. Closing the door is a way of signalling to the rest of the household that you do not wish to be distracted.

- Make the room a comfortable place in which to study. Attend to the temperature, the seating, the lighting and so on.

Organising your study area

Organise your study area to suit yourself. Regard it much as you regard your place of work. Organise your desk or table in a way that is conducive to study. Make sure your computer workstation is at the correct height and sufficiently close to a telephone point and a power socket.

Think about where you will keep your books and files. It is helpful to have dedicated shelving for these and other items. If you are not used to working with books and a computer at home, then make your arrangements provisional until your needs become clearer to you. During the first few weeks, you can try different arrangements. You can make small improvements until you find the set-up that meets your needs. Recognise, however, that you *will* need a dedicated place to study and that you will need to organise it.

By organising your study environment in this way, having a regular and appropriate place to work, you gradually create good study habits. When you sit down at your desk you will expect to start work. With your materials to hand you will not waste time looking for things. The time you give to establishing your study area will be time well spent.

Making time for your studies

How many hours of study are you required to do each week in order to complete your course? Education providers normally advise learners of the number of study hours, weekly or in total, needed to follow a course. This is usually an *average* – some people will take less time, others will take longer – so you will need to take account of your personal learning speed. Don't be unduly concerned if your personal learning speed is not very fast. Working out the meaning of what you are studying takes more time than reading to glean information. Learning through the medium of a second or third language can also take longer. If you are not sure how many hours you are expected to dedicate to your studies each week, your first step is to find out.

However many study hours are required for your course, clearly up to now this amount of time has been taken up with other activities. You must now find this time. Your next step is to analyse and record how you are presently spending your time. Until you do this, it will be difficult to fit your new studies into your life in an organised way.

Analysing the way you currently spend your time

For a week, keep a diary of everything you do. Complete a day-by-day, hour-by-hour record, for example:

	Monday	Tuesday	Wednesday	etc.
7 am				
8 am				
etc.				

When you keep your diary, make sure that you include *everything* you do, including:

- time taken up by your work
- travel time
- all your domestic commitments
- your commitments outside the home
- leisure and relaxation time.

Planning your work time

When you have completed your diary, analyse what you have recorded. In order to make space for your studies, you must switch time from one or more current uses. As you plan your study periods, choose times that will maximise the outcomes. You may have to try different times during the first weeks. If you have a tiring job you may find that the best time to study is before you start work. And although several short periods of study (say of two hours duration) are usually more effective than a single, prolonged one, you may find that you have no alternative but to set aside up to a full day sometime during the week.

Negotiating your commitments

It may appear from the analysis that there is no time in your life to study. Be ruthless about your priorities and find the time required for your studies. Remember that taking a management course is an investment in yourself. Look for additional time. Some employers are willing to give time for study; even a half-day every month to write an assignment will help. Sometimes students say that simply knowing they have this option makes a great deal of difference to their motivation!

Make space now for your studies – but reserve a little for leisure and relaxation.

Planning individual study sessions

When you have planned your studies strategically, you must then plan your approach to each individual study session to make the best use of it.

Planning your tactical approach

First decide which tasks you might most profitably undertake in a particular study session. Ask yourself, 'How can I best use the session, given the location, my feelings and the time I have available?' Adopt the formula 'Must do. Should do. Could do.' 'Must do' is obviously the first priority. But if you are tired, stressed or not really in the right mood to tackle a difficult piece of course material you consider to be a priority, then you may be better off (and become less frustrated at lack of progress) if you decide to do a different task. You could try something more active, such as to jot down some ideas for the next written assignment, or to check the latest messages in your computer-mediated conference if your course includes this feature. You may find that such activities warm you up and motivate you to the extent that you are able eventually to turn to the task of tackling that difficult piece of course material.

You should allocate approximate times for tasks – including short breaks. Do not expect necessarily to follow your plan slavishly: the path for any individual study session may profitably diverge from what you intended. But the plan will get you started and will give shape and purpose to what you intend. Consciously monitor your progress on a task. If it is not going well, then try another tack. Could the task be broken down into smaller chunks? If you are having trouble in engaging with a piece of text, perhaps you need to reconsider your reading strategy. Above all, do not prevaricate. It is easy to find excuses during study sessions – the too frequent breaks that sap concentration, the favourite television programme that comes on in the middle of your scheduled study period, and so on. These are indications that you need to reset your study priorities for that session. Finally, remember the all-important reflection at the end of the session. Was it productive? If it was not, then be sure you know what the reasons were and what the lessons are for next time.

Goals, measures and outcomes

If someone, your boss or a friend, asked you about your progress during your course, how would you respond? You would no doubt reply in a general way 'Fine', or perhaps, 'I'm finding it hard going at the moment'. You would have some criteria in mind by which you judged your progress, but the chances are they would not be very precise. They need to be more precise so that you can measure what you have accomplished and where your strengths and weaknesses lie. Study is just like any other task in the sense that you will need to monitor your progress.

Getting started

Set yourself the goal of completing the first week's work or perhaps the first two weeks' work according to the course timetable, or one you have devised for yourself if there is no 'official' timetable. Concentrate on completing the first tasks. When they have been accomplished, you will be able to say 'I've started' and you will be prepared for the next tasks. Those next tasks or goals may include the completion of a first written assignment. Once you have written the first assignment, you will feel a sense of accomplishment. You will be entitled to feel that you have passed an important marker on your route through the course.

Once you have accomplished the first goal or stage – such as completing the first week's reading or the first task – then you set up the next goal or marker post. Step by step, stage by stage, make your way from one to the other. During the process you will settle into the course, find a rhythm of study, and you will feel more confident in tackling the rest of the course.

Measures of success

There can be two broad measures of your success. 'Passing the course' can be one. 'Passing the course', may comprise passing continuous assessment and an examination. 'Becoming a more effective manager' can be the other broad measure. Think of these two measures as the axes of a matrix as shown in Figure 2.1.

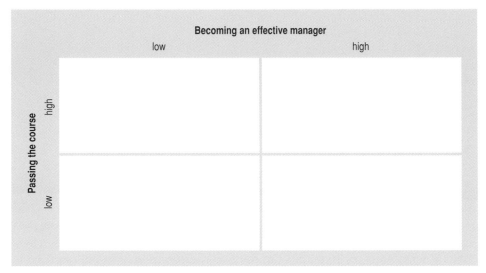

Figure 2.1 **Assessing your success**

You should complete this matrix for yourself. If you are successful in both passing the course and becoming a better manager, you will find that you occupy the high/high cell in the matrix. You will be meeting the requirements of the course and you will also be developing your effectiveness at work. More generally, the figure is a way of reminding yourself of the two ways of assessing your progress.

Monitoring your development

If you keep some kind of record of your work on the course, you will have a sense of how you have progressed. It's easy to forget how you felt at the start of the course when everything was new and strange. A record gives you a measure against which to judge your progress. When you have good records to refer to, you will no doubt be pleasantly surprised about the evidence of your progress and you will have a better idea of where you need to improve.

Keeping a learning diary

Keep a learning diary – a record of what you learn. Develop the habit, week by week, of recording the impact of the course – the reading, the discussions, the assignments – on your thinking and on your workplace practice. At the end of the course you will have a record of outcomes which you can use to assess your development.

Record in your learning diary:

■ Your study sessions, the material you studied, how long you studied for (you will be able to check your total weekly study hours), how you felt about your study session (you could give it a rating) and any major points to return to or to follow up next time. Don't forget to look back at your diary entry when you begin your next study session.

■ Your thoughts about each assessed assignment before you submit it (you could award yourself a mark). Turn to the diary entry when the assignment is returned and record your reactions to your tutor's comments and to the mark awarded for your work. Refer back to your diary before your next assignment.

■ Finally, and importantly, your thoughts on the application of your studies to your work. This will help you to monitor your development as a manager. Your record will reveal the ways in which you have changed as a result of your studies.

At the end of your course, your diary will also provide you with a strong platform for looking forward to what you need to do next. And do not forget its worth when the time comes for your job appraisal. You will have some solid evidence to call on for this and for other job-related purposes.

Setting up support at work

The whole point of learning is to hone our thinking skills and increase our knowledge to *develop* ourselves. For managers engaged in learning about management, this development has a very practical aspect: we expect to be able to use what we learn at work so that we can become better managers. Indeed, applying our learning at work is an essential part of the vocational learning process. Your learning will not be confined to the hours when you are studying. To learn in the most effective way, you will need to apply your learning at work. This, too, may require preparation.

Opportunities

Use opportunities that arise in the course of your daily work to apply your learning. You may be able to negotiate additional opportunities with your employer such as:

■ working with peers and colleagues

■ placement on special projects

- increased responsibilities – expanded role
- job rotation.

Tell your line manager that you are studying and provide a list of the topics you will cover. Your line manager may then be alert to opportunities for you to put your new knowledge into practice. For example, if your organisation is recruiting for a new or existing post, you could be involved in the process. You might be given the opportunity to draft a job description, person specification or advertisement, to organise the interview schedule or be a member of the selection and interview panel.

Being mentored

Consider finding a mentor in your work place for support and to help you apply your new knowledge as you acquire it. Mentoring is a time-honoured practice in which a relatively inexperienced person is helped by a more experienced one who provides at least some of the following:

- sponsorship – opening doors
- coaching – teaching 'the ropes'
- protection – providing support
- exposure – creating opportunities
- challenging work
- role modelling – demonstrating valued behaviour, attributes or skills
- counselling – providing a helpful and confidential forum for exploring personal and professional dilemmas
- acceptance and confirmation – support and respect
- friendship.

(Source: Kram, 1985)

Sometimes, all of these functions may be provided by one person who, in return, may expect hard work and loyalty. Good mentors are likely to have a genuine interest in the person they are mentoring, and mutual trust is important. A mentor may help you to fulfil your potential, to identify with your organisation or profession, to make sound judgements and to gain the right experience, while ensuring that you are noticed and appreciated. Ideally, your mentor should not be your line manager. It is best, too, if your mentor has experience of mentoring, works in the field of staff development and training and has recent experience of studying a management course. Above all, your mentor must be a person with whom you can establish good rapport and who is willing to make the necessary commitment. To gain the most from mentoring you should:

- Organise monthly meetings of about one and a half hours.

- Plan carefully what you want to know and the questions you want to ask.

- Share information on your progress and what you are learning.

- Discuss how you would like to apply this new knowledge and skill to your work.

But remember, your mentor will probably not be familiar with the particular course you are following and will not have all the answers!

Peer relationships

Mentoring by a more senior person at work is not always possible. You may have tried it and found that it did not work as you had hoped. Mentoring may not work when protégé and mentor are of the opposite sex because traditional gender roles and prejudices tend to come into play. There are alternatives however. We have relationships with a variety of people at work – with line managers, those we line manage, and our peers – which help to meet our development needs. Peer relationships can provide only some of the forms of support that conventional mentoring can, but they can give other, unique types of support. Peer relationships offer mutuality (both parties give and receive) through which each person can achieve a sense of expertise, equality and empathy which are often missing in conventional mentoring. Such relationships are likely to be more available, too, because we usually have access to more peers at work than any other group, and they can last far longer than mentoring relationships. A comparison of peer relationships and conventional mentoring are shown in Table 2.1.

See Being mentored, p. 30.

Table 2.1 Functions of mentoring and peer relationships	
Conventional mentoring	**Peer relationships**
Sponsorship	Information-sharing
Coaching	Career strategising
Exposure and visibility	Job-related feedback
Protection	–
Challenging work assignments	–
Acceptance and confirmation	Confirmation
Counselling	Emotional support
Role modelling	Personal feedback
Friendship	Friendship
Complementarity (mentor gives, protégé receives)	Mutuality (each party gives and receives)

(Source: Kram and Isabella, 1985)

Not all peer relationships will provide all of the functions listed. There are different types of peer relationships. The level of trust between peers will determine the level of disclosure and this in turn is likely to have an impact on how effective the relationship is.

If a conventional mentor is not available to you – or even if you establish a mentoring arrangement – you might want to consider a peer relationship. Undoubtedly, you already have a number of informal peer relationships on which you might build. Above all, remember you have a 'family' of relationships at work, all of which may provide you with support of various kinds. Nurture them.

CHAPTER 3 LEARNING SKILLS

In this chapter of *The Manager's Good Study Guide* we take you through the fundamental skills you need to learn effectively in order to succeed on your course. These skills are not just skills for *studying*. They are primarily skills for *learning* and will be of use at work where we learn much of our professional knowledge. Some skills are particularly useful for managers: for example, listening and giving feedback can help others to learn and to be more productive. What we sometimes call study skills are useful in many situations. You can practise them both when you study and when you are at work.

Reading and note taking

Your reading strategies

Almost everyone will have experienced a time when there seemed to be too much reading to do in the time available, especially when the language of the texts was technical or academic. The amount of reading required on a management course can be daunting. If you have not studied for some time, the academic language of texts may seem off-putting and difficult, and reading to learn from texts presents its own challenge. A range of reading strategies will help you to meet this challenge and, used appropriately, will ensure that you read for different purposes, in different ways, in order to arrive at different outcomes.

Identifying your own reading strategies

A reading strategy is an 'operation' you put into action according to your purposes for reading and according to your progress when you are reading. If you are asked to read and to comment on a company report, you will probably need to read that report from cover to cover. If you are reading a newspaper to catch up on recent events, however, you will probably select relevant material by looking at article titles and headings, by glancing first at opening and closing paragraphs, and so on. You will read selectively, spending time only on those articles that look particularly interesting. Deciding what to concentrate on, and what to omit or to skim read, is just one reading strategy. Deciding what action to take when you encounter difficult phrases or words is another reading strategy and one that might be particularly important when you start reading academic texts on your management course. Will you ignore them, will you re-read the difficult parts and try to understand the meaning from the context, or will you stop and consult a dictionary?

You need to become aware of your own particular reading strategies. Good readers monitor their progress as they read. Do you do this? For instance, do you sometimes pause to gather your thoughts, to relate the text to your experience, or to question your comprehension? Do you sometimes decide to re-read a particularly important or difficult part of a text? If you tend to read without monitoring your progress, make a point of monitoring your progress the next time you read something. Remember, though, that your purposes for reading will determine how much you need to understand. Always keep this in mind.

Effective readers

Effective readers decide on their purposes for reading before they start to read, and they keep them in mind as they read. They may glance through a text to see whether it is relevant to their needs; they may search a text only for specific information that they need; they may grapple with the detail of a text because it will enlarge their understanding of a topic or will provide them with new ideas. Good readers will change their purposes as they read if the text does not meet their original purpose. Effective readers do the following:

■ Read through a text once in order to get a general idea of its meaning and content. Then they re-read it, make notes or add marginal comments, and highlight particular sections of the text (assuming always that the text belongs to them!).

■ Pay attention to the structure of a text because it will help them to understand the writer's purpose and argument. They take notice of headings and subheadings, of opening and closing paragraphs and of other signposts that the writer has provided.

■ Ask questions of the text and of themselves when they read. They monitor their progress through the text and take appropriate corrective action, when necessary.

■ Know that reading for study purposes will require them to re-read in order to check their understanding, to reconsider particular points of interest or importance, and to add to their notes.

■ Speak the words in their heads or out loud as a way of unravelling the meaning when they find a text, or part of a text, difficult to understand. They also draw sketches or diagrams as a way of getting hold of the meaning.

■ Try to understand rather than just to memorise what they read. This effort to understand is itself an aid to memorising.

See Critical
thinking, p. 63.

■ Read critically. They test the writer's argument against alternative arguments and their own previous knowledge and experience.

Skim reading

Always start reading with a clear purpose in mind – even if you change it as you read – because your purpose will determine your approach to the reading task. A lack of a clear purpose will mean that your reading will be unfocused and ineffective. Remember that with many texts, apart from novels, you do not need to read everything. You are in charge of your own reading.

How skimming will help your reading

Skimming rapidly through a text is an efficient way to:

■ Decide quickly on its relevance to your informational needs.

■ Hunt for pieces of information where close reading of the text would not be an efficient use of your time.

■ Help you to organise your reading once you have decided that a text is relevant and warrants close reading.

The art of skimming

If you already know something about the subject matter of a text, carry out the following quick checks:

■ See whether the author's claim to expertise seems well founded.

■ Note the date of publication of the text and the references cited.

This information will help you to decide on the extent to which the text warrants your attention. There may be no point in reading a work that has already been superseded. But if the text is relevant to your needs, then some parts may be more relevant than others. Familiar content need detain you only long enough for you to decide whether the writer is saying something new or is providing a new interpretation of existing data.

This is just one of the reasons why you need to learn to skim. Once you have decided that a text is broadly relevant to your needs, you need to get a feel for how you will use it to best effect. Well produced texts provide you with a mine of information. To help you to extract information, read with a pencil and highlighter at the ready to mark matters of interest to return to or to record. To help you extract information:

- Examine the contents list which shows the chapter titles or section headings.

- Look for the writer's aims and objectives, whether these are formally set out or are part of the preface, foreword or introduction, or appear in the opening paragraphs.

- Glance through the text to look at the subheadings if they are not included in the contents list.

- Look for any summaries or abstracts as these are invaluable signposts to content.

- Skim read opening paragraphs and conclusions, particularly their opening and closing sentences.

Even when you have decided on content that looks relevant and interesting, you need not necessarily read it word for word immediately. First of all, let your eye run rapidly down the centre of the page to pick out key words to help you to decide whether you really need to read more closely.

Studying a text

Good learning materials are designed to help you to study them. Texts should be written in a straightforward style and well signposted to help you organise your reading and relate the content to your existing knowledge. It should be easy to find your way around the material and to refer to it again when you need to. And all the time there should be an expectation that you will be an active reader, actively and critically involved with the text.

In most good textbooks or course books you will find:

- A contents list that shows the main sections that build up the argument of the text, and their page numbers, so that you can find them easily. The contents list shows you a map of the text in advance of reading it.

- An introduction to the topic that provides an overview of the contents. The introduction answers your first question, 'What's this text about?'. It will tell you, for example, that the text is about an exploration of management from different perspectives, the roles managers are expected to play, and so on. You should know right from the start what you will read and its relevance to you.

- Clearly set-out aims and objectives. These are the writer's intentions in writing the text and they state what you should be able to do as a result of studying it. So, if a text makes a claim that adopting a particular practice will be beneficial, you can judge on the basis of experience or testing in the workplace whether the practice is successful in your own work context.

- Section headings and subheadings within them. They order the text and break it down into digestible chunks.

- Activities to reinforce your learning by prompting you to think about what you have read and how it relates to your own experience. Activities help you to grapple with the content rather than merely attempt to absorb it. Not all textbooks or course books contain activities, however. If they do not, stop reading at regular intervals and ask yourself, 'How does this relate to me, or the organisation I work for?'.

- Summaries of chapters or sections and a list of key points. These will enable you to check your understanding.

- Plenty of diagrams – a picture is worth a thousand words.

Work actively and critically with the text. Know why you are reading it (to gain fresh insight and knowledge, to track down particular information, to prepare for a course assignment and so on). Have a pen and a highlighter to hand.

Making notes

People often think of making notes as just a way to help them to recall things – rather like a shopping list. But a list is not what you will end up with if you are fully engaged with what you are reading. You will be marking key text with a highlighter pen and writing words in the margins: words such as 'Note the link with...', 'Remember for the assignment', 'No! Not in my experience', 'How does this compare with...?' and so on. You will create your own diagrams to illustrate your understanding, and your own sets of notes. In short, you will make the text your own.

Notes serve a number of purposes:

- **Understanding** First of all, your notes help you to understand the content.

- **Making connections** As you read actively, you will make connections with concepts, ideas, examples and so on, from other resources or from your own experience. Capture your thoughts and insights in your notes.

- **Aiding recall** Your notes will help you to recall content. You'll need to do this not only for assignments and examinations, if your course has them, but also to use concepts and ideas at work.

The stages of making meaningful notes

Having read a text actively with pen in hand, you can now truly transform the content and make it your own. Distil your understanding of the material into key ideas and concepts, the key authorities and examples, and connections with other material, to suit your own purposes. For example, you might reduce the author's argument to a page or so to insert at the front of the text. Your summary might take the form of a mixture of bullet lists, mind maps, cause and effect diagrams, pictures and so on, to suit your preferred approach. If you have an examination to revise for, your notes can be reduced even further to the core ideas, concepts, authorities and examples, which you can remember and use to trigger information. A single word or phrase, or a simple diagram, can act as a cue to recalling a detailed and complex idea. Finally, remember that your notes are just that – yours. Make them effective in whatever way suits you. But above all, do make them!

Writing

Effective writing – that is, getting our message across to an audience – requires practice and perseverance. Managers need to communicate with others in writing. If you are studying, you will also need to write effectively to meet the requirements of your course. Successfully conveying your message will rely entirely on your ability to express it in writing.

See Mind mapping, p. 135 and Multiple-cause diagrams, p. 137.

Whatever your message, and regardless of the way in which you convey it, you will need to use information, instructions, inquiries, ideas and decisions in a written form that is easy for your readers to understand, and that is appropriate to your audience and to your purpose.

Sometimes we write for ourselves alone, and no one else will need to understand our messages. Notes and summaries are examples of such writing. These help us to clarify our thoughts and to put complicated concepts and ideas into our own words as part of our learning process. At other times, we need to write for an audience. We may have to produce reports at work, and on formal learning courses we may be writing assignments for tutors to read. On these occasions, our writing will be read and assessed. It is important that it does us justice.

If you are writing in English as a second, or foreign, language, then you will probably feel particularly anxious about your writing. In order to prepare yourself for writing assignments you should practise writing as much as possible, preferably before you start your course.

The purposes of assignments

You may be required to carry out assignments as part of your course. If so, it is likely that they will serve two purposes: assignments are likely to be assessed and contribute to your overall mark for the course, and, importantly, they will contribute to your learning. When preparing assignments you will need to think hard about one or more ideas and, in all probability, to apply those ideas. As a result, you will come to understand those ideas more clearly and you will also be able to assess the significance of the ideas to your own thinking and practice.

When you submit your assignment to your tutor, it will be rather like giving a draft report to a colleague with the invitation to 'Please comment on what I have written'. Your tutor will comment on your argument, on the data you have used, and generally on the extent to which your assignment meets the requirements of the course or module. When you submit an assignment, you give your tutor the opportunity to teach you personally.

Allow sufficient time for writing your assignment. Regard the effort you give to the task as an investment in your own development. The more thorough the preparation, the more you will come to understand what you are writing about, and so the more you will be extending your intellectual and practical capabilities. You will soon discover the direct contribution that the writing of assignments makes to the way you do your job.

Recognise as well, that your assignments will constitute a portfolio of work. At the end of your course, you will be able to look at your collection of completed assignments and say 'I wrote them all'. You will be able to regard them as a record of achievement.

Understanding assignment questions

Whenever you write, you will be writing with a purpose. You will be describing and explaining something; you may need to illustrate a point, evaluate options, discuss, define, criticise and, sometimes, compare and contrast two or more models or systems. You will need to be clear about the meaning of each term in your assignment brief. Understanding assignment questions sounds easy. But learners sometimes do one or more of the following:

■ Answer the question they would like to have been asked.

■ Answer only part of the question.

■ Write a poor answer – one that could have been written without opening a course book.

■ Write solely about their work environment, instead of using it to show how management concepts are, or could be, applied.

Be clear about what an assignment question is asking. The following is a technique for identifying what is being asked for. Take the assignment question and a pen. Read the question carefully then underline the actions and information required.

Sample assignment question

Write a report in which you:

    (a) explain what information flows are involved in a particular aspect of your work

    (b) evaluate how sufficient and suitable this information is

(c) identify what extra information about this aspect of your work you have decided to gather and why

(d) describe how you gathered this new information, and from whom

(e) present clearly and visually the most useful findings from your information gathering

(f) set out the main lessons and implications or recommendations for future practice that arose from the investigation.

You have now identified the information needed and what you need to do. But are you clear about what the terms mean? The list below contains a number of terms you are likely to find in assignment questions or instructions.

Describe Give a detailed or graphic account.

Explain Provide reasons for something. It also means to make plain, interpret and account for.

Illustrate Illuminate using concrete examples, or to use a figure or diagram to explain or clarify.

Evaluate Make an appraisal of the worth of something.

Interpret Expound the meaning of a thing, to make clear and explicit, usually giving your judgement as well.

Discuss Investigate or examine by argument, to sift and debate, to give reasons for and against.

Define Give the precise meaning of a word or phrase (the more usual terms for concepts). In some cases it may be necessary or desirable to examine different possible or often-used definitions.

Criticise Give your judgement about the merit of theories or opinions, or about the truth of facts. You will need to support your judgement with evidence or the reasoning involved.

Compare Look for similarities and differences and perhaps reach a conclusion about which option or position is preferable.

Contrast Set two or more options or positions in opposition with the aim of revealing the differences.

Analyse Separate out a thing into its component parts to identify the components, to work out causes or to identify underlying principles.

Present and set out Terms that refer to how to convey information, points or findings. They mean that the information *needs to be included*. We can assume that the terms mean to present or set out clearly using appropriate methods – using numbered or bullet points, graphs or charts for example.

Learning what these terms mean will help you to structure a report. While an assignment question may provide an excellent guide to structure, there will be times when you have to create your own. Often, you will need to begin by defining something, for example, organisational culture, to ensure that your audience knows what you mean. Then you will need to describe or illustrate, criticise or evaluate, or compare and contrast, say, your organisation's communication methods with those of a more successful competitor. Your interpretation may be confined to a specific section in your text, or it may be required in a number of sections of your report. In the latter case you will need to use suitable 'flagging' so that your audience recognises your words as an interpretation (e.g. 'This can be interpreted as...').

Using the terms will not only aid the structure and clarity of your writing, but will help you to be more precise when you write. You will be able to distinguish between description and interpretation, for example, although it may be hard to discuss or analyse something without providing some element of description. Importantly, applying the types of thinking involved will help your critical reasoning skills.

Tackling assignments and reports

If you are unfamiliar with or uneasy about writing assignments or reports, the following process provides a way of tackling these tasks.

Gathering your thoughts

Once you are clear about the task, gather your initial thoughts. Begin by brainstorming. Write down the topic and then jot down your ideas about it in whatever order they come to you. You probably know more about the topic than you thought you did initially. Do not attempt at this stage to restrict the free flow of your ideas, or to impose any order on them, or to sort and select them. Leave such refinements to a later stage. Choose whatever method suits you to capture your thoughts: a list, a mind map or some other representation.

See mind mapping, p. 135.

Next, read about the topic. Follow any suggestions in the assignment notes. Read the course materials that you thought particularly relevant during your initial brainstorm. Then skim read the contents of other likely materials.

Consolidation and thinking

Now mull over the task and your notes for a day or two. Allow your thoughts free rein, but also take a break from thinking specifically about the writing task and content. Do something relaxing – go for a walk, for example. You will be surprised at the ideas that pop, unbidden, into your mind. Whatever you do, jot down those ideas!

Pulling your thoughts together

Now for more focused work. Glance through your initial ideas again. Fresh insights will usually have emerged from the period of consolidation and thinking. Discard anything that now seems less relevant. (But save your original notes so that you can return to them if you have second thoughts – and do check them again later to make sure you have not missed anything.)

The first draft

Organise and group your more refined ideas into an outline, or skeletal draft. Here is one way of constructing a first draft, using the assignment question to impose a structure.

1 Set out as many headings as there are parts to the assignment question, using words from it as section headings. Put an extra heading at the top titled 'Introduction'. Leave half a page or more between each heading.

2 Analyse the assignment question in terms of the *actions*. Leave the introduction aside for the moment and begin with the second heading. If the instruction is 'describe' then write 'I will describe...' under it. (If the instruction is 'explain' and you have had no prior instruction to describe, you will need to both describe and explain.) Under each heading begin a similar sentence containing the action word: 'Here, I will assess...' or 'My interpretation is...'. This will keep you focused on what you are trying to *do* with your newly acquired knowledge.

See Understanding assignment questions, p. 38.

3 Now refer to the assignment question again and analyse the information you need for each part. Under the incomplete sentences, set out *what* it is you need to describe, explain, or evaluate.

4 Now flesh out the skeletal draft with material from your notes. As you do this, you are likely to identify gaps in your knowledge which you will need to fill before beginning a full draft.

5 When you have listed your main conclusions, or recommendations, return to the introduction section. Now list the points you will need to include to introduce the topic and the reasons why it is being addressed.

See Writing reports, p. 44 and A template for reports, p. 45.

6 Convert the structure of your draft to report format, if required.

The writing process

The writing process may be summarised as follows.

(1) Start early (2) clarify the task (3) brainstorm (4) read (5) consolidate and think (6) select (7) order (8) draft.

You will need to go through this process whether you are writing an essay-type assignment for your tutor or writing a report at work.

An example of describing and explaining

In your day-to-day work and life, as well as in your studies, you will often be called upon to 'describe' and to 'explain' and/or 'interpret'.

Suppose that market researchers have asked a representative sample of adults in a locality about the way they spend their leisure time. The researchers, having completed their questioning, have collated the replies and have prepared a set of tables and charts.

Describe the results

As a first step, the researchers will be expected to describe the results produced. Their written report will contain such statements as '66 per cent of men aged between 30 and 39 years spent at least three hours a week on physical exercise', or '10 per cent of women said they had fewer than five hours of leisure time a week'. In this way, the researchers would state what the main features of the results are. These main features might be those that strike the researchers as important or, perhaps more likely, they will be the ones that the researcher knows will be relevant to the customer.

Explain and interpret

A marketing manager might say to the researcher: '*Explain* these results to me'. The marketing manager is really asking: '*Why* do 66 per cent of men aged between 30 and 39 spend at least three hours a week on physical exercise?'. The researcher will provide some known or likely causal relationships (very speculative ones might need further investigation). Now the marketing manager has another question, this time one that he must answer himself: 'What do these results *mean* in terms of our marketing strategy?'. The marketing manager needs to *interpret* them in business terms. The interpretation will be different depending on whether the organisation manufactures food or sportswear, or runs sports clubs.

The two steps

Recognise these two steps of describing followed by explaining or interpreting. Sometimes, you will be asked to describe an event. When you are, choose those features that you expect will be of the greatest relevance to the person who asked you (at work or during your studies). No doubt, you will also be asked to explain or interpret. You are being asked to look closely at something and make sense of it in particular ways. 'Analyse', 'evaluate', 'criticise', and even 'compare' and 'contrast' are other ways of asking you to do this, although the outcome of each will be different.

See Understanding assignment questions, p. 38.

Writing for your audience

When you write an assignment or a report you must know your audience and constantly bear them in mind. With report writing, the audience may be obvious – a group of senior managers, the marketing director, or perhaps your organisation's funders. It is less clear who the audience is, however, when it comes to assignments that you may be required to write as part of your course. Suppose an assignment question asks you to describe, analyse or explain some aspect of your work as a manager. The implication is that you are doing so for the benefit of someone else, your tutor. After all, you know enough about your own job already!

But do you? Such an assignment question is really asking you to write about your job by drawing on your understanding of the course material and the ideas and concepts you have read about, to show that you understand them and that you can apply them. This introduces a new perspective on the task. Before you can begin to tackle the question you have to understand the relevant course material for yourself. Then you have to step outside your everyday role of being a manager and apply the new ideas and concepts you have learned to the management job in an insightful way. By doing so, you test the material by applying it to your job and you test your job by applying it to the course material. This process is called iteration.

Writing for yourself

By looking at the task in this way, you see that your prime audience is yourself. You are demonstrating to yourself that you both understand the material and that you can apply it to a job of which you have personal experience. Remember that 'you have not understood it until you can say it'. Unless you can do that clearly, you will be unable to undertake such a task for anyone else. Your account will be muddled and unclear.

Writing for your tutors

In reality there is another audience, your tutors, who are looking metaphorically over your shoulder and who will award you a mark for your assignment on the basis of the soundness of your argument. So the dialogue that you hold with yourself must be open to sharing with someone else, someone who has read the material that you have read but who may have little understanding of your job and the way you carry it out. So your tutors, like any informed audience, may say things like, 'I'm sorry, but I do not understand that. There seem to be steps missing from your argument.' Or, 'That's not the accustomed understanding of that concept', or 'Your conclusion does not seem to follow from your evidence'.

Note that the primary purpose of course assignments is to demonstrate your knowledge and your understanding of what you have learned. As a result, course assignments of any kind will be far more explicit in their account of theories, concepts and references to other writers than most 'real-life' writing tasks that you may undertake as a manager. Even when an assignment specifies a particular format, for example, a formal memorandum or a report to a senior manager, you will need to remember the underlying purpose of assignments. A particular format guides style and language, but you will still need to demonstrate your knowledge and understanding.

Writing reports

A management report has specific purposes, for example to provide information or to make recommendations about a course of action. Organisations may have certain preferences for the style of presentation but overall there are common practices. These practices have the merit of familiarity. Writers of reports have a template to work to; readers of reports can rely on a familiar format when they read a report.

You may be required to present a course assignment in the form of a report. If you are familiar with your own organisation's preferred style, then use it. If you have not written a report before, or if you want to think afresh about the layout of a report, then there are some general rules that you can adopt. These will ensure that you set out what you want to say in a way that will help your reader to follow your argument and to know straight away what conclusions you have reached. In addition, the rules will provide you with a step-by-step checklist.

The structure of a report

The layout of a report is usually plain to see. Each section will have a general heading. There will also be subheadings. The overall structure will depend on the purpose of a report. Here are some typical overall structures:

- A chronological order to show how things or processes happened or should happen.

- A statement of the problem, analysis of the options and recommendations.

- A proposal stating the strengths and weaknesses and finally the recommended action.

Reports will usually have the following features:

- A cover page with a clear and informative title, together with the names of the addressee(s), the author's name and the date of production.

- An executive summary. This is normally a précis of the report including the main conclusions and recommendations. It is designed to persuade a busy executive to read the rest of the report.

- A contents list.

- A brief introduction which states the purpose of the report.

- The main text with the topics covered in separate paragraphs, with appropriate headings and subheadings.

- Conclusions set out the answers to the issues or problems raised, even if one or more conclusions are that further investigation is required. The conclusions follow strictly and only from the preceding argument.

- The recommendations that arise strictly and only from the preceding argument; they must be clear, specific, sensible and realistic, and must include likely costs where appropriate. Recommendations often constitute the practical interpretation of the conclusions.

- A reference section giving the sources of the information cited in the report.

- Any necessary appendices to provide important background information, including diagrams and tables, that it would be inappropriate to include in the main text.

- A numbering system throughout the report for ease of reference.

A template for reports

The following is a template for a report. Notice these features:

- presentation of the executive summary at the top of the document

- use of headings

- use of numbered sections.

Cover page Include the title of the report; addressee(s); author; date.

Executive Summary Provide a summary of your report here. By presenting your findings straight away, you release your readers from uncertainty.

Contents Insert page numbers if appropriate.

1	Introduction	5	Recommendations
2	First main section	6	References
3	Second main section	7	Appendices
4	Conclusions		

1   Introduction

1.1   Introduce your report. Explain what prompted it, and state its scope, that is, what you deal with. Conclude your introduction with a sentence that leads into the main body of the report.

2   First main section heading

2.1   First section of the main part of the report. There can be subsections to this first section.

2.2   Give each subsection a separate heading.

3   Second main section heading

There can be as many main sections as you require.

4   Conclusions

4.1   Allocate a subsection to each of the main parts of your conclusion.

4.2   Ensure that there is a correspondence between your conclusions and the summary. As a rule, the central point of a subsection forming part of a main section is expressed as one component of your summary. For instance, the central point of 3.1 should be expressed in 1.1 of your summary.

4.3   Comment on the tentativeness or strength of your conclusions.

5   Recommendations

5.1   List your recommendations as 'Recommendation 1', 'Recommendation 2' and so on. Ensure that there is a correspondence between your recommendations and the argument in the main sections and the conclusion to your report.

5.2   Comment on the appropriateness and feasibility of your recommendations.

6   References

See Citing and referencing, p. 49.

List the sources of the information you used in your report. They should be complete and follow a recognised style.

7   Appendices

7.1   List your appendices by their titles and give each a number which corresponds with the order in which they appear. It is usual to start each Appendix on a new page.

It is good practice to include a file reference so that the report can be easily retrieved from an archive – your own, or that of your organisation. It is also usual to sign the end of the report (before the appendices and references).

Writing research reports

A research report is a special kind of report that you may be asked to write. Once you have gathered all your research data and analysed them you will need to set out your findings, and explain why, and how, you conducted your investigation.

Research reports will usually have the following features:

1   Title page (including the author and date)

2   Executive summary

3   Contents list

4   Background, including aims and objectives (terms of reference)

5   Literature review

6   Data collection methods

7   Data analysis and results

8   Conclusions and recommendations

9   Critical reflection and learning

10 Acknowledgements

11 References

12 Appendices

BOX 3.1   A CHECKLIST FOR WRITING RESEARCH REPORTS

Make sure that:

- The necessary conventions have been followed in the writing up of the research.

- The references are complete and follow a recognised style.

- The tables, figures, illustrations and diagrams are properly labelled and supply the necessary information in a succinct manner.

- A detailed and precise description of the research process has been provided.

- The choice of method(s) has been justified in relation to the type of data required and the practical circumstances surrounding the research.

- The limitations of the research method(s) have been acknowledged.

Writing concisely

Writing concisely is not just about meeting word limits. It is often about meeting audience demands. How often have you heard a senior manager ask: 'I want it on one side of A4?' or 'Just give me the headlines'. But even when no limit is set, we need our text to be accessible, long enough to cover the subject but short enough to retain the reader's interest. Here are some tips to help you write concisely:

- Include only the material that is relevant to your purpose and to your reader. If your notes contain additional material you may need in the future, save them.

- Sort your material into categories, based on what your readers need to know – 'must know', 'should know', and 'nice to know'.

- Eliminate any repetitions of material or points at the draft stage.

- Cut out paragraphs, sentences, phrases and words that are just padding. Ask 'What am I trying to say here' and try to express it directly. Phrases such as 'in the near future' can be replaced by 'soon'. Also avoid what is known as tautology – saying the same thing twice as in 'new innovation', 'mutual co-operation' or 'unfilled vacancy'. In each case, one word is better than two.

■ Use diagrams, tables and graphs. Although they will need to be described, they are valuable in expressing a good deal of information in a concise way.

■ Keep the detail of examples to a minimum.

Assignments

The same tips apply when writing assignments as part of a formal course of study. In this case, however, there will be a set question to address and some conventions. The following are some additional tips to help you write concise assignments when word limits are likely to apply:

■ Use the assignment question to select content.

See Plagiarism and how to avoid it, p. 48 and Citing and referencing, p. 49.

■ Draw on and make explicit reference to relevant concepts provided in the learning material – and make sure they are properly referenced.

■ If required, draw on your own experience, work environment or situation for illustration or argument, but be relevant and brief. Well-considered examples save words.

■ Make sure your work is objective and analytical – not subjective and unduly biased.

■ Make sure you have a synthesis of theory, practice and common sense.

Writing concisely takes a little longer. As the French mathematician Blaise Pascal wrote in 1657: 'This [letter] would not be so long had I but the leisure to make it shorter.' The most common fault of inexperienced writers, and particularly of students, is to pour onto paper everything they know about a particular topic. This is tough on readers. If you are a student it will be tough on your grades too!

Plagiarism and how to avoid it

Plagiarism is the term used when a person takes the work of another person and presents it as their own. In the world of writing, it is a very serious matter. It is easy to see how it can happen, however, whether you are a management student learning from course materials, or a busy manager needing information to include in a report. On one hand, you want to show that you are making use of accepted or new ideas you have been reading about; on the other, you do not want to be accused of following them slavishly, to the point of plagiarism. You may want to put the material into your own words but you may be worried that you will not explain it correctly or as intelligently as the original writer. What should you do?

Acknowledge others

Make a simple, unbreakable rule to acknowledge your sources of information. Far from making a person appear ignorant, it shows that they are well read and well informed. There are various conventions for acknowledging the work of others, depending on the style of writing, or genre, you are using. If in doubt, you will not go far wrong by including in your text the source of information, or, in brackets, the names of authors and the date of publication, for example (Bloggs and Bloggs, 2003). At the end of your text, provide a bibliography setting out the authors' names in full, the date of the publication, its title, and the publisher. Interested readers will then be able to track down the publication for themselves.

Express it in your own way

Even when we provide a reference to the source of information, we can run into problems by using almost the same wording that is used in our source. Even if we refer to the source, we can still run the risk of plagiarism because we are presenting another person's words as our own unless we make it clear that we are quoting them. To overcome this, we need to understand as fully as possible what the writer means and then write it as *we* understand it. There is always a risk of getting it wrong, of course, but that is part of the learning process. A useful tip is to imagine explaining the idea to someone who is unfamiliar with it. How would you explain it to them? You can often spot your own misunderstandings when you do this. Revisit the text to fill in your gaps, then try explaining it again. As you do this you are both learning and developing your own style – positive gains! Better still, as you become accomplished at this, you may even find flaws in your source's argument – a basis for critique.

Quotation marks

Sometimes an idea is very elegantly expressed and we want to use the original words. In this case, use the words as a quotation from the original text, use quotation marks and acknowledge the writer. Another possibility when using long quotations is to set them apart from the body text and to display them clearly in a set quotation style. In this case quotation marks are not needed, but, of course, the source must be clearly displayed.

Referring to management models

Remember that as you make knowledge 'your own' you will shed the detail and remember only the key points or concepts. Plagiarism will become less of an issue. But you will still need to acknowledge the sources of ideas that are not your own. Try tying particular ideas to the originators' names – this is relatively easy in the field of management because it is already something of a convention. We speak of 'Kolb and Fry's learning cycle' and 'Mintzberg's managerial roles' for example. Make it a habit.

Citing and referencing

When writing a text in which you use the work of others, you will need to cite the material and provide full details in a reference list or bibliography.

You will need to do this whether you are quoting material, paraphrasing it, summarising it, referring to research findings or using statements to support an argument. It is essential to include sufficient and accurate information for others to be able to locate the paper, book, website or report cited. The Harvard system of referencing is the most commonly used. In this system, authors are cited in the text *and* a full reference is given in a references list or bibliography at the end. The Harvard system sets out the information to be given and the order in which it is given. The system remains the same regardless of any stylistic features that may be adopted. Stylistic variations will determine the use of capital letters, italics, punctuation marks, brackets around dates, whether volume numbers appear as Vol. 2, Issue 3 or 2(3), for example. As long as the style adopted is used consistently, it does not matter which you use unless you have been asked to use a particular style.

In-text citations

- Give the author's (or originator's) surname and the year of publication in the text. You can do it like this (Bloggs, 2006). Or if it can be made part of the sentence, like this: 'Bloggs (2006) has suggested...'.

- Include page numbers if necessary: As Bloggs (2006, p7) insists: 'The problem will not be resolved if...'.

- When several documents have the same date and author, distinguish them by adding a, b, c... after the year, e.g. Bloggs (2006a, p7).

- If there are two authors, give the names of both (Black and Spender, 2003); if there are more than two, give the first author's surname followed by *et al.* (Zender *et al.*, 2006).

- If you refer to a secondary source, that is, one quoted in another source, cite both in the text like this: Bloggs (2003 cited by Jergen 2006, p.9). List only the work that you have read – Jergen – in your bibliography.

- The source of diagrams needs to be cited. Under the diagram give the author's or originator's surname and date of publication, for example, (Bloggs, 2006). If you have adapted the diagram then it is appropriate to write the citation like this: (Based on Bloggs, 2006); or (Adapted from Bloggs, 2006). This indicates that changes have been made.

Bibliographies

Full references should be included in a references list or bibliography at the end of your document. The information you need to provide changes slightly according to whether you are giving details of a book, a multi-authored book (usually edited by a volume editor), a journal article, a webpage or some other source of information. Here are some examples setting out the information required, the order, and samples. Although the Harvard system specifies that, when referencing books, writers should provide the place of publication, this is not always done. Consistently applied, it is an acceptable omission in many cases – but check first! Note that initial capitals are used for the names of journals and newspapers, but not necessarily for books when their titles are long. (Titles of books and journals can be underlined or italicised, depending on style.) Note, too, how punctuation is used.

Books Author's surname, initials, year of publication, *title*, edition (if not the first), place of publication, publisher.

> Roast, E.D. and Bean, S. (2003) *Wake Up and Smell the Coffee*, 2nd edn, London, Mill.

Contribution in a book Contributing author's surname, initials, year of publication, title of contribution, in, surname of editor(s) of publication, initials, followed by ed. or eds, *title of book*, place of publication, publisher, page numbers.

> Bandit, A. (1997) 'Risky investments' in Cash, M.Y., ed., *Capital Growth*, Houston, TX, Thyme, p.10–21.

Article in a journal Author's surname, initials, year of publication, title of article, *title of journal*, volume number, part number, page numbers.

> Clevah, V.V. (1999) 'Intelligent organizations', *Smart Management*, Vol. 9 (3), p.17–23.

Newspaper article Author's surname, initials (or newspaper title), year of publication, article title, *newspaper title*, day, month and page number(s).

> The Daily News (2001) 'All systems go!', *The Daily News*, 14 February, p. 22.

Publication from an organisation Name of issuing body, year of publication, *title of publication*, place of publication, publisher, report number (if there is one).

> Academy of Accounting (2004) *Accountancy: Calculating the future*, London, Academy of Accounting, Report 77.

Webpage There is no standard method yet for citing electronic sources, but you should give the universal resource locator (URL), the date you accessed the webpage and as much other key information as possible. For example:

> Eiseburg, D. (2004) 'Intangible assets', London, Academy of Accountancy. http://www.academy.org.uk/publications/report_4.html [accessed 3 July 2006].

Diagrams The source of diagrams should be cited in your bibliography. How you do this will depend on where the diagram came from (a book, contribution in a book, journal article and so on). Use the appropriate referencing system for the source. You need not indicate in the bibliography that you are referring to a diagram or that you have adapted it in some way: that will be clear from your in-text citation.

Other media The Harvard system covers all types of media, from personal communications to business conferences and television programmes.

Organising the references

List the references in alphabetical order of authors' names. If there are several items by one author, start with the earliest and list them in chronological order. If two or more have the same date, order them by the letter (a, b, c) that you used in the in-text citation.

Polishing your writing

If you read a management report with poor grammar and spelling mistakes, how does it affect the way you feel about the report? Do you take it as seriously as you might a better written report? Even experienced writers make mistakes but you, as a reader, probably never see them because experienced writers read their work through and correct their mistakes or seek help to ensure that the final product is of a high quality. Always read through your work – twice if possible (the first time to check the clarity of the message and structure, and the second to check grammar, spelling and consistency of style or format). Try reading out the text to another person, or ask them to read it.

Remember, readers are human – they may 'switch off' if your message is confused, your text is poorly structured or is full of mistakes. You will keep your readers interested if you learn to write logically, clearly and accurately. So, if you have not had recent experience of writing an extensive piece of text for others to read, try not to let your first course assignment be your first attempt.

Active and passive voices

'Choosing your voice' is not about the way you speak, it is about the choice of writing in an active way or a passive way. Look at these two sentences:

1   The IT manager authorised the purchase of three additional PCs.

2   The purchase of three additional PCs was authorised by the IT manager.

Both sentences convey the same information. When you read them, you know what was authorised and by whom. Yet they convey the information in different ways. In (1), 'The IT manager' is the subject of the verb 'authorised'. There is a sense of directness about the sentence. In (2), 'the IT manager' is no longer the subject of the verb (which has now become 'was authorised'). Instead, the subject has become 'The purchase of three additional PCs'.

The two sentences represent two different 'voices'. The first sentence is in 'the active voice'. This term describes a sentence in which the action is undertaken by the subject of the sentence. In (1), 'The IT manager' is the subject of the sentence as it was the manager who authorised the purchase. The second sentence is an example of 'the passive voice'. The subject of this sentence is no longer 'the IT manager'.

The difference in the way that the information is conveyed will be relevant to your writing. You may be accustomed to writing your internal documents in one form only. Or you may not have thought about the matter. Consider the effects of each. The passive voice is associated with impersonality, with the reduction or the elimination of a sense of the personal from the writing. It also involves using more complicated sentence constructions that will make your writing less easily understood. Look again at the two sentences with these thoughts in mind. In most cases when you write, you have the choice between the two voices. If you want your text to come over as direct, choose the active voice.

Using similes and metaphors

Senior managers, experts, gurus and writers on management often use similes and metaphors. The reason is simple. A complex issue or idea can be communicated clearly and succinctly when it is explained in terms of something familiar. When someone is speaking of, for example, a progression towards a goal they may explain the steps in terms of the rungs of a ladder or stages of a journey. Constructing similes and metaphors can also help a person understand a complex idea in addition to communicating it. The ability to say something like 'My organisation or my unit is like a ...' or 'My organisation or unit is a ...' will help you to understand your organisation or unit and to convey that understanding to other people.

A graphic example

At the end of a management course, students were asked to 'Draw a cartoon which shows you before you began your course and which shows you now, close to the end of the course'. Figure 3.1 shows one student's cartoon.

Figure 3.1   Before and after studying a management course

The student imagined that his organisation was like a maze. He, like everyone else, was working day after day in an organisation in which it was difficult to know where to go, what was happening, how to progress and how to reach a destination. In the student's mind, working in the organisation was a constant challenge in terms of trying to make sense of what was going on.

Towards the end of the course, the puzzlement had gone. Instead, the student had a guide. Indeed, he had guides to give to other people in the organisation. He had the means to make sense of the maze. The inference is that working in the organisation was still puzzling, but less so for the student and others who had guides.

That understanding of the organisation and of the student's relationship to it was achieved by the imaginative act of likening the organisation to a maze. Another student imagined their department to be a gambling casino where the rewards depended not just on skill but also on luck, and where there was constant competition for those rewards. When you express your understanding of your organisation or situation in this way you will reveal what you see as the dominant feature or features. Using similes and metaphors can be useful for clarifying your own perceptions and, when expressed in words, they are a way of conveying a perception to others in an economical and readily-understood way. The danger lies in over-simplification.

Similes and metaphors are close to each other. The sentence 'My organisation is *like* a maze' is a simile. But the statement 'My organisation *is* a maze' is a metaphor.

Using an apostrophe

Misunderstandings about the use of the apostrophe are all too evident. It is not unusual to see public advertisements that mistakenly add an apostrophe to the word *its* in sentences such as 'The product comes complete with it's own carrying case'. And some writers seem to assume that every *s* on the end of a word should have an apostrophe, either before it or after it.

The first barrier to overcoming problems with using the apostrophe is knowing that you have a problem with it! Here is a quick diagnostic test. Place a tick or a cross by each apostrophe in each sentence, indicating whether you think the apostrophe has been used correctly or not.

BOX 3.2   USING AN APOSTROPHE: A QUICK DIAGNOSTIC TEST

1   It's stark exterior looked forbidding.

2   The womens' cloakroom is over there.

3   The red coat is her's.

4   I work for a not-for-profit organisation. My organisations' logo is a black and white shield.

5   The manager's were furious about the change's.

---

6 There was a long queue for the lady's changing rooms in the fashion store.

7 I always think of accountancy primarily as a mens' profession.

8 This building was designed in the 1820's.

9 I have lots of CD's at home.

10 The management consultancy company Joop Coopes has relocated to a larger site. Coope's old office block is for sale.

There were eleven apostrophes in the ten sentences. For each tick you made score one mark and for each cross score zero. Add up your total score. If your total score was one or more, you need to read this section. All eleven apostrophes were wrongly used!

The apostrophe signals missing letters

The apostrophe is used to show where letters have been missed out from a word. *It's* has an apostrophe when it is the shortened form of *it is* or *it has*, as in 'It's plain to see that...' or 'It's been months since I last heard from you'. Other examples are: *who's* (who is), *they're* (they are), *there's* (there is), *I'll* (I will), *wouldn't* (would not), *don't* (do not), *you're* (you are), *she's* (she is), *we're* (we are), *I'm* (I am), and so on.

The apostrophe signals possession

The apostrophe causes the most confusion when it is used as a possessive, denoting *of* or *belonging to*. For example:

1 John's new car was red. (The new car belonging to John was red.)

2 The purchaser's complaint was upheld. (The complaint of the purchaser was upheld.)

3 Purchasers' statutory rights are not affected. (The statutory rights of purchasers are not affected.)

Note the two different positions of the apostrophe. In (1) and (2), there is just one John and just one purchaser, so the apostrophe goes before the *s*. In (3), there are two or more purchasers, so the apostrophe goes after the *s* (*purchasers* is plural: putting the apostrophe before the *s* would make it singular).

Note two special cases. The first is when a word is singular but ends with an *s*. This often happens with surnames. Suppose you had a colleague called Jones, then his desk would be *Jones' desk* or *Jones's desk*. It would never be written as *Jone's desk*. The second special case is that of plurals which do not end in an *s*. Some examples are *women, men, people* and *staff*. Here, an apostrophe and an *s* are added, as in *the men's cloakroom* (the cloakroom of the men).

You may have wondered why *its* doesn't follow the possessive apostrophe rule. The answer is that, like *hers, ours, yours* and *theirs, its* is a possessive pronoun. Possessive pronouns are *already* possessive and need no indication of possession. You must write *hers, ours, yours, theirs* and *its* without an apostrophe. The remaining possessive pronouns – *mine* and *his* – do not cause a problem.

Revisit the diagnostic test at the beginning of this subsection and correct each sentence. The correct versions, with explanations, are given in Appendix 2.

Common spelling errors

Words that sound alike

Words such as 'principle' and 'principal' sound exactly the same but they mean different things. You will not be able to rely on computer software tools for checking spelling and grammar: they are simply not smart enough. There is really no alternative to knowing what you mean and which word to use to express your meaning. You probably expect no less from others, especially your tutors. If you really struggle with spelling and grammar, then use an electronic dictionary, or have a good paper dictionary and a hand-held electronic spelling aid nearby when you write. (Use the 'sound like' function on the hand-held device to establish correct spellings before looking up word meanings in the dictionary.) Word games such as crossword puzzles are a good way of improving spelling, and learning a foreign language can improve your understanding of grammar.

- compliment, complement

I considered it a *compliment* to be *complimented* on my assignment.

Without Chris, we were one short of a full *complement*.

His study of the course *complemented* his natural ability.

- effect (noun), affect (verb)

The *effect* of climate change has been widely felt.

Climate change will *affect* us all.

- flout, flaunt

If you continue to *flout* the rules, you'll be in trouble.

If you continue to *flaunt* your recent success, people will think you are boasting.

- lead, led

Water pipes used to be made of *lead*.

The rescuers *led* them from the building.

■ practise (verb), practice (noun)

You must *practise* your speaking skills.

Without *practice*, your foreign language skills will decay.

Note: American English uses *practice* as both a verb and a noun.

■ principle, principal

The organisation was committed to the *principle* of equal opportunities.

The college *principal* gave the idea her support.

An aid to memory: The principal was my pal.

■ proceed, proceeding, precede, procedure

We *proceeded* to interview the candidates immediately after they made their presentations.

The company began legal *proceedings* to protect its intellectual property.

The *preceding* month's figures showed a 10 per cent increase.

It is standard *procedure* to ask candidates to make a presentation

■ stationary, stationery

The vehicle was *stationary* when the other vehicle collided with it.

The shop sold *stationery*: paper, pens and so on.

■ their, there, they're

Their understanding of the meeting was not the same as mine.

There are not sufficient funds for the project.

They're expected on the next flight.

Note: *theirs* (denoting that something belongs to them) must be distinguished from *there's* (the shortened form of *there is* or *there has*).

■ who's, whose

Who's that at the door?

Whose book is this?

Other words commonly misspelled

■ *Accommodation* is spelled with a double 'c' and a double 'm'.

■ *Height* includes a letter 'e'.

■ *Liaise, liaison* – note the second letter 'i' in each case.

■ *Pursue, pursuit* but *persuade, persuasion.*

■ *Recommend* and *recommendation* are spelled with a double 'm' but not with a double 'c'.

Experienced writers read their work through or seek help from a colleague or editor. You should do the same. If, in particular, your grammar is poor ask someone to help you correct your text. Do not rely on the spelling and grammar checker on your computer – it will add to your confusion!

Some rules of thumb for spelling

■ 'I' before 'e' except after 'c'.

Examples are: *friend, receive, brief, receipt achieve*. There are exceptions however: *neither, weight, seize, weird, counterfeit, leisure.*

■ Verbs ending with one 'l' have a double 'l' when a suffix is added.

Examples are: *model, modelling, modelled; compel, compelling, compelled; propel, propelling, propelled.*

■ The endings of comparatives and superlatives change according to how they end.

To one-syllable words add 'er' for comparatives and 'est' for superlatives. Examples: *fast, faster* (than), *fastest; slow, slower* (than), *slowest; simple, simpler* (than), *simplest; large, larger* (than), *largest.*

For words ending in 'y', drop the 'y' and add an 'i'. Then add the 'er' or 'est'. Examples: *lucky, luckier* (than), *luckiest; lazy, lazier* (than), *laziest.*

For words ending in a single vowel followed by a single consonant, double the last letter, then add 'er' or 'est'. Examples: *hot, hotter* (than), *hottest; fat, fatter* (than), *fattest; big, bigger* (than), *biggest.* Exceptions to the rule are words ending in 'w': *slow, slower* (than), *slowest.* Words with a double vowel also have only the 'er' or 'est' added: *cool, cooler* (than), *coolest.*

■ The usual way of denoting the past tense or past participle is to add 'ed'. The exceptions are words that already end in 'e' or 'y'.

For words ending in 'e', simply add a 'd': *live, lived; save, saved.* For words ending in 'y', drop the 'y' and add 'ied': *hurry, hurried; cry, cried.*

The English language has many irregularities. If you are unsure, consult a dictionary.

A writing checklist

Often, we need to correct or edit our own writing. This may take more than one reading of the text. The first reading may be to ensure that what you have written makes sense, that it is well-structured, sound and suitably indicated with headings and subheadings. The second reading may be to check spelling, grammar, punctuation and consistency of style.

Checklist

Content

- Have you kept your audience in mind throughout your text?

- Have you said what you meant to say? Does your text convey what you intended?

- Are your arguments logical? Have you supported them with evidence?

- When the evidence supports more than one interpretation, have you acknowledged this?

- Have you used enough evaluation? Is it clear and precise?

- Have you arrived at a conclusion and made recommendations?

See Logical reasoning and critical thinking, p. 60.

Style and structure

- Have you been consistent in the style or genre you have chosen (e.g. report style)?

- Have you organised the text in a way that makes the structure clear to readers?

- Are your sentences consistent in terms of tense (past, present, future) and person (I, we, you...)?

- Are your bullet point or numbering systems appropriate, correct and consistent?

- Are your diagrams, tables, graphs and other textual aids properly labelled?

- Have you acknowledged your sources of information, using the conventions of the genre (e.g. academic references or acknowledgements list)?

See Citing and referencing, p. 49.

Spelling, grammar and punctuation

- Does every sentence have a subject and a verb?

- Do your verbs agree with your subjects?

- Have you checked your use of apostrophes?

- Are all the words spelled correctly?

- Have you checked your punctuation – full stops, commas, question marks, hyphens, colons and semi-colons?

See Using an apostrophe, p. 54, and Common spelling errors, p. 56.

Logical reasoning and critical thinking

Logic

The use of logic is essential in thinking and constructing arguments or cases. Logic refers to the rules we need to apply in relating one statement to another. We use logic to distinguish between good reasoning and poor reasoning. Consider the statement: 'I do not think these time management courses teach anybody anything – look at the two people we sent on one'. You need to be able to identify the faults in this kind of reasoning.

Formal logic

There are two kinds of formal logical reasoning: deductive and inductive. You are probably familiar with them without realising it.

Deductive reasoning

An example of deductive reasoning is:

> All dogs are animals. (All Xs are Ys.)
>
> Ben is a dog. (Z is an X.)
>
> Therefore Ben is an animal. (Therefore, Z is a Y.)

If we look at the structure of the argument we can see that there are two statements and a conclusion, and we can see the relationship between them. The two statements are the *premises* of the argument on which the final, conclusive, statement rests. We would find it hard to disagree with the argument. Now consider the next argument:

> All managers have blue fingers. (All Xs have Ys.)
>
> Ben is a manager. (Z is an X.)
>
> Therefore Ben has blue fingers. (Therefore, Z has Y.)

The argument is sound! Why? It is because the conclusion is correctly drawn from the two premises. The rules of logic have been obeyed so the argument is *valid* or *sound*. But it doesn't mean that it is *true*. A conclusion is true *only* if its premises are true. Another way of expressing this is: If P is true, then Q is true. P is untrue, therefore Q is untrue. Let's look at the 'blue fingers' argument again. We have the equivalent of two Ps in this argument (two premises):

> $P1$ = All managers have blue fingers. (All Xs have Ys.)
>
> $P2$ = Ben is a manager. (Z is an X.)
>
> Q = Therefore Ben has blue fingers. (Therefore, Z has Y.)

Clearly, $P1$ is not true. How do we know? We have not seen all the managers in the world, but we do not have to: we know that such a statement containing the word 'all' must be wrong. Even *one* manager without blue fingers will overturn the premise.

Inductive reasoning

Inductive reasoning is very different from deductive reasoning. While deductive reasoning starts with some general statements and moves through to a particular conclusion, inductive thinking does more or less the opposite. It starts with particular information, observations or evidence, and moves through to a conclusion which is often general. In doing this, a conclusion may well go 'beyond the evidence'. For example, a generalisation about all or most people, or a group of people, made on the basis of observing just a few people (the 'evidence'), will clearly go 'beyond the evidence'. But we often accept generalisable conclusions because they are useful: they help us to know what to expect in similar situations. We use them to *predict* what might happen. Here is an example of inductive reasoning:

> I timed 1,000 people to see how long it took them to reach the emergency exit nearest to their desks. I found it took an average of three minutes.
>
> I selected the 1,000 people on the basis that they were representative of the total workforce.
>
> Therefore, it takes an average of three minutes to reach an emergency exit.

This conclusion predicts that *any* person walking from their desk to an emergency exit will take, on average, three minutes. But is the argument sound? Consider the next example:

> I've just timed myself to see how long it took me to walk to the emergency exit nearest my desk. It took me three minutes.
>
> I'm no different from other people.
>
> Therefore, it takes three minutes to reach an emergency exit.

Of the two arguments, which are you most likely to believe and why? Both have some *objectivity* about them because the observation was based on a formal measurement (time). If we study the arguments, we find that one of the conclusions goes much further 'beyond the evidence' than the other. In the first example, the conclusion is based on 1,000 observations. In the second it is based on just one. The greater the evidence for a conclusion (provided the evidence is relevant!), the more sound the argument is likely to be. Thus, with arguments based on inductive reasoning we need to assess not only whether they are sound or unsound, but *how sound* and whether one argument is *more sound* than another. The greater the supporting evidence, the more sound an inductive argument is likely to be. However, soundness is not based purely on the amount of evidence provided but also its quality and relevance. For example, if the sounder argument set out above were part of a larger argument in order to plan for fire hazards in the building, what would we think of the evidence? The *average* time to reach an emergency exit is not wholly relevant – we would want to know how long it took the *slowest* person to reach an emergency exit too!

Logical reasoning in action

See Logic, p. 60.

In everyday life, arguments are not set out neatly for us. We need additional skills to 'unpack' an argument and often to extract it from the rest of what a person has said, to recognise the weak and strong points of an argument, to analyse the evidence behind the claims made, identify the conclusion, and to question the claims. Consider Argument 1:

Argument 1 'A number of research studies have shown that the power of money as a motivator for increased work performance is short lived and has less effect the more comfortable people are financially. Thus, increases in pay cannot be relied upon to improve productivity.'

This is the kind of argument you are likely to find in your learning materials. It is based on *inductive* reasoning. Say I want to use this information in a work situation. I might use *deductive* reasoning as set out in Argument 2:

Argument 2 'I want to increase productivity – it can be improved by various means. However, productivity is not improved by raising pay. Therefore, I will not increase pay to try to improve productivity.'

Look closely at each argument, starting with Argument 1. The research studies into pay as a motivator of productivity will (or should!) have been carried out using systematic observation in a number of settings with different groups of employees. Data will have been gathered and analysed. The conclusion that pay cannot be relied upon to improve productivity will have been drawn on the basis of these data. However, it does not necessarily mean that money never motivates people whatever they are paid and whatever their work context. For *some* people pay will be a motivator of productivity, it is simply that it cannot be *relied* upon as a motivator.

Now look at Argument 2. In building my argument I set out my premises, then I drew a conclusion which will not be true if one of my premises is not true. One of them is not entirely true. It would have been better for me to have investigated a little further to find out if pay motivates people in specific contexts. Say I read the course book again more carefully. I see that there are research studies which show that money is a motivator when it visibly rewards performance, but that this direct relationship is unnoticeable in many jobs. This means that workplace factors will influence whether or not a pay increase has an effect. Rather than hastily dismissing a pay increase, I might scrutinise the context of the group of workers whose productivity I want to increase. Depending on what I find, I might or might not increase pay, or I might introduce some kind of profit- or gain-sharing system.

When considering or constructing arguments, we need to pay particular attention to the following:

- The *premises* of an argument: are they true?

- Where the premises are *evidence*: how good is the evidence? Has it been systematically collected from many observations; how comprehensive is it; has it been interpreted properly?

- The *conclusion*: is the conclusion a valid one to draw from these premises? Could some other conclusion have been drawn?

When a person simply states 'I think that applying Concept X will solve this problem', this is not setting out a case or an argument. It is simply a statement, unsupported by any reasons why Concept X might work. By using 'the rules' of argument, people are able to judge the soundness of an argument. You will be able to assess other people's arguments, and, most importantly, your own!

Critical thinking

Critical thinking is the kind of thinking we use when we are being analytical: it is informal logic but embraces the rules of formal logic. Critical thinking involves *critique*, *questioning* or *scepticism*. In order to learn more and manage better we should use critical thinking in four main areas:

1 **Rhetoric**. Assumptions and premises used in a case or argument; the form of an argument; the language used. The questions to ask here are: 'Do the conclusions follow from the premises?' 'Are the premises justifiable?' 'Is the language fair?' 'What is the purpose of adopting this particular attitude?' 'Why am *I* adopting this particular attitude?'.

See Logic, p. 60 and Logical reasoning in action, p. 62.

2 **Tradition**. The taken-for-granted traditional ways of doing things or conventional wisdom. Relevant sorts of questions here are: 'Why are things done this way?' 'Is the situation the same now as in the past?'.

3 **Authority**. The dominant or privileged position. Here, appropriate questions are: 'Why is one view dominant or privileged?' 'Are there other perspectives?' 'What kinds of experiences inform those perspectives?' 'Are other perspectives invalid?'.

4 **Objectivity**. The idea that knowledge is value free, objective, disinterested and is not shaped by the structures of power. First, one needs to realise that knowledge is *never* value free and objective. While we may rely on the science of aerodynamics to fly to a business meeting, most knowledge we will deal with as managers is not of this sort. Seemingly objective 'facts' are not what they appear to be, but are generally interpretations by people and are biased by self-interest, power, contexts and assumptions. The questions to ask here are: 'Why has *this* problem been raised?' 'Why has *this* decision been made (or put off)?' 'What factors are promoting or suppressing particular information?' 'What is shaping the agendas of discussions or meetings?'.

(Source: Mingers, 2000)

Building sound arguments

When you are preparing an argument – a case that you want to put to your colleagues or to a supplier or customer, or an assignment that is part of your course – you will want to think about:

1   the data and the assumptions that will constitute the foundations of your case

2   the inferences you will be able to draw from the data

3   the conclusion you will be able to reach.

These elements are portrayed in Figure 3.2.

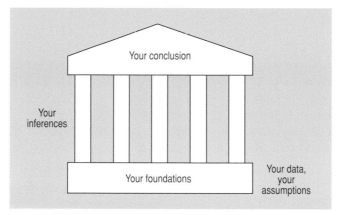

Figure 3.2   Building a case

The foundations The foundations of your case will comprise your data and your assumptions. Suppose you wanted to change the organisation's pricing policy. No doubt, you would present some data about the effects of the present policy, the data being drawn both from within and outside the organisation. The foundations would also include the assumptions you made. The assumptions, in this instance, would certainly be about the responsiveness of the market to price, and the response of the organisation's competitors.

The inferences Once you have set out the data, the premises they support, and any assumptions, you can then draw inferences. Here is an example: 'The recent promotional price reduction in our main competitor's product was extremely successful. The market conditions do not appear to have changed since then and we have the resources to run a good promotion. I expect that if we had a similar promotion it would be equally successful.' The final inference here is that what worked for the competitor will work for us. An inference can be one step in an argument, like a link in a chain, or it may be the final one – the conclusion.

The conclusion This will be the main assertion of the argument. We usually want the conclusion to stand out. In that sense, the conclusion is an eye-catching part of the building that rests on the main structure.

As you construct an argument, remember that you can be challenged about any part of it – about the data and the assumptions and about the inferences you have drawn.

Critical dialogues and inquiry

Arguments have a goal: to build or refute a case. The context may be an educational one, or one in which you are trying to persuade another person to accept your argument. A dialogue is an exchange, usually verbal, between two or more people. A person's case or argument may have to be 'discovered' from what they say in a dialogue, typically through the use of questions and responses. This is because in the world outside books, people do not often set out their arguments formally. They are more likely to say: 'I think Sam is the best person for the job'. You might respond: 'Why, exactly? Sam doesn't have much experience of that particular technology. Bernardo would be the better person for the job.' The response to this might be: 'Why is experience of the particular technology so important? Sam can pick it up easily. We need his project management skills.'

Clearly, there is more than one 'argument' going on here. If there were no real exchange of views, no exploration or critique of them, then we would have two separate arguments as depicted in Figure 3.3. This sometimes happens of course! But both at work and when we are learning, we need to hear and question the views of others, and have our own views questioned if we are to improve our knowledge and understanding and make better decisions.

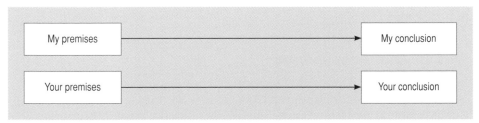

Figure 3.3 Two separate arguments

This is done by asking questions and replying to questions to explore arguments as depicted in Figure 3.4. There are some rules, of course: the rule of relevance (neither of us must wander too far from the point), the rule of co-operativeness and the rule of informativeness (we must try to formulate our responses using our understanding of each other's knowledge of the topic under discussion). In a persuasive dialogue – one in which I try to persuade you that Sam is absolutely the best person for the job – you and I engage in a series of questions. We ask one another: 'What's your thinking on this?' 'Why?' 'How so?' 'How come you're very sceptical of that?'. As we move through our discussion, you might find that one of my premises is irrelevant or at least open to reasonable criticism; you might find that another seems very solid. I concede one of my premises and you adopt one

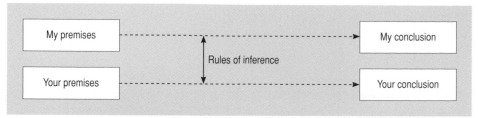

Figure 3.4   **The critical dialogue**

of mine and modify your own. We may decide that neither of us has sufficient, or sufficiently sound evidence or facts to come to a conclusion. We might decide to seek more information. Using the rules of inference, we scrutinise each other's arguments.

As we each ask and respond to questions, we reformulate our arguments. I hope you will reformulate yours to be more like mine. If the dialogue is one in which we are expected to reach agreement, one argument will prevail. If we had been equally persuasive (or equally open-minded) and equally co-operative, this argument might be a consensus. We would reach a single conclusion from an agreed set of premises as shown in Figure 3.5.

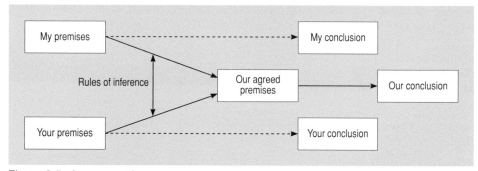

Figure 3.5   **Agreement by consensus**

See The constructivist model of communication p. 77, and Active listening, p. 79.

A consensus is ideal in many situations, of course. But sometimes the point of a discussion is to 'establish the facts'. This is the case in an *inquiry*, in which people want to investigate, in a fairly neutral way, the soundness of premises. The goal is to overcome some lack of knowledge. More co-operative than adversarial, the emphasis of inquiry dialogues is on 'testing' the evidence on which premises rest. However, they are conducted in much the same way as other dialogues: by questioning. The important point about what are known collectively as 'argumentative dialogues' is the use of searching, purposeful questions which reveal one's own and other people's thinking, and 'test' arguments. If you 'win' simply because everyone else has accepted the argument without question, it may be a hollow victory. If poor evidence is accepted without inquiry, no additional knowledge has been gained. Sometimes, such dialogues can be difficult if there are differences in status between people, unless those who are more senior, are alert to the potential difficulties and make it clear that incisive questions are both acceptable and expected. In educational settings, dialogues with tutors and peers are a *vital* part of learning. Such settings provide a 'safe' context for learning how to question.

Developing your thinking

Great importance has been attached to the development of critical thinking by philosophers and educators alike. It is considered essential to the development of personal autonomy and independence: by thinking critically people are in a better position to assess arguments, standards and principles that are presented to them. This is important if people are to protect themselves and others from the consequences of flawed thinking or misinformation.

Critical thinking cannot be taught. It can be encouraged but, like many skills, learners need to *practise*. Only then will it become second nature. We can map the development of critical thinking as a series of steps. These are set out in Table 3.1.

Table 3.1	Developmental stages for critical thinking	
Stage 1	The unreflective thinker	We are unaware of significant problems in our thinking
Stage 2	The challenged thinker	We are becoming aware of problems in our thinking
Stage 3	The beginning thinker	We try to improve our thinking but without regular practice
Stage 4	The practising thinker	We recognise the necessity of regular practice
Stage 5	The advanced thinker	We advance in accordance with our practice
Stage 6	The master thinker	Skilled and insightful thinking become second nature to us

(Source: Paul, 2000)

A strategy for improving your thinking skills

Table 3.2 contains some useful strategies for improving your thinking skills in general and getting used to being *mindful*.

Table 3.2	Useful strategies to develop thinking skills
Use 'wasted' time	Catch yourself wasting time, then use that time to ask yourself: 'What did I think about today?' 'If I had to repeat today what would I do differently?' 'Did I do anything to further my long-term goals?' 'Did I act according to my values?' 'If I spent every day in the same way as today, what would I have accomplished in ten years?'.
Work on problems	Choose a problem to dissect and work on it in free moments: State the problem as precisely as possible. Figure out what kind of problem it is. Set aside problems over which you have no control. Work out the information you need to solve the problem, and seek it. Analyse and interpret the information; draw inferences. Plan your options for action. Evaluate the options, recognising your limitations of money, time and power. Work out a strategy for action. Monitor the implications of your actions; adjust your strategy, analyse your representation of the problem itself, as necessary.
Internalise intellectual standards	Focus in turn on each of the following intellectual standards week by week: clarity, precision, accuracy, depth, breadth, logic, significance. Taking clarity as an example: Are you understanding clearly what you are saying, reading or hearing? Practise stating, elaborating what is meant, giving examples and using analogies, metaphors, diagrams or pictures.
Develop your intellectual traits	Work on one intellectual trait each month, striving to develop: intellectual perseverance, autonomy (recognise how your behaviour is influenced by others), empathy (try to understand the perspective of others), courage and humility (notice when you are being defensive – it is a barrier to learning).

(Source: based on Paul, 2000 and Elder, 2000)

Problem-solving

An important part of a manager's role is to solve problems. Problem-solving involves logic but it also involves *field-specific* knowledge of different kinds. For example, managers need knowledge of the standards that are normally applied to the judgement of statements in management (as opposed to, say, medical research) and knowledge of how much evidence is normally sufficient to solve the problem. Standards and evidence differ according to discipline or profession, and to the nature of the problem.

The basic skills required for problem solving are much the same, however. Beliefs – yours or those of others – must be properly justified in order to distinguish knowledge from opinion. If I say: 'I believe we can save on production costs' you will expect my statement to be supported by a set of reasons that stand up to careful scrutiny by you. The reasons may challenge accepted thinking or existing beliefs – yours or those of others. If they do, then there could be something wrong with the accepted thinking or with the argument put forward. Either way, it means that a person needs to understand how beliefs (and reasons for them) relate to one another. (People who learn by rote rather by trying to understand the connections between statements and the evidence for them often have trouble with this synthesis and cannot solve problems with the 'knowledge' they have acquired!) Listening carefully to the reasons put forward also involves a suspension of belief for a short time in order to avoid *prejudice*. For example, if you have just spent six months working meticulously to reduce production costs, you may not be willing to listen to me when I claim that we can save yet more money.

Not all problems are of the same type, of course. Sometimes logical thinking, critical thinking and existing knowledge are sufficient to solve a problem. Sometimes, a problem cannot be resolved until more evidence has been collected to support statements: this may be the case, for example, in marketing problems where more knowledge of competitors or customers may be required. It is not easy to distinguish between different kinds of problems but the use of logic and questions will often provide the clues for how to solve them.

A method for solving problems

See Logic
p. 60

There is broad agreement on the basic method for solving problems. Some methods are simply more elaborate than others, or more demanding. The one we have chosen is a sound method suitable for solving practical management problems. Called the IDEAL method, it has steps that are easy to remember – each letter of the work IDEAL stands for one part of the process:

> I – Identify the problem. Often a problem is identified for us, but not always. Some problems are accepted as 'facts of life' or 'the ways things are' when, conversely, they can and should be resolved.

D – Define the problem. Identifying a problem and defining it are different. Here is a simple example. The problem might be that certain types of food splatter fat when they are fried in a pan. This identifies the problem. Then we need to *define* the problem by asking *precisely* what it is. Is it that the food splatters when the heat is too high, or that splatters of hot fat burn people, or that the splatters of hot fat travel too far? Each definition of the problem leads to a different approach to a solution: the first definition might lead, simply, to turning the heat down; the second to the development of hand/arm protectors; the third to the development of a device for preventing droplets of fat travelling too far (a splatter guard).

E – Explore alternative approaches. Analyse the problem systematically by breaking it down into its components parts (the heat, the food, the pan, the fat, etc.). If the problem is more abstract then the use of diagrams can be valuable. Another way is to work on a simpler, practical version of it.

A – Act on a plan. Devise a plan for action based on the most promising approaches and work out how to implement the plan.

L – Look at the effects. That is, look at the implications of your plan(s). Are you creating a further problem or problems in the future? Which plan appears to provide the best solution to the problem? (In the example above, the problem solution was the splatter guard. This was an inventor's solution, however. A cook's solution might have been to turn the heat down or to change the cooking method.) Working systematically through potential solutions will reveal the adequacy of the problem definition and approach to a solution: you may have to start again!

(Source: based on Bransford and Stein, 1993)

The problem-solver's checklist

When presented with a problem – or when one presents itself – do these five things:

1   Check the factual accuracy of any information. Scrutinise the evidence for any claim, just as you would if you were to read an advertisement for a photocopier that purported to operate 40% faster. The question that is probably in your mind is: *40% faster than what: the previous model; equivalent models; a much cheaper model?* Sometimes when people provide information they *intend* us to make inferences, e.g. 40% faster than other equivalent models. Take care, too, when people use analogies to set out a problem: they may describe a situation by drawing on the working of a machine, for example. We need to question whether the analogy used is appropriate – it may not be, but it may bias our thinking.

2   Check your own and other's reasoning – is it logical and consistent? Don't forget, though, that while reasoning can be logical and consistent, the premises can be wrong. This is why you need to check the factual accuracy of any statements.

3 Explore assumptions. When we solve problems, often we do not have all the information we need and so we make *assumptions*. Consider the statement: *The staff didn't have time to fulfil the order.* There are a number of assumptions that could be made: the staff were already overworked; they did not have the appropriate equipment to fulfil the order; they were not trained for the task; the order was too large; the order was more complex than usual; the Marketing Manager was too optimistic; there were equipment failures. Each assumption, if acted on without exploration, could lead to a solution that might be wholly ineffective. Make sure you are aware of the assumptions that you are making and that they are reasonable ones.

4 Put pen to paper. Write down the IDEAL steps you took. This should make it easier to spot flaws in your thinking.

5 Seek feedback. Ask others to critique your approach to the problem and your solution. If you are studying a management course, you and your fellow students can learn a great deal from each other – it is a powerful learning technique!

Improve your problem-solving: debug your thinking

There are some widely-recognised sources of bias in thinking and reasoning (and problem-solving). Awareness of these biases and a willingness to avoid them will improve your cognitive skill.

1 **Something out of nothing.** Human beings are natural pattern-spotters – we have a predisposition to impose order, to 'see' relationships between things and make cause-and-effect conclusions. It is fundamental to learning. However, we can too readily discern patterns where none exists.

2 **Too much from too little.** It is easy to misinterpret incomplete and/or unrepresentative data: be aware of the completeness or representativeness of information. It is also easy, when assessing a 'fact' or belief, to simply try to confirm it rather than to refute. This is the same as asking a one-sided question. Some classic examples concern 'rule tests' such as: *If a person is drinking alcohol then that person must be over 18 years old.* We can write this as: If p (drinking alcohol) then q (over 18 years old). To test the rule people are given four cards with the names of drinks on one side and ages on the other. The four cards are presented with the name of a drink or an age showing, as set out in Table 3.3. Note that each drink represents p or *not-p* and each age represents q or *not-q*.

Table 3.3 The display of cards				
Card shows	COKE	BEER	16	23
Card represents	not-p	p	not-q	q

You are allowed to turn over only two cards. Which cards would you choose to turn over to confirm *and* refute the rule? First you should try to *confirm* the rule by testing *p* (that is, turning over the 'beer' card). You want to see if the reverse side shows an age over 18. Then you should try to *refute* the rule by testing *not-q* (that is, by turning over the '16' card). You want to see if the reverse side shows a non-alcoholic drink. If you chose both p ('beer') and q ('23') you would be trying only to confirm the rule rather than to refute it too, since both 'beer' and '23' are 'confirmation' choices. You may need to think about this!

See Logic
p. 60

3 **Seeing what we expect to see.** We often accept information that is consistent with our existing beliefs even if the information is ambiguous or inconsistent. This is because our existing beliefs influence our interpretation of new information. In the worst such cases, our prejudices may make us selective about the information we attend to and bias our interpretation of information.

4 **Seeing what we want to see.** We are inclined to adopt self-serving beliefs about ourselves and to adopt comforting beliefs about the world. Thus we often believe in things that are not true. Some common beliefs of this sort are: that the world is 'just' and that somehow a bad event will be balanced out by a good one; that failure is the result of 'bad luck' while success is attributed to positive personal qualities.

5 **Believing what we are told.** Much of what we know does not come from first-hand experience but from books and from what people tell us. Inevitably, such information is simplified by the writer or speaker who emphasises or underemphasises some aspects of the information to make a point, to entertain, to make the information more plausible, or to make it more understandable to the reader or listener (this book is a good example!). Sources of information are not equally reliable. 'Urban myths' are created by people believing without question what they are told and which may have been passed from person to person, group to group. Always check the accuracy of important information before acting on it.

6 **The imagined experience of others.** We tend to believe that others share our views, habits and beliefs more than they actually do. We overestimate similarities and often continue to do so because people are reluctant to openly question or challenge our views and beliefs. After all, tact is considered a social virtue. People prefer to feign agreement even if, privately, they disagree. In organisations and other group settings, this leads to 'group think' in which maintaining the consensus in the group becomes an important aim, with the result that poor (or disastrous) decisions can be made. When good, clear thinking is required, questioning and argument are vital.

(Source: based on Gilovich, 1993)

CHAPTER 4   WORKING WITH OTHERS

In our working lives we are often required to work in groups on a common task. The goal is to produce an outcome which we could not have produced if we had worked alone. In a management team each member will have something individual to contribute to the completion of a task. The result of these different contributions will be a collective outcome that none of the members could have achieved without the others. When the practice works well, each group member will have contributed and each will recognise that the collective result is an optimum. But that is not the only outcome of group work. A key advantage to working with others is the knowledge that people gain through the process of discussion while working together on a task. This is why, on many formal learning programmes, opportunities are provided for learners to work in groups. But to maximise the benefits learners need to understand how best to work together, to develop communication skills, and to acquire some of the basic techniques that groups can use to ensure that they achieve their goals.

Working in study groups

If you are following a formal course, whatever the arrangements are for group work, there are ways in which you can create additional opportunities to aid your learning. Learners often arrange their own informal face-to-face or electronic study groups in order to work together on their course.

Common activities are:

- discussion of course topics
- discussion of a current assignment question
- review of a previous assignment
- revision for an exam.

Setting up a face-to-face study group

Setting up face-to-face study groups is easy if you are a full-time student who sees fellow students on a regular basis. But there are a variety of ways of studying, and part-time supported distance learning is a popular option. With this system, students may meet formally face to face for regular tutorials, or may be in touch with their tutors and fellow students electronically, or both. The guidelines below can be used in a variety of study contexts, although the importance of each will vary according to your study circumstances.

As early as possible in the course, do the following:

■ Confirm and exchange names and contact details.

■ Find out more about each other's management experience and explore the benefits members expect to gain from the group.

■ Establish a convenient place to meet and agree a date for the first meeting.

■ Agree an outline agenda of suitable items for discussion at the first meeting and a suitable way of working to help the group to gain momentum. (People will need to take on team roles such as convenor, chair, note-taker and so on.)

■ Decide how to communicate, for example by circulating electronically the agenda and any notes taken during meetings.

The first meeting

If people find that the first meeting does not address their needs, they will soon drift away. So it is important to get it right. While informality is a keynote of a study group, a degree of structure will be needed to help it along. The outline agenda will help people to know what the meeting aims to achieve. However, group members must come prepared to contribute actively to the meeting according to their strengths:

■ Accept that you will need time to form yourselves into a fully-functioning group – effective performance may only come after working through stages of uncertainty towards general agreement on how to work together.

■ Structure the agenda to follow a cycle of opening, developing and closing phases – the opening phase should deal with minor matters and help everyone to get on track; the developing phase is where the business should be done; and the closing phase should round off the business and bring the meeting to a satisfactory conclusion. The individual agenda items should follow a similar pattern.

■ Someone will be needed to chair the group with a light touch to help the proceedings along, and someone will be required to take note of any points that should be recorded.

■ Arrange a date for the next meeting; suggest likely items for the agenda and agree how to keep in touch with each other.

Discussing a current assignment

Students are often anxious that discussing an assignment may constitute cheating. However, the risk is slight if assignments require students to draw upon their own experience. Moreover, there is nothing wrong with discussing and clarifying approaches to an assignment in your study group. If you are instructed to produce *individual* work, you must not write your assignment as a group or copy chunks from each other's answers. That would constitute cheating. When you write your assignment answer, you must do so alone.

Communication

The foundation for working with others is communication. Clearly, it is hard *not* to communicate – even saying nothing communicates something! We all communicate but do we know what communication is, and what it means to communicate? The basis for improving communication skills is knowing something about how communication 'works'. A general definition of communication is 'social interaction through messages'. People use the term communication in many ways ranging from, for example, the rate of transmission of information through a channel, to interactions that involve intention and understanding.

The information theory model of communication

The most widely-known perspective on communication is based on information theory, developed by Shannon and Weaver (1949). This approach has had a huge impact on the design of telephone and computer systems, and also on how people view the communication process. The basic idea is shown in Figure 4.1.

The model has three basic components:

1   A sender or source of an encoded message – for example, a person or a television camera.

2   A medium or channel of transmission – for example, signals running along cables or sound waves travelling through the air.

3   A receiver which decodes the message – for example, a person, a television or a radio receiver.

An additional feature is noise in the channel which restricts the amount of information that can be transmitted. Imperfections or noise in the telephone wires between two handsets can distort sound as it travels to the receiver; other people in a room may interfere with the exchange of messages between two people face to face.

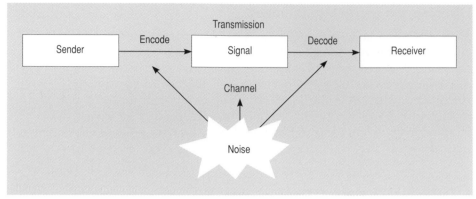

Figure 4.1   **A simple model of communication**

How the model works

1   The sender (source) wants someone else (receiver) to know or do something.

2   This information can only be conveyed to the receiver as some type of message.

3   The message is encoded by the sender (source). It is structured into a form of code, such as language, gesture or action, designed to get the message across.

4   The message is transmitted through the particular channel – face-to-face, remote, electronic, textual – that best serves the purpose.

5   The message passes from the sender to the receiver. The message is now out of the control of the sender and may be influenced by noise in the environment.

6   The receiver attempts to decode the message by deciphering the code that runs through the words, action or gesture that were sent by the source.

7   The message has reached its destination when the receiver attributes meaning to it and acts accordingly.

This traditional model of communication has since been modified to acknowledge the roles of redundancy and feedback.

■   The certainty of receiving a message is increased if some elements of the message are not critical to understanding. About 30 per cent of the words in any English language text could be eliminated, yet most readers would still understand it. This is referred to as redundancy.

■   Communication is an interaction between two parties, both of whom have sending and receiving roles, rather than a one-way process. Sending and receiving may be contemporaneous rather than sequential. (For example, in a face-to-face encounter, a receiver may smile or frown while listening to a speaker/sender.) This is known as feedback.

The information theory model of communication is easy to apply and useful in some contexts where the sender and receiver are very similar. With people, this means they must share certain rules, beliefs and presuppositions. But this is not always the case. The model does not address issues of meaning, understanding or interpretation. It does not guide us when we are trying to develop messages for recipients who are different from us, for example, those who belong to different cultures or who have different assumptions or perspectives from our own.

The constructivist model of communication

The constructivist model of communication is so called because it sees people as constructing mental images and models which they use to understand and make sense of the world. Language gives form to our experiences because, as we learn language, we develop a system of categories or names to describe our perceptions. Each person constructs their understanding by fitting labels to raw experience. One person's constructions will differ from those of another person. Unlike the information theory model, the constructivist model places central emphasis on the differences between individuals.

Does this mean that we all possess 'separate realities'? The answer is yes, but there are limits. The 'raw data' of our experiences are quite similar – physically, water is water wherever you live, although its significance and use are influenced by ethnic culture. A common language is usually a feature of an ethnic culture, so people learn and use the same language to construct their understanding of the world.

Of course, people do not always share precisely the same experiences – a person who works in a small organisation will experience something different from a person working in a large one. And when they do have 'the same' experience, their views of it may differ. Consider shopping, for example. Do you love it or do you regard it as a grim chore? When we meet people from other cultures, differences in perspectives and meaning can be a lot greater. So what guidance does constructivism give us on communication? It suggests we need empathy – the use of one's intellect and emotions to understand another person's view.

Six steps to empathy

The following list sets out six steps to achieve empathy:

1 **Assume difference** This means being actively vigilant and seeking out differences in how another individual views a situation.

2 **Know self** To be receptive to another, we need to realise that our own view of a situation is just that – a view – and that there may be alternative views that will enrich our knowledge or understanding.

3 **Suspend self** To be receptive to another person's views, we need to put our own ideas aside and try to enter the world of the other person. This is known as switching frames of reference.

4 **Allow guided judgement** Because we will not be sure that we have understood the other person's viewpoint, we need to be guided by feedback on our understanding. This is likely to involve asking the other person questions like 'So your view is...' and allowing the person to correct us.

5 **Allow empathetic experience** With the information given, we can then construct the alternative view that the other person holds. This knowledge is valuable when, for example, we need to predict how the person will respond to a future message or situation.

6 **Re-establish self** We can now return to our own view of a situation, but it is highly likely that our own view will have changed because we have incorporated new knowledge of and from another. In attempting to understand someone else's view we have extended our knowledge, whether this be social, emotional, cultural, practical or scientific.

(Source: based on Bennett, 1987)

Seeking to understand another's view in this way is the basis for constructing a dialogue in which mental models, understanding and meanings can be shared. We are then better able to choose the most appropriate behaviour to convey our intended meanings. We are also better able to interpret the intended meanings of messages from others.

Choosing between models of communication

The information theory model of communication comes from engineering and was developed to address problems such as how noise and limited channel capacity influence the sending and receiving of messages. It assumes similarity between sender and receiver. In contrast, the constructivist model draws our attention to the process of how we form categories and create knowledge from our experiences. It assumes that people are different and reminds us that others may interpret our words and actions differently from how we had intended.

Is each model equally useful in communication? In assessing this, we can think of a vertical continuum between the two theories. This is shown in Figure 4.2.

The bottom end of the vertical continuum in the diagram represents the assumption of similarity. The top end represents the assumption of difference. It is safe to assume similarity when we are considering identical machines sending information. As we travel up the continuum, we can think of increasing degrees of difference between people. An identical twin is likely to be more similar than a close friend, and a close friend will be more

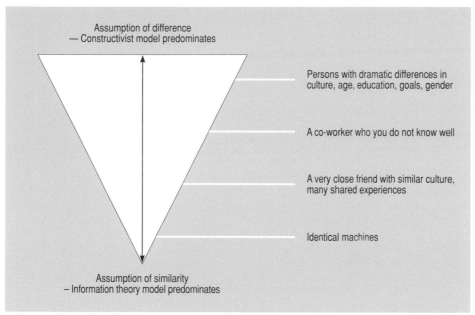

Assumption of difference
— Constructivist model predominates

Persons with dramatic differences in culture, age, education, goals, gender

A co-worker who you do not know well

A very close friend with similar culture, many shared experiences

Identical machines

Assumption of similarity
– Information theory model predominates

Figure 4.2   When to assume similarity or difference

similar than a colleague or co-worker. At the top end of the continuum we can think of people from very different cultures from our own.

The width of the inverted triangle represents the *effort* required to achieve good communication in those situations. Because of the greater effort and time required to communicate effectively and empathetically with people who are very different to ourselves, we do not want to go any 'higher' than necessary in any situation. But judgements about how much effort to put into communication will need to take account of the greater effort needed to correct misunderstandings and repair poor relationships if the initial effort proves insufficient. There will be many occasions in your life as a student and as a manager when you will need to make such judgements.

Active listening

Listening is essential to communication. Much of our listening is half-hearted. Attention can wander so that the mind leaps to the next question, or makes judgements before the other person finishes what they are saying. When working in groups, we are often so concerned with getting our own views across that we do not make the space to hear what others are saying. There are many workplace situations where active listening is particularly important. Examples include situations where you are: giving or receiving instructions; disagreeing with a colleague; discussing a problem; coaching or mentoring a new colleague; conducting an appraisal interview.

Active listening means:

■ giving whole-hearted attention to the person speaking

- demonstrating, or checking, that you have understood
- not doing anything else!

Reasons for using active listening are:

- to avoid misunderstandings
- to build relationships by giving respect to and demonstrating acceptance of the other person
- to encourage people to say more and to speak frankly
- to enable people to become clearer in their own thoughts about an issue, by allowing them to articulate what is on their minds.

Guidelines for active listening

1 **Give people your attention** Face them and make eye contact. Indicate that you have *time* for them too.

2 **Be ready to paraphrase or 'play back' what they have said** Use expressions like 'So you are saying...' or 'I'm hearing you say that...'. Use summaries to check your understanding and to demonstrate this to the other person.

3 **Use questions if you do not understand** 'Can you say a bit more about...?' or 'I'm not sure I understood the point about...'. Do not ignore things you do not understand. That can simply infuriate the other person.

4 **Acknowledge the other person's feelings** This may be included in your paraphrase or can be done separately, for example 'I can see that you feel very angry about that'. Acknowledging feelings can be a way of demonstrating your understanding of the situation.

5 **Encourage if the other person appears uncertain** Ask open-ended questions such as 'So what happened next?' or make supportive comments 'It sounds very difficult'. Simply nod and say 'Uh–huh'. Silence can also encourage people to say more.

6 **Do not react or respond in other ways until it is clear that the other person has finished** Do not leap in with an answer or tell someone that their worries are unnecessary; both these reactions are ways of being dismissive. This may be difficult if you are hurt, frustrated or angry about what is being said.

The degree of difficulty you experience in using these guidelines will be affected by the situation in which you are using them. The more tense the situation, the harder you will have to work to use these principles. Active listening can also be inhibited by unequal relationships. When one party considers the other to have some kind of power or authority over them, it can be harder for them to feel comfortable enough to communicate openly and honestly.

Communicating assertively

Many people have difficulties explaining their viewpoint, communicating unpopular messages or simply saying 'No'. Techniques of assertive communication can help by enabling people to communicate effectively in ways which are more easily heard by others.

What is assertiveness?

Assertive behaviour means standing up for yourself, but in ways which respect the rights of others. This distinguishes it from *aggression* (fight) which involves violating the rights of others, and from *evasion* (flight) which involves respecting the rights of others at the expense of your own.

Contexts where assertiveness is useful:

- stating your own views
- disagreeing with others' views
- making a request
- refusing a request
- offering criticism
- responding to criticism
- giving praise
- responding to praise.

Scripting an assertive response

Often the reason why people have difficulties in responding assertively lies in their lack of technique. *Scripting* is an assertive technique that can be particularly useful. Its elements are the building blocks of assertive communication:

1 **Prepare** Clarify your purpose and ensure that you approach the other person and the situation in a positive frame of mind. If you can't do this, then the best thing is probably to pause and allow time for the situation to calm a little.

2 **Identify the problem and state how you feel and your wants** This involves explaining to the other person what you perceive the problem to be, how you feel, what you want and what consequences are likely to follow if these needs are not met:

Observation	When you do [specific action]
Feelings	I feel [unwanted feelings]
Needs	I want or don't want [specific things] because [give reasons]

Consequences If you do what I want [positive outcomes] and if you don't do what I want [negative outcomes].

3 **Respect the other person** Recognise their needs by showing *empathy* with their situation: 'I realise you have put a lot of work into this'. Seek their views: 'Please tell me what you think...'. If you include some form of recognition or acknowledgement in your four-point statement your views are likely to be better received and your needs are more likely to be met.

Limits to assertiveness

Many communication techniques have their roots in European or North American culture. They are based on the belief in self-determination and focus on one-to-one communication. As such, these techniques have limitations:

■ They take no account of *structural and political imbalances* in organisations or society at large, for example in hierarchical organisations a manager may not expect someone in a clerical position to be assertive about their needs.

■ *Dominant or powerful groups* may interpret assertion from members of other groups as aggressive even if no hostility or offence is intended. Gender, ethnicity and disability can all affect interactions in this way.

■ Individuals may be encouraged to take on responsibility for *righting wrongs that are outside their control.*

■ Assertiveness can ignore *collective* virtues such as the solidarity of working for a cause.

■ Some cultures have more respect for *tact* than honesty and may expect deference on both sides.

Assertiveness may not be universally appropriate.

Negotiating

In any group situation, understanding the principles of negotiation can assist the group's functioning and will help you to achieve satisfactory outcomes for all. A key feature of successful negotiation is the attempt to take an all-round view of the desired outcomes and to seek to understand the perspectives of others that affect their approach. Successful negotiators try to find *win–win* solutions in which both sides benefit and to avoid *positional bargaining* in which each side becomes locked into apparently entrenched and escalating demands.

Four things that assist negotiations

1 **Separate the people from the problem** Tease out the relationship issues from the substantive issue to be negotiated.

2 **Focus on interests not positions** Try to identify the more general interests and concerns of the parties involved rather than specific positions.

3 **Generate options for mutual gain** There is no one right solution. Search for alternatives and mutually advantageous outcomes. Be prepared to develop and explore innovative options and suspend judgement until late in the process.

4 **Agree criteria for solutions** Try to establish a set of essential and desirable criteria that the outcome of the negotiation should meet.

Behaviours that affect negotiations

In any negotiation, there are behaviours that hinder and those that help the negotiation. Skilled negotiators avoid the following negative behaviours.

■ **Irritators** Words and phrases which add nothing to the content and serve to irritate the other parties should not be used.

■ **Defence/attack spirals** Sequences of attacking statements and aggressive defences are unhelpful.

■ **Argument dilution** Don't clutter your argument by including too many points or digressions. Identify and adhere to the main, strong points of your case.

■ **Behaviour chains** In behaviour chains someone asks a question, summarises and puts some information into the proceedings, all in one statement. Others do not know which bit of the input to respond to and get confused.

■ **Counter proposals** When one party immediately responds to a proposal from the other side with a proposal of their own, little is achieved. The effect is to signal that 'I haven't listened to a word you have said'.

Skilled negotiators demonstrate the following positive behaviours.

■ **Test understanding and summarise** Check that everyone understands the things in the same way and clarify the structure of any agreement. These behaviours will also help you to build relationships by demonstrating that you have listened and that you appreciate what others have been saying.

■ **Flag or signal** Tell people what sort of behaviour you are going to use next, for example 'Could I ask you...' followed by the question. This is easy to analyse and indicates that you are communicating clearly. It also controls the listening and perception of the audience.

- **Ask lots of questions** This helps you to identify other options to create a win–win situation and gives a deeper understanding of the other parties' constraints.

- **Explain how they feel** Openness helps to create trust and enhances relationships between people.

- **Review their performance** Reflection after the negotiation with a colleague will help you to identify the strengths and weaknesses of your approach.

Dealing with difficulties

If your negotiation seems to be failing because someone else is being difficult:

- **Do not react** Deal with *your* behaviour, not your opponent's. Keep focused on the desired outcomes and concentrate on securing agreement.

- **Look at the situation from the other person's viewpoint** It is harder for a person to be hostile if you are listening to them and acknowledging what they say and feel.

- **Do not reject – reframe** Take whatever the other party says and direct it against the problem. Try to engage them in a problem-solving approach by offering new ways of looking at the problem.

- **Make it easy to say 'Yes'** This is more than offering an attractive deal. Involve the other party in crafting the agreement. Look beyond immediate interests and seek to meet more intangible needs, such as recognition. Help them to save face and find ways of presenting the solution as a victory.

- **Make it hard to say 'No'** Educate the other party about the costs of saying 'No'; warn, do not threaten; exercise restraint and make sure there is always a path to 'Yes'.

Giving and receiving feedback

We are often asked to provide feedback on other people's performance of various activities. As a manager, you need to give feedback to those who work for you and with you. As a management student, you may also be asked to provide feedback to your peers. Many people find giving appropriate feedback difficult. There are a number of techniques that you can use to help others to absorb the messages you are trying to communicate.

Being positive

Here are some tips on giving positive feedback:

■ **Give praise where it is deserved** Many of us live in quite negative cultures. From schooldays we are conditioned to believe that offering criticism means telling other people what is wrong with their work or their actions. This is not so. In literary criticism you are asked to highlight the strengths *and* weaknesses of a book or a play. So should it be with criticism in management. Often managers spend a lot of time telling people who report to them what they should have done, and neglect to offer praise for the things that were done well. People are much more willing to hear justifiable negative feedback if they are confident that you will also praise them when they have done a good job.

■ **Be positive about yourself** Being a manager can be an isolating experience in many organisations. Many new managers are promoted from a team into a management position and find themselves with pressures from above without the supportive network of colleagues they have been used to. It is important to recognise any sense of isolation and develop awareness of when you are feeling (or being) defensive because of this. It is important to develop support mechanisms, which will enable you to deal assertively (rather than aggressively or passively) with your colleagues.

■ **Give compliments** As a general rule, people are receptive to compliments. Look for opportunities to praise a person's work.

Giving feedback

Although we do not always do it, giving positive feedback is relatively easy and rewarding. Most of us like to be praised. When you have to communicate something more negative to colleagues, however, it can feel much more difficult. Without preparation, you may offer inappropriate comments and may feel anxious. Here are some tips:

■ Give positive feedback first.

■ Say things in a supportive way. Soften the negatives.

■ Criticise only behaviour that can be changed.

■ Suggest ways in which performance might be improved.

■ Place the feedback in the context of a relationship.

■ Make your feedback well-timed, clear and direct.

(Source: Piccinin and Mason, 1991)

Receiving feedback

Receiving feedback can be as difficult as providing feedback. However, feedback is a rich source of learning if we are able to handle it well. Some tips for receiving feedback are:

- Listen actively.

- Ask for precision. 'Who said that?' 'What was the specific behaviour?' 'When?' 'What are the consequences?'

- Agree/disagree with criticism. Acknowledge what is true. State your disagreement with anything you consider invalid.

- State what you have learned for future action or behaviour from the feedback.

- Give information to correct misunderstandings.

- Set limits. Tell the critic how you want to receive feedback if you have been criticised inappropriately.

(Source: Piccinin and Mason, 1991)

Working with others in a computer-mediated environment

The fundamental mechanisms of learning and communication are the same whichever way a person learns. However, the *medium* of learning and communication has an impact. There are many different ways in which people are able to work and learn together using computer-mediated technologies. Some examples include: computer-mediated conferences hosted by the internet or delivered using specific commercial software packages, internet forums and even simple email communication. The advice and guidance which follows is intended to be general in nature and not specific to any particular technology or software platform.

'E-learning' in its most basic form is simply a way of delivering educational or training materials electronically. It may or may not involve interaction with the materials, or support from tutors. But learning via computer-mediated conferencing and computer-supported collaborative learning can be incorporated into courses of study whether these are delivered predominantly online or face to face, or as distance-learning programmes. Many informal learners also make use of computer-mediated forums, including specialist conferences that professional bodies make available to their members.

Participating in a computer-mediated discussion or conference

The computer-mediated environment provides the opportunity for learners to socialise, exchange information, work co-operatively, or work together in a fully collaborative way. *Collaborative learning* refers to the active construction of personal knowledge as learners work with and discuss their understanding of concepts, and transform their understanding as a result. *Co-operation* refers to working together. Both co-operation and social interaction are essential, not only to achieve a goal, but for people to gain one another's trust to be able to collaborate (just as in any team or group situation). The extent to which learners will be able to work collaboratively will depend on the purpose of the computer-mediated facility provided and the size of groups. Facilities may range from large-scale computer-mediated conferences to smaller areas dedicated to group work.

Advantages of the medium

A particular advantage of computer-mediated communication is that it can allow *asynchronous* communication between two or more people. You can send a message at whatever time suits you. The message will be delivered almost instantly, but people can respond when it suits them. In this way a cumulative dialogue on a topic can be built up and be available for participants to read and re-read as and when they wish.

In many ways it is easier to participate in a computer-mediated discussion than in a face-to-face one. You have more time for a considered reply and personal characteristics, such as shyness, are not obvious. Indeed, it is a surprisingly friendly medium for communication. And as the informality of computer-mediated interaction is somewhere between writing and speaking, you do not need to spend undue time in polishing your reply provided that it is clear.

In order to benefit from a computer-mediated discussion, you must join in frequently. As in a face-to-face meeting, if you miss an opportunity to make a contribution at the appropriate time, the discussion will move on and the chance of useful interaction will be lost. *Timely* contributions are needed to make the activity worthwhile.

Rules for computer-mediated discussions or conferences

As in any social situation, there are certain rules that people need to respect, to ensure the smooth running of a computer-mediated conference or discussion. Someone may act as controller or moderator of the conference, to introduce the participants, to get the conference going and to keep it on track. Others may undertake roles such as timekeeper or summariser. All such conferences are dependent on active participation. If people do not join in, then a learning opportunity is missed.

All participants need to be aware of the need to follow protocol, make their messages easy to handle, and observe the rules of courtesy. The following lists provide some guidance in these areas.

Protocol

- Think about the purpose of your intended message, about your intended audience and about the likely impact of your message. Decide on the most appropriate medium for it – email, a computer-mediated conference, conventional mail or a face-to-face meeting.

- Use email to communicate speedily with people who must take action; copy your message 'for information' to those who should know about (but not act on) its contents.

- Use computer-mediated conferences to communicate publicly with conference members and to encourage public responses.

- Be strict about message content – social messages belong in conferences for socialising and not in task-oriented ones.

- Use the appropriate 'Reply' button. Decide beforehand whether to reply solely to the originator of a message; to the originator and to those who also received the message; or to the whole conference when the message originated within a conference.

- In group environments support and encourage others ('Good point. I hadn't thought of that.' 'Are there any other views?' 'I'd like to support Mary's point...', and so on) to help the interaction along.

Making messages easy to handle

- Give each new message (one that is not a reply) a short, informative title.

- Keep the message length short to help the reader (about one screen as a maximum).

- Use attachments for longer contributions, giving a brief description of the attachment in the message text.

Courtesies

- Think carefully before you 'forward' messages to others. If in doubt, seek permission from the originator to avoid potential embarrassment.

- If you use a quotation, then follow the normal rules and acknowledge your source. Copyright applies to electronic media as it does to other media.

- Understand the importance of 'netiquette'. Although the style of messages tends to be more informal and immediate than in much traditional writing, common courtesy and good manners apply as much in a computer-mediated environment as elsewhere.

Development of computer-mediated learning

Learners appear to go through a series of developmental phases when they work together in large computer-mediated conferences, moderated by tutors. Phases move from getting to grips with the electronic medium through to learning independently of tutors.

1 **Access and motivation** Feeling comfortable and competent with the medium is the first step, together with a willingness to expend time and effort.

2 **Computer-mediated socialisation** A sense of belonging grows. Establishing norms so that trust can develop is important. The lack of physical cues and clues – body language, voice intonation and so on – can be both a barrier and an advantage. It may take longer to get to know people in a computer-mediated environment, but there are sufficiently few cues and clues to trigger prejudices.

3 **Information exchange** Co-operative tasks are achieved by information exchange. The information exchanged may be from course learning materials, or from external sources such as internet websites.

4 **Knowledge construction** Participants take more control, relying less on the tutor, and start to become *authors* rather than transmitters of information.

5 **Development** Participants take control of their own learning and that of their group, developing *metacognitive* knowledge.

(Source: Salmon, 2002)

These stages have been idealised to help tutors and, in practice, they may not be so evident. What happens in a carefully monitored computer-mediated learning environment may be less apparent in such a group working outside the bounds of formal education.

See Knowledge types and processes, p. 8.

Critical success factors in computer-mediated learning

Any group of people that wants to work well and achieve its goals will pay attention to processes and protocol. Critical success factors in small-group computer-mediated working include the following:

■ team formation as an activity in its own right

■ competence among team members

■ shared understanding of the goal

■ structuring the activities needed and attending to process

■ mutual respect and trust

■ creation and organisation of shared work areas

■ clear lines of responsibility

- selective use of outsiders

- realisation that collaboration ends when the goal is achieved.

Most of these may strike you as essential to professional team working. What underlies most of the critical success factors is *responsibility*. This does not change in a formal learning situation in which the group goal is knowledge gain. Learners often rely too heavily on the tutor and can be passive. Taking responsibility for your own learning and its outcomes is essential to the success of the *group*. It will mean making use of your tutors as knowledge resources and as guides, rather than as *the* source of knowledge and procedures. Reluctance by learners to make this shift in perspective can lead to resistance to peer collaboration. But there are other reasons for resistance too.

Resistance to collaborating with peers

Learners may feel uncomfortable with or resist working collaboratively in computer-mediated groups for various reasons:

- If learners are following a formal course of study they may think of collaboration with peers as cheating rather than gaining from being exposed to different perspectives and approaches.

- Learners may regard collaborative work as an additional course requirement rather than an integrated component.

- Computer-mediated working takes time.

- Computer-mediated working requires more organisation than learners anticipate.

See Organising computer-mediated group work, p. 91.

- Lack of attention to trust-building early on can prevent a group 'getting off the ground' or working productively.

- If only one or two individuals in a group are motivated to collaborate, the group is unlikely to succeed.

(Source: Tyler *et al.*, 2001)

On formal courses of learning, tutor support can help learners to surmount barriers and resistance. Computer-mediated collaborative group working offers you an alternative approach which you should try for yourself. You should make time, make efforts to ensure the success of the collaboration, and then judge for yourself whether this more overtly social form of learning enhances your knowledge and understanding. It is worth trying more than once or twice: every group is different according to the experience, capabilities and social skills of individual members. The needs and behaviour of a group are also influenced by its task and context.

Computer-mediated working and stress

Working collaboratively in a computer-mediated environment can be stressful. By now, you can probably make an intelligent guess as to what the main sources of stress are. We have just seen that when working collaboratively learners cannot rely on tutors as much as they do in more traditional forms of education. Consider, too, that most computer-mediated work is *asynchronous* – learners are contributing at different times. This is ideal if people are learning in their own time (as part-time learners) or are geographically distant and live in different time zones. But it does mean that responses to messages will not be immediate. Research shows that stress in pairs of learners results from:

- having to take greater responsibility for their own learning

- waiting for responses

- the pressure of tight timescales for 'cycles' of sharing and responding.

(Source: Allan and Lawless, 2003)

Causes of stress are likely to be similar for learners in larger groups. A stress *reducer* that has been identified among groups of four learners is the ability to organise.

Organising computer-mediated group work

An advantage of working collaboratively in a computer-mediated environment is that the medium is primarily an *asynchronous* one, making it possible for members of a group to contribute to a task or discussion at different times. However this distinct advantage can quickly turn to a disadvantage unless the group is organised, co-ordinated and managed. Groups working in such an environment need a greater level of organisation than those that work face to face.

First, we will assume that you and your fellow group members:

- have a common task or objective, you see yourselves *as* a group distinct from other groups

- are interdependent to some degree – your task or learning goal is not achievable by any one person in the group

- have agreed the values and norms which are going to govern your interactions and conduct – for example, that everyone will have an opportunity to contribute and that common standards of politeness will prevail.

Now what do you do? As managers or aspiring managers, you probably already know the answer! Group members need to ask the question: 'How much management and by whom?'.

The group will need to do five things:

1 **Generate a list which links individuals with tasks and responsibilities** This will mean developing a shared understanding of what is needed to achieve the task or outcome the group has been set. To do this, all members of the group must do some background work as individuals, they must know what kinds of roles are required, and they must all have some knowledge of their strengths and weaknesses in these roles – or graciously be prepared to find out!

2 **Schedule the tasks** This also involves understanding the overall task and agreeing when stages need to be completed in order to meet the deadline – a deadline should be agreed if none has been imposed externally.

3 **Agree on what will be collectively acceptable as the outcome** This may be a document or a learning outcome.

4 **Work out a process for the task** The medium will have an impact here for several reasons, primarily the asynchronous nature of the medium and the constraints of the software you are using. When you need to work on documents, some software may allow you to create communal folders, work on a single stored document, and so on. In other cases, files may have to be circulated and exchanged along with messages. Decisions then need to be made about how individual group members should work on such documents (simultaneously or consecutively) and whether they are best circulated as attachments or in the body of a message.

5 **Work out a process for working together** In a face-to-face situation, a chairperson or co-ordinator will ensure that everyone has an opportunity to contribute; it will be clear when decisions have been made and, usually, it will be evident whether the project or task is on schedule. When working in a computer-mediated environment, things are a little different. People can indicate their presence and progress only by posting electronically a message or document, so a *synchronising structure* needs to be adopted by the group.

The best way for a group to get started is for members to meet face to face first. If this is not possible a round of telephone calls or emails can be organised, and one person may need to assume the role of temporary co-ordinator. Failing that, everything will have to be discussed in the computer-mediated environment. It is likely that the fifth activity mentioned in the list – working out a process for working together – will be given least attention until, that is, the group hits its first crisis! One way of adding a synchronising structure to asynchronous collaboration is known as the virtual circle procedure.

The virtual circle

First, the group must break down its planned discussions or deliberations into stages or rounds. Then it must decide on a time frame for each round – say, four days, although some rounds may need to be longer than others depending on the nature of the discussion. Each day should be reserved for new contributions. The virtual circle sequence then operates as follows:

1   On the pre-agreed 'start' date, the chairperson (or co-ordinator) posts an initial message asking for discussion.

2   All group members contribute to the discussion, every day if possible, posting new points and responding to those posted by others.

3   To mark the end of the discussion period, the chairperson summarises the discussion and (if appropriate) proposes a decision.

4   Each group member responds to the summary and the proposed decision if there is one, by voting or by consensus. The chairperson then notifies members of any result.

(Source: based on Johnson-Lenz and Johnson-Lenz, 1991, modified by Einon, 1997)

Groups must incorporate these virtual circles into their task schedule. They can be set up as milestones – dates by which events such as decisions or contributions must happen. This strategy is commonly used in project management. An example is shown in Table 4.1.

Table 4.1 Example of milestones for a decision and a task					
February 1–8			**February 9–21**		
Period for achieving Decision A			**Period for achieving Task B**		
Discussion period	Voting period	Notification period	Work period	Submission period	Notification period
6 days	1 day	1 day	10 days	2 days	1 day
Feb 1–6	Feb 7	Feb 8	Feb 9–18	Feb 19–20	Feb 21

(Source: Einon, 1997)

Like all tasks in which contributions need to be synchronised, there is an administrative overhead. This is much better appreciated by group members when the virtual circle and milestones are used.

Practical tips for computer-mediated group working

■   **Roles** Successful groups often include individuals with roles such as chairperson, secretary, progress chaser and mediator. Each group needs to decide which roles are required and to allocate them. More than one role can be allocated to a person; roles can also be rotated.

■   **Making contributions** Holidays and work routines may prevent some group members contributing as often as others. It is best to address these issues early on. Such individuals may be happy to contribute more at other times, or to take on a group role which involves less computer-based work, for example, seeking outside help or information, or constructing summaries. Discuss expectations about how often group members will enter the computer-mediated environment and make contributions.

■ **Dealing with non-contribution** Decide on the sanctions that will be put into place in cases where an individual does not contribute. Should non-contributors be allowed to remain in the group? Should they be allowed to share the outcome of the collaboration – particularly if the task is an assessed assignment? You may need to discuss this with your course tutors.

■ **Tolerance and support** Group members will differ in their abilities and social confidence. Failure to contribute may reflect a person's lack of belief in their own ability or their social shyness. Groups need to be supportive and caring, and to avoid exclusion. Remember, helping another person to understand something that you do already will help you to understand it more deeply, will identify areas that you need to work on yourself *and* will fix it better in your memory. (It is said that if you want to learn – teach!) Conversely, if you lack confidence in your abilities, find out what happens when you say, explicitly: 'I'm not sure I understand. Please could someone explain?' It would be unusual if someone *didn't* offer their help.

■ **Professionalism** Adhere to high standards of behaviour. Be professional and friendly – the computer-mediated medium is quite informal. Use good-natured humour if it helps social interaction but take care, especially if you are working in a cross-cultural group. Avoid causing offence, and be prepared to explain your jokes!

■ **Individual effort** The essence of collaboration is the construction of new knowledge. To do this, each group member should be prepared to work at an *individual* level at appropriate times, both before and during the group work. This is because each person will need to make *active*, real contributions based on their knowledge and understanding, and not simply *react* to others. Collaborative learning is not an alternative to individual learning: learners present their individual understanding of something to a group, group members respond, explore, question, critique, reinterpret and so on. During this process individuals reconstruct the personal knowledge *that they acquired in their individual learning sessions*. Think of these individual learning components as preparation for collaborating and contributing.

■ **Plan B!** Technology is great – till it breaks (and it always seems to). Always have an alternative plan to ensure communication does not break down completely when technology fails. Use telephone, fax, email or face-to-face communication *in emergencies*, and exchange sufficient information (early on) for those routes to be used rapidly when needed. To be fair to your fellow group members you should not agree to work in a computer-mediated environment if you know you are going to experience on-going technical difficulties that will also make life difficult for them. Plan Bs are for exceptional circumstances.

■ **Study the software** The software you are using will influence the way you work. Look at what your software supports are before making firm plans about how you intend to collaborate on documents. If you have to work on the same document individually but simultaneously, label each version of the electronic file clearly.

■ **Use your judgement** When you or your fellow group members have found new information or material, evaluate its status before using it – does it constitute a personal opinion or is it the work of an acknowledged expert? Question both source and content. Academic journals, including those covering management, usually have a peer review system by which articles and papers are scrutinised by others in the field. This acts as a quality control mechanism – but isn't fail-safe! Other material may be very useful but you must exercise your critical judgement about its quality and how you will make use of it – for illustration purposes, perhaps.

Techniques for group work

A key advantage of group work is not simply that several people can achieve more than one. Effective group work benefits from bringing together different experiences and perspectives. Many techniques for group work are structured ways of drawing on these.

Brainstorming

Brainstorming is a way of quickly generating ideas, usually in a group setting.

Two principles apply to the process:

1 **The separation between being creative and being judgemental** The generation of the ideas must be kept separate from the assessment of the ideas. It is sensible to keep the assessment until after the creative (the brainstorming) phase.

2 **Quantity breeds quality** There are two parts to this principle. First, the generation of ideas is cumulative: one idea will stimulate another which will stimulate another and so on. Second, as good ideas are rare, the more ideas that are generated, the more likely it is that the collection will contain a good idea.

These principles lead to four practical rules:

1 **No criticism** This rule is the most important one. There must be no criticism of an idea. This rule is just a particular expression of the first principle, the postponement of judgement. The prohibition of criticism applies both to what is said and what is signalled by gestures or other actions.

2   **Freewheel** The expression of ideas must be uninhibited. Whatever comes to mind should be welcomed, including random thoughts, images that are funny, ideas or possibilities that in other meetings or circumstances would be unwelcome, ideas that are apparently irrelevant as well as those that seem to be relevant, and so on.

3   **The more ideas, the better** The more ideas there are, the more likely it is that there will be one or more good ones.

4   **Hitch-hike** The brainstormers must look for opportunities to build on each other's contributions. One idea 'hitches a ride' from another. Hitch-hiking will improve the quality of the ideas and also contribute to a sense of team working.

A helpful process

A brainstorming session can be enjoyable and productive. The process will require the brainstormers to set aside what may be a normally cautionary (or inhibited) approach to proposals and ideas. At a first meeting, in particular, the manager or co-ordinator must ensure that there are no barriers to the process of generation. The ideas will flow when there is a shared sense that the purpose of the session is to generate ideas. Once the participants have experienced the process, then that shared sense will be in place for subsequent sessions.

Running a brainstorming session

See Brainstorming p. 95.

When running a brainstorming session, well before the meeting draft a statement of the problem and choose the participants. Five to ten people are likely to provide sufficient diversity and energy in the session. If there are too many participants a session becomes difficult to run. Closer to the meeting, perhaps two or three days before, circulate the statement of the problem, the background to it, and a note on the running of the session, including the four brainstorming rules. The session will require a facilitator and a recorder. Think about finding people to take on these roles. In a first meeting, you might be the facilitator; the recorder's job can be passed from one participant to another during the session.

Running the session

Begin the session with a review of the brainstorming process. Remind the participants of the four rules, particularly the prohibition of criticism. Then run a warm-up session. Distribute a statement of a problem (which is unrelated to the main problem) and nominate a recorder. Allow some time to clear up any uncertainties about the statement of the problem. Allow the recorder time to prepare and initiate the warm-up. Let the participants become familiar with the process of calling out ideas as they occur to them. The recorder's job will be to record every idea (including quiet asides, jokes, etc.) in the contributor's own words or in an agreed rephrasing. As the warm-up continues, the contributors will learn to speak their ideas clearly and to pace their contributions to the recorder's ability to record them. It is usually best to confine the recorder to the task of recording; in a small group, though, the recorder may also be able to contribute. Let the warm-up run for 10 minutes. At the close, give the participants a chance to talk about the experience.

Then initiate the main session. Follow the procedure that you followed for the warm-up. Close the session when the ideas cease to flow. In any case, close after 30 minutes.

As a separate activity, collate, sort and evaluate the ideas. Provide the participants with copies of the results.

Clustering ideas

Clustering is a way of grouping different ideas so that the different groups, or clusters, exhibit themes or generalisations. Clustering is a way of handling the many ideas that may have resulted from a brainstorming session.

See Brainstorming p. 95.

The process

1   The various ideas are written onto separate cards or adhesive notes. Each card or note should carry just one idea. The idea could be an issue, a possible course of action, an idea for a product or service, and so on.

2   The cards are formed into groups or clusters. The clustering can be done by one person, but it may be more productive for two, three or four people to share the task. The cards are attached to a tabletop, wall or whiteboard.

3   Clusters of similar ideas are formed, and each cluster is given an agreed label.

4   There is no ownership of the clusters or labels. As the group members study the cluster, any one of them is able to move a label or move a card. A duplicate card will allow an idea to be part of two clusters.

5   The clustering continues until a stable set of clusters and labels emerges.

This process will lead to an agreement or convergence among the group, and so the stable pattern can be presented as a collective view. That view can be contrasted with the views of other groups.

In the same way, the clustering can be undertaken not by groups but by individuals. When completed, the individual patterns can then be presented and compared.

Once there has been a presentation, there can be an opportunity for the groups or the individuals to review their clusters and, if they wish, to amend them in the light of what they have seen.

Buzz groups and snowballing

Buzz groups are used to provide a change of pace and activity in order to aid thinking or to encourage consolidation after a discussion group, for example. Buzz groups are so called because of the buzz of conversation that ensues when they begin.

How buzz groups work

People are asked to form into pairs to discuss some important input that has been made. Even a couple of minutes' activity can be useful. It is sometimes helpful if people are asked to spend a short time collecting their own thoughts beforehand. The discussion in pairs, often as a preparation for a fuller group discussion, will loosen up and develop the pair's thinking. Each pair is asked to record one or two major points for subsequent contribution to the discussion, which should be richer as a result of the activity.

Besides their more general use, buzz groups can be a useful way to help move an idea forward. They can also be used in appropriate circumstances to help even large audiences to become more actively involved in the subject matter of a talk or presentation.

Snowballing

Snowballing is a development from buzz groups and is used to refine thinking and develop ideas further. Each pair is asked to join another pair and a further round of discussion ensues, each pair contributing points from their initial discussion. The four record the main points from their fuller discussion, perhaps on a flip chart as an impromptu visual aid for a brief subsequent presentation of their findings. Their presentation or report then becomes input for a full group discussion.

Round robins

When a group gets stuck or needs a fresh input of ideas to tackle a problem or to establish a way to proceed, a round robin may help. This is a simple but effective way of giving everyone in the group an equal chance to contribute their ideas or comments on an issue, irrespective of their status in the group. If the group generates many ideas it has the added advantage of focusing attention on the ideas rather than on the individual who suggested them, and so the ownership of ideas is more easily shared. It provides a relatively safe format for collecting ideas because the first step is to gather views not to judge them.

How to organise a round robin

There are six steps in the round robin process:

1   The group leader asks each member of the group to spend a few minutes thinking about the problem or issue if they have not already done so.

2   Each person jots down any points or ideas that they want to raise.

3   The group leader goes round the group members in turn asking each person for one idea from their list, avoiding repetition.

4   The ideas are recorded on a flip chart.

5   The process continues until all the ideas are listed.

6   There should be a period of reflection when people consider the ideas and absorb them. There can then be a further discussion and some assessment of the ideas.

Giving presentations

In group working, a presentation is a way of communicating the group's views or findings, and it can be used to generate ideas and gather valuable feedback. In management, it is a useful skill to develop because the ability to communicate verbally in an interesting, informative and convincing way can help to persuade others to follow your leadership. Many people find the prospect of making a presentation to an audience somewhat daunting. If you have never made a presentation before, you may well be nervous. However, this is definitely a skill which improves with practice. A management education environment provides a safe context in which to do this.

Steps in preparing a presentation

1   **Plan** Identify the message you wish to communicate. What are you trying to achieve? Are you intending to inform people or to persuade them? What do you want people to do as a result of your presentation? What are the main points you wish to get across? Have you all the information you need? For how long should you speak?

2   **Audience** Try to put yourself in your listeners' situation. How much are they likely to know about the topic? What kind of presentation would arouse their interest?

3   **Teamwork** If you are one of a group making a presentation, agree on how to divide up the topic and who will say what.

4   **Prepare** Decide on the information, evidence, examples and arguments you will need to convey your key ideas. A good rule is to identify no more than three key ideas or points and just enough information to support them (it is easy to include too much). Decide, too, on the most useful visual aids (graphs, diagrams) to use. Work out a logical flow for all the content. Then decide on how you will begin and end. How you decide this will depend on the purpose of the talk. Typical 'openings' include: relating the subject of the talk to something within the listeners' experience or interests; setting out your overall message; explaining how your audience will benefit from your talk. The aim of your opening

statements is to get attention and arouse interest. Typical conclusions include: repeating the main points; summarising the overall message; posing a challenging question or urging/calling for some kind of action. Always try to finish boldly and conclusively and with the same energy and enthusiasm with which you began. Then prepare your notes for the presentation, including any additional material, handouts for example, that might be helpful to your audience. Often, the first set of notes will be detailed ones, but if you rehearse what you want to say you will probably find that you can summarise your notes and reduce them to a series of headings, sub-headings and key points. Some speakers then transfer these on to small cards as an aid to memory. (You can always have a full set of notes to hand in addition to the cards.)

Keep any visual aids as clear and as simple as possible: make sure content always triumphs over style. If you are making a PowerPoint presentation using a digital projector, prepare a set of overhead projector transparencies or printouts of the slides just in case the technology fails you. Check that any equipment you plan to use is in working order and is set up correctly before the start of your presentation. Check that your voice can be heard at the back of the room (remember that your voice will travel less far when your audience is present): use a microphone if necessary. And finally, think about the room and its layout – is the seating arranged appropriately; is it too hot or cold; does the layout create the right impression?

The presentation

1   **Relax** You will give a better performance if you feel comfortable in front of your audience. Do not try to force yourself into a presentation style with which you feel uneasy. Consciously slow your pace, particularly if you know you have a tendency to speak quickly when nervous.

2   **Get attention and arouse interest** Wait until the audience is quiet, look directly at your listeners and make your opening statements with enthusiasm and energy without referring to your notes. This way, you will appear more confident and your audience will be more 'forgiving' when you later refer to your notes.

3   **Tell listeners when they can ask questions** If you are putting forward an argument you may not welcome interruptions. However, if you are delivering a training talk it is important that your audience understands each point as you proceed, so you may welcome questions during the presentation. Tell your audience in advance whether you will take questions during the talk or at the end.

4   **Be easy to listen to** Try to use a conversational way of speaking. It is hard to listen to someone if they are speaking too fast or delivering lists of points. (These are problems that can arise through trying to cover too many points and too much information to support them). If you are referring to notes, look at your audience as often as possible. Check your voice regularly (and your breathing: inhale quickly but deeply). It's easy to begin using a confident and resonant voice and then gradually speak

more quietly in a flat tone. Modulate your voice (alter the pitch and pace, and use emphasis) so that you highlight the important words and phrases to help your audience comprehend what you are saying. If you are prone to hesitation when speaking, remember that a short pause is better than an 'um' or an 'er' although an occasional 'um' or 'er' can endear a speaker to an audience. Check your body language, too: it should convey confidence in what you are saying (if it doesn't your audience may think you are concealing doubts) and it should match your voice. It is easier to listen to a person who is not displaying signs of nervousness or uncertainty: these can distract listeners from the content of a presentation.

5   **Monitor your audience** Watch for signs that your audience is not fully engaged, for example, people may look puzzled, bored or restless. If you see any of these signs, don't be afraid to respond appropriately. For example, you might say: 'I see one or two puzzled faces; perhaps I haven't explained myself clearly. Are there any points you would like me to go over again?' Or faced with a bored or restless audience, you might stop and ask people for their opinion on the argument or information presented so far. It may be, of course, that it's been a long day or that it's almost time for a coffee break. If the initial energy and enthusiasm with which you began has tailed off into a dull delivery of information, then re-energize your voice and attend to your body language. While it's best not to distract your audience with too much physical movement, if you have been standing very still you could try moving a little, or sitting, or using more hand gestures to emphasise points.

6   **Watch the time** In most circumstances there is a fixed amount of time for a talk. If you spend more time than you intended on some parts of your presentation, you may have to hurry through other parts of it. This can reduce the impact of what you want to say, especially if your conclusions are rushed. It will also leave less time for questions from the audience. Questions give you the opportunity to support what you have said by expanding on or exploring important points. It is usually possible to identify in advance which parts of a presentation should not be shortened or hurried through and which parts can be treated in less detail if necessary. You can indicate that you have more information if your audience requires it.

7   **Dealing with questions** Many speakers dread questions from the audience because they fear they will not be able to answer adequately. It is a good idea to anticipate difficult questions you think may be asked and rehearse some responses. But when faced with a question to which you don't know the answer, it is best to be honest. You can suggest sources of information or, if appropriate, you can offer to find out the answer and let people know by email. Another way of dealing with such questions is to 'throw the question open to the audience', that is, ask the audience to answer the question. You do not *necessarily* have to answer every question asked. Some questions may not be of general interest. For example, one listener may have a particular problem with understanding how you arrived at a particular figure. You can offer to discuss the matter

after the talk. This is also a useful tactic if a questioner is hostile. Other methods include rephrasing the question and answering with a question. Rephrasing the question is useful when the question asked is a poor one, that is, it is too narrow, or it can be answered with a simple 'yes' or 'no' which may close-off rather than open-out discussion. You can say: 'That is a valid question but one that might lead us further is...' Answering a question with a question is useful when the first question is based on a wrong assumption, or appears unconnected with what you have said. You can point out and question the assumption being made or ask the questioner to provide a little background to the question. A small but important point is that questioners may not be heard by the rest of the audience, so repeat the question before you answer it to retain listeners' interest. It is also a good idea to signal when time is running out and say how many more questions there are time for so that you can end the presentation on a high note. Remember that, for the audience, a lively question-and-answer session may be the high-point of a presentation during which they learn as much from the exchanges as from the content of the presentation itself.

Planning

Planning well is particularly essential when working with others. All members of a group or team need to be working in a co-ordinated way toward the same goal. It is hard to achieve anything without being clear about *what* you are trying to achieve, some idea of *how* to achieve it and some idea of establishing *whether* you have achieved it. The following plan gives eight stages which should be considered before undertaking a group activity, to ensure that the group's objectives will be accomplished.

BOX 4.1   THE EIGHT STAGES OF A PLAN

1   Define the objectives – and your measures of success

2   Generate and evaluate the options

3   Identify the activities

4   Sequence the activities

5   Identify the resources

6   Review the plan

7   Prepare action plans, schedules and progress markers

8   Monitor and control – adjust tasks, re-plan or revise objectives, if necessary.

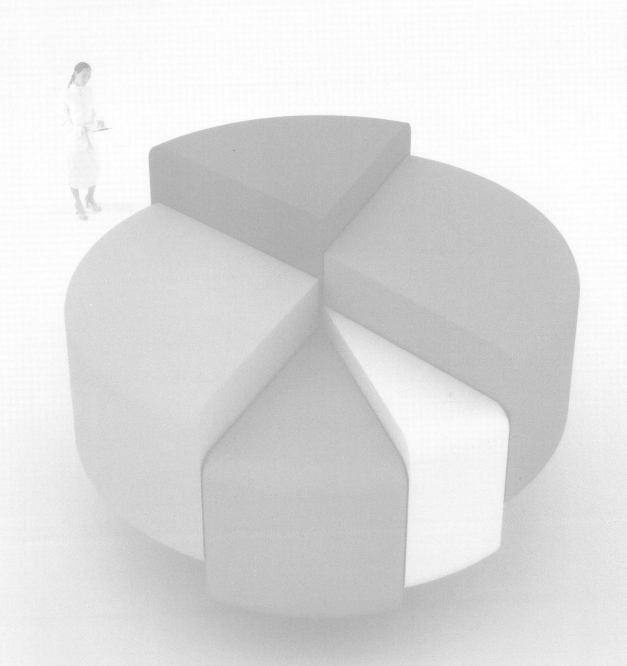

SECTION 2 MANAGEMENT TOOLS AND TECHNIQUES

This section of *The Manager's Good Study Guide* deals with tools and techniques for gathering, using and presenting information in a management context. Every manager will encounter situations in which:

■ facts or ideas need to be communicated

■ information needs to be obtained from investigation

■ data need to be organised, analysed and interpreted.

Information is required to make decisions on which actions are based. This ensures that decisions made and actions carried out are informed. Informed actions are more likely to be effective than those based on an opinion that may be biased. Sometimes information is readily available but needs to be put into a form that is easily communicated in order to support a case or argument. At other times, data will need to be gathered systematically for a particular purpose. Then, the data collected will need to be analysed and interpreted to turn the 'raw' numbers or words into information – a transformation process.

Section 2 is organised by themes: working with numbers, effective ways of displaying information, investigative methods, and working with data. Like other sections of the Manager's Good Study Guide, it is designed for your reference and each of the tools and techniques presented can be looked up independently of the others. Margin notes guide you to related tools and techniques to aid your understanding.

CHAPTER 5 WORKING WITH NUMBERS

The world is full of numbers, perhaps especially so for managers. Almost daily we are presented with graphs, charts, tables, budgets and financial statements, information about inputs and outputs, customers and clients. Not only this, there are times when managers themselves will need to generate numerical information which must be processed and interpreted. There are many tools available to help us work with numbers, from simple calculators to the sophisticated spreadsheet software packages on our computers. But to use them effectively, we need to understand the basics of how to represent numbers and carry out arithmetical operations. Many of us learned these numerical skills early on in school and believed we would never forget them. For some of us, arithmetic may have been something of a mystery which we put aside, perhaps hoping that the need to understand it would fade over time along with the pain of those early experiences! This chapter of *The Manager's Good Study Guide* is for those who need to remind themselves about numbers and arithmetical operations, or need to understand them for the first time. You may be surprised that you can now more easily grasp concepts that were previously elusive. Later chapters in this section assume you have a basic understanding of numbers and arithmetic.

Number representation

We are familiar with how to write numbers and the fact that there are *place values* for units, tens, hundreds, thousands and so on. Each place is a multiple of ten larger than the preceding one. Consider the number 2,563. The four digits would read as 'two thousand, five hundred and sixty-three'. In the UK, a comma is used to separate the digits into groups of three. In a larger number such as 2,524,173 the comma is used twice; this allows us to easily identify the number of millions and thousands. This visual indicator makes the list of digits easier to analyse; without it we would have to cope with interpreting 2524173.

We can show the number 2,563 in a simple table.

	Thousands	Hundreds	Tens	Units
2,563	2	5	6	3

There is one further symbol, the decimal point. This is used to show the transition point between units and tenths, and is usually denoted by a full stop. The standard decimal notation for a number such as 251.32 can be represented as in the table below.

	Hundreds	Tens	Units	Decimal point	Tenths	Hundredths
251.32	2	5	1	.	3	2

Note that a zero (0) in a number is simply holding a place: 100 means 1 hundred, 0 tens and 0 units.

	Hundreds	Tens	Units
100	1	0	0

There are some other terms you may find useful which refer to types of number. Common ones are listed below.

Natural numbers

Natural numbers are 'counting numbers', the ones we know and use everyday: 1, 2, 3, 4, ... The list goes on forever. If we include zero, we call these numbers 'whole numbers' (0, 1, 2, 3, 4, ...) because they have no digits to the right of the decimal point which is invariably omitted when we write them.

Integers

Natural numbers are examples of integers or 'whole' numbers. We can place whole numbers in a list that *ascends* from zero: 0, 1, 2, 3, 4, ... The list goes on forever. Numbers above zero are known as positive numbers.

Negative numbers

These are numbers with a value of less than zero: −1, −2, −3 and so on. They are known as negative numbers, indicated by a minus sign in front. Negative numbers can be integers (whole numbers). When they are whole numbers they can be placed in the list of integers, *descending* from zero: ..., −4, −3, −2, −1, 0. You will have encountered negative numbers if your bank account has ever been overdrawn!

Operations: adding, subtracting, multiplying and dividing

There are four operations that you will use most frequently. These are listed below along with their individual symbols and an example of use.

Operation	Symbol	Example
Addition	+	6 + 21 = 27
Subtraction	−	27 − 6 = 21
Multiplication	×	15 × 4 = 60
Division	÷	24 ÷ 3 = 8

If you are not sure how to perform these operations, seek more help as soon as you are able to. The internet is a particularly good source of aid. This is because the demand is great: you are not alone in needing help with some of the concepts at whatever level!

Manipulating positive and negative numbers

Adding and subtracting

When we add two *positive* numbers together, the answer is a *positive* number: 2 + 2 = 4. When we add two *negative* numbers together, the answer is a *negative* number: (−2) + (−3) = −5. (The brackets are used to show that we mean 'minus 2' and 'minus 3', rather than 'subtract 2' and 'subtract 3'.)

When we add a negative and a positive number, we get a positive or a negative number depending on which number is 'bigger'. For example, if we add 3 to (−1) the answer is 2, a positive number: (−1) + 3 = 2. If we add −3 and 1, the answer is −2, a negative number: (−3) + 1 = −2.

A simple way to understand the addition of numbers of different signs is to use a number ladder. Take the example $(-1) + 3$. Find -1 on the ladder and then move UP the ladder 3 steps (because 3 is a positive number). You will arrive at 2. Now consider $(-3) + 1$. Find -3 on the ladder and move UP 1 step (because 1 is a positive number). You will arrive at -2. This method also works when adding numbers with the same sign. Consider $(-2) + (-3)$. Start at -2 and move DOWN 3 steps (because -3 is a negative number). You will arrive at -5.

| 8 |
| 7 |
| 6 |
| 5 |
| 4 |
| 3 |
| 2 |
| 1 |
| 0 |
| −1 |
| −2 |
| −3 |
| −4 |
| −5 |
| −6 |
| −7 |
| −8 |

Subtracting numbers with the same or different sign is slightly harder but is more easily understood if you allow the numbers to represent money. With two positive numbers, the calculation is straightforward. Say you had €2 in the bank but needed to pay a bill of €7: $2 - 7$. You would have a debt of €5 (-5) after paying the bill. On the number ladder you would start at 2 and move DOWN 7 steps, arriving at -5.

Now consider the calculation $2 - (-6)$. The idea to follow here is to treat -6 as a cancelled debt, from which you gain. In this case you had €2 and a debt of €6 was cancelled (you 'gained' €6). Thus $2 - (-6) = 8$. That is, subtracting -6 involves having *more* money because a debt was cancelled, so you start at 2 and move 6 steps UP the number ladder, arriving at 8. Similarly, if you had €6 and a debt of €2 was cancelled (you 'gained' €2) the answer is the same: $6 - (-2) = 8$. On the number ladder you start at 6 and move UP two steps.

When *both* numbers are negative you can treat both numbers as cancelled debts from which you gain. Thus $(-2) - (-6) = 4$. On the number ladder you start at −2 and move UP 6 steps, finishing at 4. Perplexing as it may seem, subtracting negative numbers is the same as treating them as positive numbers and adding them. If you remember this rule, calculations with negative numbers will be straightforward.

Multiplying negative and positive numbers

When we multiply a positive number by a negative number we *always* get an answer which is a negative number, for example:

$$(-1) \times 12 = -12$$
$$(-3) \times 4 = -12.$$

It doesn't matter how the numbers are ordered, the answer will be the same. When we multiply two positive numbers, the answer is *always* positive, for example: $4 \times 4 = 16$. Similarly when we multiply two negative numbers the answer is *always* positive:

$$(-4) \times (-4) = 16.$$

The rules are as follows.

$$+ \times + = +$$
$$- \times + = -$$
$$+ \times - = -$$
$$- \times - = +$$

Dividing negative and positive numbers

First of all divide the numbers and then determine the sign of the answer as follows: if the signs of both numbers are the *same* (negative or positive), then the answer is *positive*. If the signs of the two numbers are *different* (one is negative and one is positive), then the answer is *negative*.

The rules are as follows.

$$+ \div + = +$$
$$- \div + = -$$
$$+ \div - = -$$
$$- \div - = +$$

Multiplying any number by zero

Whenever you multiply a number by zero, the number is *always* zero. It is impossible to *divide* a number by zero.

Order of operations and brackets

When more than one type of operation is used, the order in which the calculation is performed is important. Brackets are used to separate a sequence of operations into smaller, unambiguous parts. This is necessary when you are presented with what looks like a complicated calculation.

Consider $3 + 14 \div 2 - 2 \times (2 + 1)$. Work through the calculation in the following order.

1   Carry out any calculations in brackets.

2   Do any divisions and multiplications.

3   Calculate any additions and subtractions.

In the example $3 + 14 \div 2 - 2 \times (2 + 1)$, the steps will be as follows.

>   Step 1: $3 + 14 \div 2 - 2 \times \mathbf{3}$
>
>   Step 2: $3 \mathbf{+ 7 - 6}$
>
>   Step 3: $\mathbf{4}$

To test the importance of brackets and rules, work from left to right through the calculation $2 \times 2 + 1$. The answer is 5. Now try calculating $2 \times (2 + 1)$. The use of brackets and the rules gives a different answer: 6.

Rounding

Rounding is about presenting a number that is suitably precise – that is precise enough for the purpose.

Suppose that a manager of a small organisation wanted to compare the average monthly salary in the organisation with monthly salaries in other local organisations. The manager, having compiled the data and made the appropriate calculations, found that the average monthly salary was £2,347.89.

You probably realise that this number is too exact for the manager's purposes. No doubt, the manager would ignore the 89 pence and take the average salary to be either £2,347 or £2,348. In the first instance, the manager would have rounded down to the nearest pound; and in the second instance, the manager would have rounded up to the nearest pound. The mathematical convention is that values of 0.5 and above (in this example, amounts above 50 pence) should be rounded up, while amounts below 0.5 are rounded down.

In fact, even this way of expressing the average salary would probably be too exact for the manager's purposes. The manager might be content to round the amount to the nearest 10 pounds, that is, to take £2,350 as the average salary. As you can guess, if the actual average had been closer to £2,340 than to £2,350, then rounding to the nearest 10 pounds would have led the manager to take £2,340 as the average salary.

Rounding is about reducing the precision of a number so that the number is suitable for the intended purpose but has the benefits of being easier to handle than the original, exact answer. Two common ways in which numbers can be rounded are by presenting the number to so many significant figures or so many decimal places.

Significant figures

One way of rounding a number, or presenting the number in a suitably precise form, is to give the answer to so many 'significant figures'.

When £2,347.89 is presented as:

£2,347.89 – the answer is correct to six significant figures

£2,347.9 – the answer is correct to five significant figures

£2,348 – the answer is correct to four significant figures

£2,350 – the answer is correct to three significant figures

£2,300 – the answer is correct to two significant figures

£2,000 – the answer is correct to one significant figure.

Decimal places

A third way to round a number is to give it so many decimal places.

When 3.245 is presented as:

3.245 – the answer is correct to three decimal places

3.25 – the answer is correct to two decimal places

3.2 – the answer is correct to one decimal place.

Remember that the reason for rounding a number to so many decimal places is so that the answer that is presented is suitably precise for the purpose for which it is intended.

Squares, cubes and roots

Squares (and cubes)

The square of a number is that number times itself once, e.g. 10×10. This is usually written as 10^2. (We can also refer to this as '10 to the power of 2'. 'Perfect' squares are the squares of the whole numbers 1 (1×1), 4 (2×2), 9 (3×3), 25 (5×5), 36 (6×6), 49 (7×7), 64 (8×8), 81 (9×9), 100 (10×10) and so on. The cube of a number is that number times itself twice, for example $10 \times 10 \times 10$. This is usually written as 10^3 ('10 to the power of 3'). When we refer to office space, we often measure in square metres (m^2); and when dealing with building materials such as timber or bricks, we often calculate in cubic metres (m^3).

Square roots

The square root of a number (call the number n) is the number which, when multiplied by itself produces the number n. The square root sign is written as

$$\sqrt{n} \quad \text{or} \quad \sqrt{n}.$$

The square roots of the 'perfect' squares (see above) 1, 4, 9, 25, 36, 49, 64, 81 and 100, for example, are, respectively, 1, 2, 3, 4, 5, 6, 7, 8, 9 and 10. *Every* positive number has a square root because the square root need not be a whole number. When calculating the square roots of numbers which are not perfect squares, however, it's best to use an electronic calculator!

Fractions

Many adults dislike using fractions although the concept is very straightforward. Take 1/2 a bar of chocolate (the shaded part in the diagram).

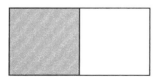

The bottom number in the fraction (the denominator) tells you how many parts or pieces there are in the whole bar of chocolate. The top number (the numerator) tells you how many pieces you've eaten. If you had eaten both parts you would have eaten 2/2, i.e. the whole bar.

Look at the bars of chocolate below. The bars are all the same size but the pieces are of different sizes. You have eaten the shaded portions.

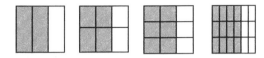

The portions you have eaten are, from left to right, 2/3 (two thirds), 4/6 (four sixths), 6/9 (six ninths) and 12/18 (twelve eighteenths). If you look at the bars again, you'll see that you have eaten the same proportion of each. So 2/3, 4/6, 6/9 and 12/18 represent the same value. There is a way to see this equivalence clearly. In the case of 4/6, both the numerator, 4, and the denominator, 6, can be divided exactly by 2, leaving a whole number as a result. The number 2 is called a *common factor* of 4 and 6 – in this context a 'factor' is a whole number that divides another one exactly. So 2 is a *common* factor of 4 and 6 because it is a factor of both of them. Dividing the numerator and denominator by their common factor, 2, gives the following.

$$\frac{\cancel{4}\;^2}{\cancel{6}\;_3}$$

The fraction 4/6 *reduces* to 2/3. If you carry out the same operation for each of the other fractions, dividing each numerator and denominator by a factor common to both numbers, you will find that each fraction reduces to 2/3. (Divide the numerator and denominator in 6/9 by their common factor, 3, and the numerator and denominator in 12/18 by their highest common factor, 6. Note that numbers can have more than one common factor: choose the highest one to reduce the numerator and denominator as far as you can.)

Equally, if you *multiply* the top and bottom of any fraction by the same number, the fraction is *equivalent* to the old one. If you had 4/5 of a bar of chocolate, but wanted to know how many fifteenths are equivalent to 4/5, you multiply both numbers by 3 (because 5 × 3 = 15).

$$\frac{4 \times 3 = \underline{12}}{5 \times 3 = 15}$$

Converting fractions to decimals

Converting fractions to decimals is not very difficult. Take the fraction 7/8. Divide the numerator, 7, by the denominator, 8, working through the process systematically.

Step 1: Write this as a division: $7 \div 8$ or $8\overline{)7}$.

Step 2:   Put a decimal point after the 7 (the units digit) and another one directly above, where you will write the answer.

$$8\overline{)\ 7.}$$

Add zeros after the decimal point after the 7 as necessary, as you divide out.

$$8\overline{)7.^70^60^40}$$

0. 8 7 5

So 7/8 = 0.875.

In all cases where you want to convert a fraction to a decimal number, divide the number *above* the line by the number *underneath* it. (Indeed, a horizontal line between a number above and a number below *means* 'divide'. You could also calculate that 7/8 is 0.875 by dividing 7 by 8 on a calculator.) If there are any whole numbers before the fraction, place them to the left of the decimal point. For example, 1 7/8 when converted to a decimal number would be 1.875.

Converting decimals to fractions

Recall that digits to the right of the decimal point have place values. Thus, converting decimals to fractions is quite easy: 0.1 is 1/10, 0.03 is 3/100 and so on. When converting a decimal number, for example, 0.23, first consider the place values of the digits.

	Units	Decimal point	Tenths	Hundredths
0.23	0	.	2	3

Then choose the place value of the digit furthest to the right as the denominator (bottom number) and write the fraction, which will be 23/100.

When converting a decimal number such as 0.35, the fraction will be 35/100. However, 35 and 100 have a *common factor*, 5, so we divide both numbers by 5 to arrive at a fraction that can't be reduced any further: 7/20.

Percentages

The use of percentages is one of the most common ways of enabling people to understand the relationships such as changes in costs, clients or improvement in production after staff training, for example. Per cent simply means 'out of 100'. So when we say: 'Costs increased by 13 per cent', we mean that costs increased by £13 for every £100 or by 13/100, that is, by this proportion of the whole cost.

In essence, when you use a percentage you are changing the base of the fraction (the denominator) to 100. Instead of stating: 'The cost of the service has increased by a fifth', you are saying: 'The cost of the service has increased by 20 per cent' (meaning, by twenty hundredths).

Suppose that the cost of a service increased from £5 an hour to £6 an hour. This increase can be expressed as a fraction or as a percentage as shown below.

As a fraction

Original cost = 5

Final cost = 6

Increase in cost = (6 – 5) =1

Increased cost as a fraction of original cost = 1/5.

The cost of the service has increased by one fifth.

As a percentage

Increased cost as a percentage of original cost

= increased cost ÷ original cost × 100%

= 1 ÷ 5 × 100%

= 20%.

The cost of the service has increased by 20 per cent.

Note: To convert a fraction to a percentage, simply multiply the fraction by 100% as shown below.

The fraction 1/5 expressed as a percentage

= 1 ÷ 5 × 100%

= 20%.

The fraction 7/8 expressed as a percentage

= 7 ÷ 8 × 100%

= 87.5%.

Percentage points

Suppose the average mark in a health and safety test was 50 per cent and the average mark after a training initiative was 95 per cent. The change in the average mark, from 50 per cent to 95 per cent, can be expressed in the following two ways.

As a percentage

Follow the steps in the normal way (increase in mark ÷ original mark ×
100%) and you will discover that there has been a 90 per cent increase in
the average mark. So a health and safety manager could say: 'There has
been a 90 per cent increase in the average mark'.

As a change in percentage points

There is a difference of 45 percentage points between the average mark
before the training initiative (50 per cent) and the average mark after the
initiative (95 per cent). So the manager could say: 'There was an increase of
45 percentage points between the two average marks'.

Notice the two different ways of expressing the change, and the difference
in meaning between 'an increase of 90 (or whatever the number) per cent'
and 'an increase of 45 (or whatever the number) percentage points'. Choose
the way that best suits your purpose.

Ratios

Ratios are a way of comparing two quantities; for example, the number of
front office staff to back office staff. Say there are 15 front office staff and
21 back office staff. We would express this as 15:21 or, after reducing each
number by a factor common to both numbers (in this case 3), as 5:7 ('five to
seven'). If the numbers have more than one common factor, choose the
largest so that the resulting numbers cannot be reduced any further. Ratios
are not the same as fractions but can be converted to fractions easily. In the
example above, the total number of staff is 36. So 15/36 of the staff are front
office staff and 21/36 are back office staff. Note that these fractions reduce to
5/12 and 7/12 respectively.

CHAPTER 6

EFFECTIVE WAYS OF DISPLAYING INFORMATION

The value of *graphics* can hardly be underestimated. Graphs, charts,
matrices, tables and diagrams are like pictures: they can 'speak a thousand
words'. They are useful for expressing information clearly and simply, and
they can be used as a visual-thinking tool – for yourself and for groups.
There are a number of techniques and types, each suited to different tasks.
This chapter covers two groups of devices. The first deals with graphs,
charts and matrices; the second covers the kinds of diagrams that are useful

for identifying and solving problems. Note that the word 'data' is plural (the singular of data is 'datum'), so you will come across phrases such as 'these data ...' or 'data are ...'.

Graphs, charts and matrices

Line graphs

A line graph is a method of showing a relationship between two variables, such as the output of an organisation and the associated costs. There are some special terms that you need to understand in order to create and interpret line graphs. These terms include: the axes, the origin, the intercept and the slope (or gradient).

Table 6.1 contains data about the output of an organisation and the associated total costs. The relationship between the output and the total costs of producing the output is as expected, that is, the costs rise as the output rises.

Table 6.1 Output and total costs	
Output	**Total costs (£)**
0	10
10	30
20	50
30	70
40	90

These data can be displayed in a line graph as shown in Figure 6.1.

The horizontal and vertical axes

The total costs depend on the output, so the output is the 'independent variable' and the total costs are the 'dependent variable'. When there is a dependence of this kind, the independent variable is plotted on the horizontal axis, which is also called the x axis. In the graph, output has been plotted on the horizontal axis. The dependent variable is plotted on the vertical axis, also called the y axis. The total costs have been plotted on the vertical axis.

The origin

The origin is the point on the graph where the x axis value (the output) and the y axis value (the total costs) are both zero.

The intercept

When a line cuts an axis, the line is said 'to intercept the axis at' [the particular point]. In this example, the line cuts the vertical (y) axis at £10, so

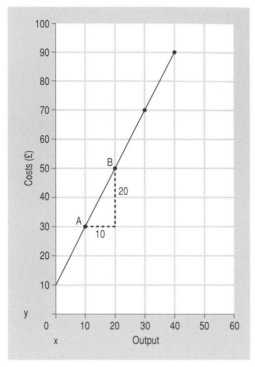

Figure 6.1 **Output and total costs – a line graph**

'the line intercepts the y axis at £10'. It can also be said that 'the intercept with the y axis is £10'.

The slope

The slope (or gradient) of the line describes its steepness. The steepness is measured by considering two points on the graph, A and B. The vertical distance between the two points is 20; the horizontal distance between them is 10. The steepness of the line is the ratio of these two distances:

$$\text{vertical distance} \div \text{horizontal distance} = 20 \div 10$$
$$= 2$$

In the example the slope is 2. This tells us that for every change of one unit in the value of x, there will be a change of two units in the value of y.

When you know the intercept and the slope, then you have a complete picture of the line. The particular graph in the example can be described mathematically as follows:

$$y = 2x + 10$$

In this equation the slope of the line is 2, and the intercept on the y axis is 10. The equation shows that the total cost (y) of an output can be found by multiplying the output (x) by 2, and then adding 10.

Time series line graphs

In time series line graphs, data are plotted or organised along a time dimension. Time series graphs are used for displaying data that show cyclical fluctuations or changes, such as growth, over time. Suppose that you wanted to present the data shown in Table 6.2 as a graph.

Table 6.2	Number of staff in an organisation					
Year	1	2	3	4	5	6
Total	10	25	40	55	60	65

You would plot the data in a line graph like the one shown in Figure 6.2.

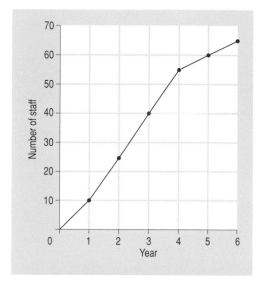

Figure 6.2 Number of staff – a time series line graph (large scale)

As a rule, the variable plotted on the horizontal (x) axis is the interval of time, for example years, months or minutes. This rule leads to the use of 'time series' to describe this kind of chart. The other variable, in this instance 'Number of staff', is plotted on the vertical (y) axis. The points are then joined up to form a continuous line, which shows how staff numbers have changed in the organisation over the years.

Selecting the scales

The scales that are used determine the look of the graph. For example, if the horizontal distance between 'Year 1' and 'Year 6' shown in Figure 6.2 were doubled, the line would be stretched to double its present length. If the horizontal distance were halved, then the length of the line would be halved. Each of the graphs would be mathematically correct.

Now suppose that you had to draw a line graph of the staff in a second organisation using the data shown in Table 6.3. Figures 6.3 (a) and 6.3 (b) show two ways of presenting the data.

Table 6.3	Number of staff in an organisation					
Year	1	2	3	4	5	6
Total	200	220	240	255	270	260

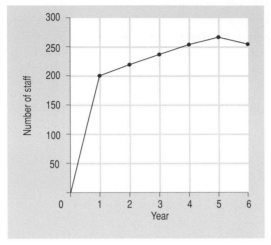

Figure 6.3 (a) Number of staff – a time series line graph (small scale, compressed)

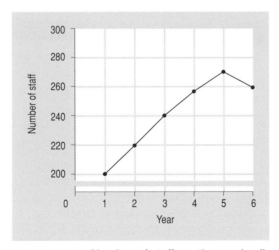

Figure 6.3 (b) Number of staff – a time series line graph (small scale)

Although both of the line graphs are mathematically correct, they look different. The effect, in Figure 6.3 (a), of beginning from zero has been to compress the data shown on the y axis (from 200 to 260) and so make it harder to understand the graph. In Figure 6.3 (b) the vertical scale begins at 200 and the scale has been extended so that the information presented in the graph is much clearer.

The presentation of data – the 'picture' of the data that is presented in a graph – varies according to the scales selected. Choose scales that are appropriate. As you examine a graph, pay particular attention to the scales.

Pie charts

A pie chart is a way of presenting *proportional* data in the form of a circle – the 'pie'. Each 'slice' shows its proportion to the whole. The whole itself must be finite and known, for example, the total number of staff in an organisation or the total IT maintenance budget.

Suppose that the staff of an organisation are comprised as shown in Table 6.4.

Table 6.4 The composition of staff in an organisation		
	Number	**%**
Senior managers	20	10
Other managers	30	15
Administrative	70	35
Clerical	80	40
Total	200	100

You could show this composition in a pie chart like the one in Figure 6.4.

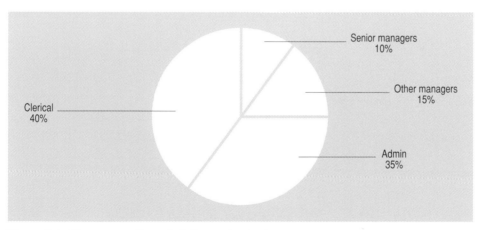

Figure 6.4 The composition of staff – a pie chart

The area of a segment (or 'slice') of the pie chart corresponds to the proportion that the category occupies in the whole. For instance, the segment marked 'Other managers' occupies 15 per cent of the whole pie.

You can use a pie chart when you want to show the components of a whole. It is possible to use a pie chart to illustrate the composition of the staff in an organisation because the data describe the whole organisation. Notice that the percentages add up to 100.

You could also use pie charts to show the composition of staff in an organisation in two (or more) years. Data are shown in Table 6.5, and data for each year are shown in two pie charts, Figures 6.5 (a) and 6.5 (b).

Table 6.5 The composition of staff in an organisation in Year 1 and Year 2				
	(a) Year 1		(b) Year 2	
	Number	%	Number	%
Senior managers	20	10	35	14
Other managers	30	15	25	10
Administrative	70	35	60	24
Clerical	80	40	130	52
Total	200	100	250	100

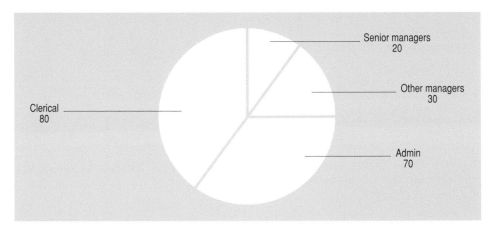

Figure 6.5 (a) Composition of staff in Year 1 – a pie chart

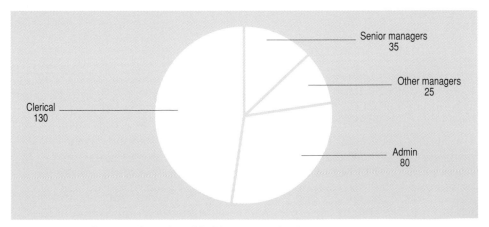

Figure 6.5 (b) Composition of staff in Year 2 – a pie chart

The Year 1 pie chart (Figure 6.5 (a)) is the same as Figure 6.4 because the data are the same. The proportion of senior managers is 10 per cent. Their number increases in Year 2, so in Figure 6.5 (b) which represents that year, they account for 14 per cent of the staff compared with 10 per cent in Year 1. The 'Senior managers' segment is proportionately larger. The 'Other managers' and 'Admin' segments are smaller compared with Year 1, and the 'Clerical' segment is larger.

Bar charts

A bar chart is another way of presenting data. It is designed to show *frequency distribution*, for example, the number of staff in each of four categories in an organisation. You could present the data given in Table 6.6 in a bar chart as shown in Figure 6.6.

Table 6.6 The composition of staff in an organisation	
Senior managers	20
Other managers	30
Administrative	70
Clerical	80
Total	200

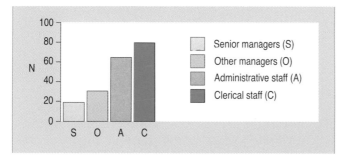

Figure 6.6 Composition of staff – a bar chart

You can see how the bar chart has been created. The four categories are marked on the horizontal axis, so the chart is built on that axis. An appropriate number scale is marked on the vertical axis. A vertical bar is drawn for each of the categories. The height of each bar represents the number of staff in that category. The width of each bar is the same. In the resulting chart we can see that the bar representing 'Senior managers' measures 20 on the vertical scale; that representing 'Other managers' measures 30; that representing 'Administrative' measures 70; and that representing 'Clerical' measures 80.

Of course, you can show more than one set of data on a bar chart. Suppose that you wanted to present the data shown in Table 6.7.

Table 6.7 The composition of staff in an organisation		
	Year 1	Year 2
Senior managers	20	35
Other managers	30	25
Administrative	70	60
Clerical	80	130
Total	200	250

Then the bar chart could be shown as Figure 6.7 (a) or as Figure 6.7 (b).

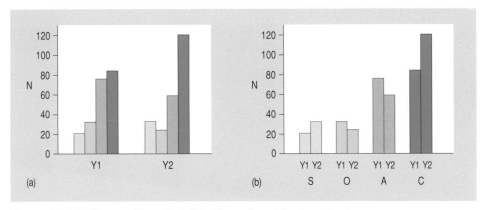

Figure 6.7 (a) Composition of staff in Years 1 and 2 – bar chart

Figure 6.7 (b) Composition of staff in Years 1 and 2 – bar chart

Notice the difference between the two bar charts. In Figure 6.7 (a) the dominant relationship, the one that will catch the reader's eye, is the one between the four categories in each of the two years. The emphasis remains on the composition of the whole staff in each of the years. In Figure 6.7 (b) the dominant relationships are between each of the four categories. If you wanted to emphasise how the numbers in the four categories had changed during the two years, you would choose the type of representation shown in Figure 6.7 (b).

Matrices

A matrix is an arrangement of 'cells' in rows and columns. A spreadsheet is a simple example of a matrix. Each cell is described by its position in a column, normally denoted by an alphabetical letter, and in a row, normally denoted by a number. So 'cell B6' on your spreadsheet is the one which occupies column B and row 6. The size of a matrix is described by the number of rows and the number of columns (in that order).

A 'two-by-two' matrix has two rows and two columns. A 'three-by-two' matrix has three rows and two columns.

Using matrices

A matrix can be a useful way of organising your thinking about a topic. Suppose that you were asked: 'How will you know when you have written a good assignment?'. Suppose as well that you thought 'usefulness' and 'mark' were the two measures by which you would judge an assignment. You could use a two-by-two matrix like the one shown in Figure 6.8.

Figure 6.8 **A matrix for judging an assignment**

The labels on the two axes of the matrix (the rows and the columns) are your two criteria, 'usefulness' and 'mark'. Each of the criteria can be divided into 'low' and 'high' so that you now have four cells each of which describes a particular combination of 'usefulness' and 'mark'. The four combinations represented by the matrix are: low usefulness/low mark, low usefulness/ high mark, high usefulness/low mark and high usefulness/high mark. You would know that you had written a good assignment if it could be placed in the high usefulness/high mark cell of the matrix.

This two-by-two matrix describes the possibilities in a simple way ('high/ low') and so enables you to think about them. The criteria ('usefulness' and 'mark') are the boundaries. Whenever you can confine the criteria (the boundaries) to just two, you can construct a two-dimensional matrix. You could also expand 'high/low' into three or more categories, or you could number your axes, for example from 1 to 9, if you wanted to create a larger matrix than the two-by-two matrix in the example.

Evaluation matrices

When there are several courses of action, then one way of thinking clearly about the advantages and drawbacks of the different courses is to compile an evaluation matrix.

BOX 6.1   SIX STEPS TO CREATING AN EVALUATION MATRIX

1 List the various options.

2 Identify the criteria by which you will judge the options.

3 Give an importance weighting to each of the criteria. (The preferred option will be the one which has the highest weighted score.)

4 Give each option a raw score from 1 to 5 under each criterion. Write the raw scores in each 'raw score' column.

5 Multiply each raw score by the weight of each criterion in turn. This gives a weighted score for the option under each criterion. In the example below, the walking holiday is given a raw score of 1 for 'Happy children'. That raw score is then multiplied by the weight of the criterion 'Happy children' (5), to give a weighted score of 5 in that column.

6 Add the weighted scores across the row for each option. The option with the highest weighted score is the winner. If two options tie, then the choice must be made either (i) randomly between the tied options, or (ii) in some other way (perhaps by a review of the matrix).

The example

Suppose that a couple who have children are thinking about the next family holiday. They list five options, including staying at home. They also list four criteria and they give each an importance weighting on a scale of 1 to 5, where 5 is the most important and 1 is the least important.

The evaluation matrix would look like Table 6.8.

Using the matrix

The results of the evaluation reflect the scores that are awarded to each option and the weightings that are attached to the different criteria. A change in one or the other (or in both) will lead to a change in the results. Accordingly, when you construct a matrix of this kind be sure to think hard about the scores and weightings. A matrix like this can be used in many ways, for example, when interviewing applicants as part of a selection process.

Table 6.8   An evaluation matrix

Options	Criteria and their relative weighting									
	Happy children		Low cost		Happy adults		Easy travel		Totals	
	Weighting = 5		Weighting = 3		Weighting = 2		Weighting = 1			
	Raw score	Weighted (x5)	Raw score	Weighted (x3)	Raw score	Weighted (x2)	Raw score	Weighted (x1)	Raw score	Weighted
Walking holiday	1	5	3	9	4	8	4	4	12	26
Cruise	2	10	1	3	2	4	3	3	8	20
Beach holiday	4	20	1	3	3	6	2	2	10	31
Stay at home	1	5	5	15	2	4	5	5	13	29
Holiday camp	5	25	1	3	1	2	2	2	9	32

Diagrammatic representations

Force-field diagrams

A force-field diagram shows the opposing pressures (or forces) that are
bearing on a situation. Within the context of planning and managing
change, the diagram shows the forces which are supportive of change (the
driving forces) and the forces which are likely to be unhelpful or resistant
(the restraining forces).

The diagram

Suppose that a manager is planning or exploring the possibility of a change
(in working practices, for example). The manager can represent the current
situation as a horizontal line. The driving forces, those forces or reasons that
are supportive of a change, can be represented as downward-pointing
arrows that are seeking to push the line. The restraining forces, those forces
or reasons that are likely to resist the change, can then be represented by
upward-pointing arrows that are supporting the line (the current situation)
and are seeking to keep it where it is.

A general force-field diagram is shown in Figure 6.9.

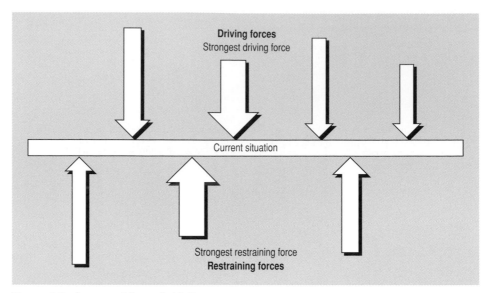

Figure 6.9 **A general force-field diagram**

The thickness of an arrow can be used to show the strength of a force. The length of an arrow can be used to show how difficult it would be to modify the force. However, these conventions are not hard and fast. You can adopt them or you can use your own. It is usual to explain your conventions in a note below your diagram.

How a force-field diagram can help

■ The diagram is a useful expositional or presentational device. When you are presenting an analysis or proposal, the diagram will enable you to describe (and distinguish between) the reasons for a change. It will enable you to do the same for the reasons why a change may be resisted.

■ The diagram will be an explicit prompt for exploring the restraining forces. The more a manager finds out about these, and the earlier, the better placed the manager will be to find a way to deal with them. The idea of the restraining forces reminds a manager to look for and identify them.

Input–output diagrams

An input–output diagram shows the inputs to a system or to an operation and the outputs from it.

A first diagram

For example, think about the inputs to the running of a commuter rail operation and the outputs from it. The diagram might look like the one in Figure 6.10.

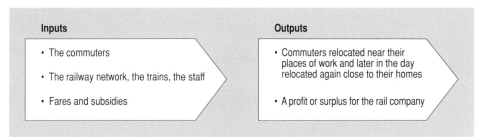

Figure 6.10 Inputs to and outputs from a commuter rail operation

The advantage of portraying inputs and outputs in this way are as follows:

■ The portrayal will show the inputs and the outputs in a way that emphasises the flow of inputs into the operation and the subsequent flow of outputs from it. The use of the arrows will establish this sense of movement.

■ At the same time, the diagram will provide the benefits of the two matching lists, the inputs and the outputs. You will gain a sense of the transformation of the inputs into outputs.

A second diagram

This first representation can be developed in the way shown in Figure 6.11.

Figure 6.11 Inputs, transformation, outputs

Figure 6.11 includes a general representation of the process that transforms the inputs into outputs. In the example, the transformation is the movement of the passengers, the customers, from their home railway stations to the stations close to their work. The diagram can help your thinking in two ways:

■ It emphasises the need for a transforming process. Something must be done with the inputs in order to achieve the outputs.

■ The transformation process is the reason for the existence of the organisation. It is the value that the organisation adds to the inputs.

You can apply an input–output diagram to an organisation or to a part of an organisation. You can apply it to your own work or to your activities outside work.

When you identify the inputs and the outputs, identify those ones that are sufficient for your purposes. Sometimes, it will be appropriate to identify a relatively long list of both. At other times, it will be sufficient to identify just the major inputs and outputs.

Influence diagrams

An influence diagram shows the influences, from within the organisation or from outside it, which bear on a person or unit.

The model

Figure 6.12 shows some of the influences which bear on an organisation. These influences, of course, are felt not by 'an organisation' but by people within the organisation. It is sensible, therefore, to talk about the influences on the management or on the manager within the organisation. Thus, Figure 6.12 shows the firm as the main system, while the manager and the other staff are shown as two subsystems within the main one.

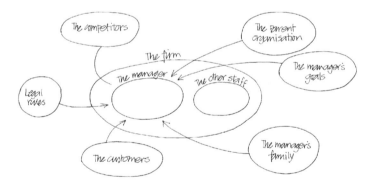

Figure 6.12 **Influences on the manager of a firm – influence diagram**

The diagram provides the opportunity to identify the external systems or bodies which influence the manager's thinking. Some of those external systems are to do with the organisation's business. They include the competitors, the customers, and the legal rules within which the firm must operate. If the firm is a subsidiary, then the parent organisation will be a powerful influence. But other influential systems lie outside what is probably understood as the business. For example, it is sensible to include the manager's family (as an influence to represent the whole of the manager's private life). It will be equally sensible to include the manager's goals.

These two latter influences, the manager's family and the manager's goals, express the strength of this way of portraying the influences on a person's (in this instance, a manager's) behaviour. The range of the analysis is entirely up to the analyst – the person who draws the diagram – to decide. In the example, any system or body can be represented on the diagram if it exerts an influence on the person whose behaviour is being examined. Perhaps one member of the manager's family is particularly influential; in that instance, that one person can be represented, along with or to the exclusion of the rest of the family. In the same way, the manager's goals could be amended to show a particular goal to which the manager was strongly committed. An influence diagram can also be used to explore and identify the extent to which the powerful people within the organisation (the senior managers) are sensitive to the forces outside the organisation which are bearing on the organisation.

Systems thinking

'The whole is more than the sum of its parts' is a good place to start thinking about systems. A car is more than its individual components. We can think of a football team as being more than a collection of individual players or a family being more than a group of people who share the same name.

Each of these examples – the car, the football team and the family – can be seen as systems. Individual parts of a system are connected together in some way for a purpose.

Examples of other systems include the local hospital, or the hospital catering system with the purpose of providing food for the patients and staff as part of the hospital system for helping the sick and injured. But the idea of systems goes beyond collections of tangible components such as people, equipment and buildings that form part of various systems. Systems also include intangible items such as ideas, values, beliefs and norms. These intangible things are factors in a system.

We can see that families have beliefs and behaviours that guide how they interact with each other and with those outside the family. Football teams and their football clubs have strong bonds of beliefs, loyalties and aspirations, and they show these in how they behave when they appear in their club colours. Their systems have tangible elements such as the playing field, the seating areas, the players, officials and supporters but also intangible elements like their hopes and fears, their history and songs, and their reputation.

We also think about a boundary around each system. This defines those things that are part of the system and those that are outside it. *Each element* of the system is connected to every other, affects how the system behaves, and is affected by it. *All members* in a family system are connected with the other members of the system (both the people and the intangible values and beliefs) and are affected by them, and affect them too. The camera that takes the family photographs can see the tangible parts but cannot see intangible parts of the system.

In the family photograph we can see grandparents, parents and children. We can see within the larger family system a number of smaller systems. These are systems too but are part of the larger family system. We think of subsystems within systems.

Five key ideas about systems

Systems thinking will enable you to analyse complex issues in an illuminating way. It takes a whole (or holistic) view of a situation.

When you think of a system, bear in mind the following five ideas:

1   **Everything in a system is connected** The elements of a system are interconnected. The members of a department or a voluntary group constitute a system. There are connections between the members. A system can comprise people, material objects, and even such intangible elements as ideas or common sets of beliefs. The idea of a system emphasises the interconnections between the elements.

2   **A system does something** A system is defined by what it produces. Every system has an output of some kind. Once again, the outputs may be tangible or intangible. When you think of a hospital as a system, then the outputs will include measurable improvements in health as well as immeasurable outputs in the improvements in people's feelings about themselves. The only valid components of a particular system are those that contribute to the specified output.

3   **Systems have a boundary and an environment** The system boundary encloses those elements that make up the system. Think of the hospital again. The boundary of the system will separate the elements that make up the system and interact with each other, from the elements that are outside the boundary. The elements that are outside the boundary constitute the environment in which the system operates. Elements in the environment affect the system but are not affected by it.

4   **The system is defined by your interest** What goes into and what remains outside a system is decided by your interest. In the local hospital, the system that provides care for accident victims may include counselling support if you feel it is important. Your system may differ from someone else's if they feel counselling is not essential. The way that you express the local hospital as a system will reflect different understandings and different points of view.

5   **Systems and subsystems** A system can have one or more subsystems within it. Your local hospital, for instance, could include a catering subsystem (a tangible subsystem), as well as a subsystem which encompasses 'the values and standards that inform the medical practice in the hospital' (an intangible subsystem).

A systems map

Mapping a system is like mapping a town. First we define the boundary and draw it on paper. The boundary separates those places inside the town from those outside. We do the same with the system. We show the system boundary with rounded corners to emphasise the imprecise nature of the boundary that separates those things that are interacting inside the system from those outside in the environment that have an effect on it.

We become selective when we draw a map. We consider the purpose of the map and choose a suitable scale. We include on the map only those things that are useful to our purpose.

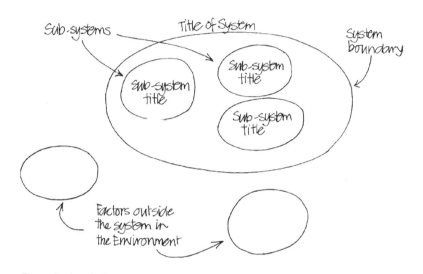

Figure 6.13 A typical systems map

Figure 6.13 shows the system boundary and the smaller subsystems inside the boundary. We include all those things that help our use of the map. A system is defined by what it does and shows only those components (those subsystems) that contribute to this output.

The environment of the system lies outside the system boundary. In the environment of our system, we include all those things that are outside the system but have an effect on it.

In reality, the systems you consider at work may reside within your team and the near environment of the system will be the organisation you work for. Your system may be influenced by the structures and organisational cultures that surround you. Further away there may be important environmental factors such as national economic conditions or the legal and political framework.

Systems diagrams can become impossibly complicated if you try to include too many elements. Show only the most influential ones.

BOX 6.2   IMPORTANT POINTS ABOUT SYSTEMS MAPS

1   A system map shows the boundary of the system and the different subsystems inside the boundary. It may also show important influences outside the boundary, that is, in the external environment.

2   A map is a map. It does not have arrows showing relationships or influences between the subsystems.

3   The scale and the detail depend on the purpose of the system map. Keep the map as simple as possible to aid clarity.

4   Ensure the map is clearly labelled. All boundaries and subsystems need to be clearly identified.

5   In changing a system, we have to draw the existing real-life system and the new system we would wish it to be. To transform the existing system into the new one requires systems interventions.

Fishbone diagram

There are times when management problems seem too complicated and 'messy' to analyse. A technique, the fishbone diagram, can be used by both individuals and groups to help to clarify the causes of a difficult problem and capture its complexity. The diagram will help provide a comprehensive and balanced picture and show the relative importance and interrelationships between different parts of the problem.

BOX 6.3   DEVELOPING A FISHBONE DIAGRAM

1   On a wide sheet of paper, draw a long arrow horizontally across the middle of the page pointing to the right, and label the arrowhead with the title of the issue to be explained. This is the backbone of the fish.

2   Draw spurs coming off the backbone at about 45 degrees, one for every likely cause of the problem; label each at its outer end. Add sub-spurs to represent subsidiary causes. Highlight any causes that appear more than once – they may be significant.

3   Consider each spur and sub-spur, taking the simplest first, partly for clarity but also because a good, simple explanation may make more complex explanations unnecessary.

4   Circle anything that seems to be a key cause so that you can concentrate on it later. Finally, redraw the fishbone diagram so that the relative importance of the different parts of the problem is reflected by its position along the backbone. Draw the most important at the head end.

Figure 6.14 shows the possible causes of failure to meet project deadlines.

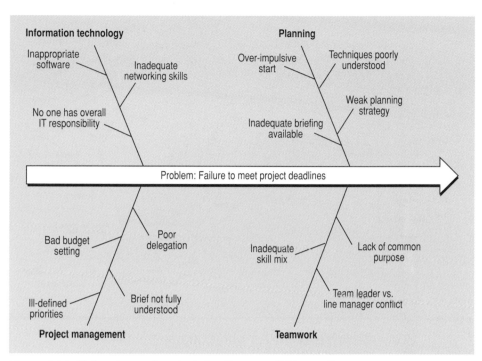

Figure 6.14 Failure to meet project deadlines – a fishbone diagram

We can see there are four main causes. These are the lack of teamwork, project management, information technology and planning. Each of these has been developed to show greater detail.

It is often helpful to develop the fishbone diagram with a group, as the analysis and consensus may provide a basis for group action and learning.

Mind mapping

The term mind mapping was devised by Tony Buzan for the representation of such things as ideas, notes and information, in radial tree diagrams – sometimes also called spider diagrams. These are now very widely used – try a web search on 'Buzan', 'mind map' or 'concept map'.

Figure 6.15 shows an example taken from a real problem-solving session.

Figure 6.15 **An example of a mind map from a problem-solving session**

(Source: Buzan, 1982).

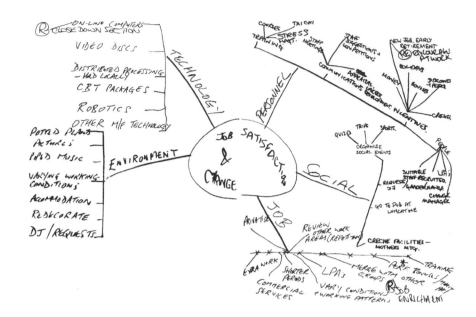

BOX 6.4   HOW TO DRAW A MIND MAP

1   Put your paper (ideally a large sheet) in landscape format and write a brief title for the overall topic in the middle of the page.

2   For each major subtopic or cluster of material, start a new major branch from the central topic, and label it.

3   For each sub-subtopic or sub-cluster, form a subsidiary branch to the appropriate main branch. Do this too, for ever finer sub-branches.

Tips

■   You may want to put an item in more than one place. You can copy it into each place or draw in a cross-link.

■   Show relationships between items on different branches by coding them using a particular colour or type of writing, for example.

■   Identify particular branches or items with drawings or other pictorial devices to bring the map to life.

There are several mind mapping software packages available. They make it very much easier to edit and rearrange the map; they can sometimes hold notes and documents associated with labels (so that they can act as filing systems), and some can switch between map and text outline formats.

However, computer-based maps have the disadvantages of the small screen, and are less adaptable than hand-drawn versions (for example, you can't usually make cross-links).

Multiple-cause diagrams

As a general rule, an event or outcome will have more than one cause. A multiple-cause diagram will enable you to show the causes and the ways in which they are connected. Suppose, for example, that you were asked to explain why a work group was under-performing. You could use a multiple-cause diagram both to help you to construct the explanation and to present it.

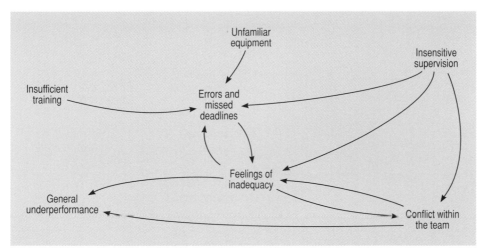

Figure 6.16 Why a work group is under-performing – a multiple-cause diagram

Figure 6.16 presents a picture of the problem. The eye can move from one element to another and can see the connections between the elements. From that point of view, a multiple-cause diagram is rather like a road map. If you can look at the diagram and say 'I can read that diagram, I can see how it explains the underperformance of the work group', then the diagram will have been effective as a means of exposition. If the diagram has been effective, then a similar one may be equally effective in explaining an event or outcome.

Using a multiple-cause diagram will help you to think about a problem, to explain the problem to other people, and to decide what to do about it. It will expose the connections between the events (including the loops – the occasions when one event leads to another which, in turn, reinforces the first). It will show you the possible routes into the problem. It will remind you of the complexity of the problem and it will help you to guard against taking an inappropriately narrow view of it.

As you construct and revise a multiple-cause diagram you will be reaching your own view of the problem. If someone else studied the problem they would probably draw a diagram that differed from your own. Different views, or different understandings, of the nature of a problem mean that there will be different ways of handling the problem.

Drawing a multiple-cause diagram

We can draw a multiple-cause diagram to explore and to communicate the complexity of a system, and to recognise that the effect of a particular system is normally the result of a number of different causes.

Examine the example shown in Figure 6.17 of the multiple causes of poor sales performance from a team.

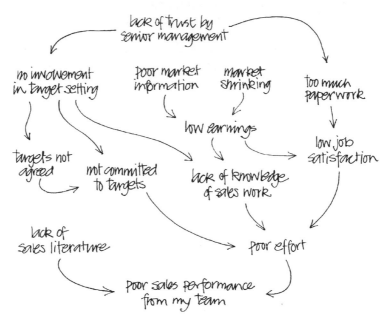

Figure 6.17 **Causes of poor sales performance – a multiple-cause diagram**

The first task in drawing such a diagram is to identify the output in which you are interested. Generally we take a single output or effect and examine the several causes leading to it. We could try to draw a multiple-cause diagram for two or more effects but the diagram would quickly become impossibly complex.

Having identified the effect we are exploring, we then add the first, or primary, causes of that effect. In this case, we have established two primary causes. These are lack of sales literature and poor effort. We then consider each of these and add their causes. Three causes of poor effort are shown in the diagram. We then move backwards through the different levels of causes until we are satisfied that we have a comprehensive diagram to explain the multiple causes of the poor sales performance.

BOX 6.5 IMPORTANT POINTS ABOUT MULTIPLE-CAUSE DIAGRAM

- We are examining the multiple causes of a single output, so all arrows lead along a path to the output.

- There needs to be a logical cause and effect relationship between each link. For example, the link between low earnings and lack of knowledge of sales work may not be clear, and another element such as high staff turnover could be included in the path.

- A single cause can have a number of effects. An example in the diagram is low earnings that lead to lack of knowledge of sales work and to low job satisfaction. Often these points are the key ones to address: an improvement (on low earnings) will lead to multiple benefits.

- Consider how the diagram can be developed to make it more effective. Important paths can be highlighted – perhaps the lines can be coloured or made thicker. Key elements can be underlined or bordered.

Drawing multiple-cause diagrams helps in exploring and in communicating complex issues. Practice improves drawing skills and deepens understanding. Draw one today!

Network analysis

One of the weaknesses of simple charts for planning and control is that they do not show how tasks are dependent on each other. Network analysis (or critical path analysis) seeks to overcome that drawback, particularly where large or specialist projects are concerned. The critical path is found as a result of the analysis of the network. There are many computer software packages which can help a manager to carry out a network analysis.

A case study

Figure 6.18 (overleaf) shows part of a critical path for converting surplus retail space into a warehouse. Each task is represented by an arrow; the length of an arrow does *not* relate to the duration of the task. The junctions (called nodes) where arrows meet would normally be numbered. You may come across other formats which use slightly different terms from those we have used.

The numbers on the arrows represent the number of working days it will take to complete each task. As you can see, there is one critical path highlighted. This is because each of the critical tasks depends on the completion of the previous task before it can start. If you add up the number of days for these tasks (2 + 20 + 10), you will see that stock cannot be received until 32 working days have elapsed. Only by changing the timescales for the highlighted tasks can the overall timescale be reduced. Gaining time on other tasks will not affect the calculation.

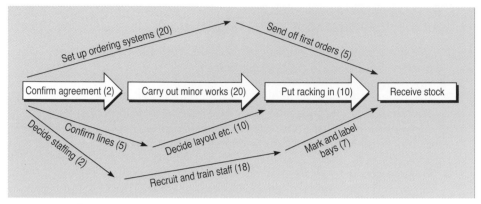

Figure 6.18 Converting surplus space for warehousing – a preparatory diagram for a network (or critical path) analysis

---

BOX 6.6   NETWORK ANALYSIS: SOME KEY POINTS TO BEAR IN MIND

■ Some tasks depend on the completion of other tasks to enable them to start.

■ A string of such tasks makes a path through your plan, and that path has a very significant effect on the timescale for your project.

■ The path will tend to define the shortest feasible timescale for the accomplishment of the project, irrespective of the tasks elsewhere.

CHAPTER 7 INVESTIGATIVE METHODS

Research design

As a manager, you will need to be able to produce sound evidence for any course of action you recommend. You will need to assemble evidence for a variety of reasons. These include the exercise of control through monitoring and evaluation, recruiting and supervising staff or market research. These can seem quite diverse activities but all involve finding out about activities, staff or markets.

The methods you adopt need to be appropriate for the circumstances you wish to explore. In order to decide which methods to use you need to think about *what* you need to know and *why*. What are the things you need to know about? If, for example, you are conducting an evaluation then you need to know about three things:

1 **The baseline information** What did you set out to do? Here you need to consider background documents; accounts of the history of the project from those involved at the time; and any records about why the project was established.

2 **Results** What information on achievements have you got or can you get from monitoring and other means? This could include monitoring records, reports from staff or feedback from customers.

3 **Context** What other information do you need in order to understand why the project is as it is? This could range widely and might include, for example, demographic changes such as a large ageing population and its impact on sales of various items, or the way in which changes in government policy affect your organisation.

Often the approach you take to finding out information and views is determined by the availability of resources and/or data. You need to consider your choice of methods against:

■ **Cost** of obtaining useful information.

■ **Time** it will take to obtain and analyse the information.

■ **Reliability** of the information obtained.

■ **Politics** of the research process – how can the methods you select help in building support for the project?

You will also need to take into account the ethics of the approach and the advantages and disadvantages. For example, in asking hospital patients about their illnesses and treatment, you would have to consider the effects on their relationship with their carers and any issues your questions might raise.

When undertaking research, you would usually not rely on a single approach but use a variety of sources. What matters, in the end, is not the validity of *individual* sources of information so much as the coherence and consistency of the information from different sources *taken together*. On their own, one person's impressions or recollections carry very little weight. But if they are corroborated by comments from several other people *and* by apparent trends in the data from records *and* by observations of staff, then the information gathered is regarded as altogether more robust.

Quantitative and qualitative data

There are a number of ways in which information can be collected. These will result in data of two different types – quantitative and qualitative.

Quantitative data

Quantitative data describe measurable or countable features of whatever has been investigated. The distances that the lorries in a transport fleet travelled between major services; the number of single-parent families; the amount of glass that will be used in the construction of a block of flats; the prices that were charged in a market on a particular day – these are all examples of quantitative data. As long as the measuring or the counting has been accurate, then there can be little scope for disagreement about the data. There is a hardness, a reliability, about the data.

Qualitative data

Qualitative data, in contrast, refer to intangible qualities or features. Customers' views on the look of a company's advertising brochure are an example of qualitative data. So are the opinions of diners in a restaurant on the quality of the food and the service. The subject of the investigation – in these instances, the look of the brochure, and the quality of the food and service – cannot be measured in a standard, objective way. Different people are likely to assess the look of the brochure differently. Different people, having eaten the same food and received the same service, may give different assessments of them. Qualitative data may describe measurements or assessments of qualities for which there are no standard, objective measures.

Using both kinds of data

Quantitative data are easy to use. A transport manager, for instance, can record the distances that the lorries have travelled. The data will be easy to display: they can be charted, the averages can be calculated, and so on. There will be a sense of precision about the data. Qualitative data, in contrast, are more difficult to handle. Diners in a restaurant are unlikely to share the same view – that is, use a common measure – of unsatisfactory service. This will be the case even if the restaurant manager says: 'Use a scale of 1 to 5, 1 being excellent and 5 being unsatisfactory'. The replies will look like quantitative ones but they cannot be measured with the same objectivity because people are likely to interpret excellent and the other categories in different ways. The quantitative look of the data can be misleading unless care is taken. In the restaurant case, it might be better to ask specific questions such as: 'How long did you wait for service?' and 'Was the wait acceptable?'. In cases where greater specificity is not possible, interpreting the data can be difficult. Nevertheless, qualitative data will complement the quantitative kind. Taken together, both kinds will present a richer and more complete picture than either kind alone could do.

Selecting your sample

Sampling is helpful to us because we can investigate a sample (a part) of a larger population in order to learn not just about the sample but about the population from which it was drawn.

Sampling is part of our everyday experience. Television companies monitor the viewing habits of a sample of the population and, using data about the sample, the companies draw conclusions about the viewing habits of the whole population. Polling organisations collect the opinions of samples of the population and use the data to present the opinions of the population as a whole.

To do this with confidence, however, means taking great care in identifying your sample. This is because it is easy to build in some systematic bias resulting from the way a sample is chosen.

For example, a sample of customers in a store might well be representative of all the customers in the store. But it is less certain that the sample would be representative of all the shoppers in the city centre, and it is even less certain that it would be representative of a nation's shoppers. The inferences you could draw about customers in a single store would be less and less convincing the more you went beyond your sample.

There are two basic methods of drawing a sample: the random and the quota methods.

Random sampling

In the case of a random sample, the individuals to be interviewed are selected at random from a list of the population (for example by using a random number-generating program).

The sample must be representative if it is to be of any use. Suppose that you wanted to talk to a random sample of the staff in an establishment that was operating three shifts over 24 hours. A member of staff, whatever the shift, must have an equal chance of being selected. It would be appropriate to select one-third of your sample from each of the shifts. Or if 80 per cent of the staff were men and 20 per cent were women, it might be appropriate to take four-fifths of the sample at random from among the men and one-fifth at random from among the women. A 'stratified random sample' of this kind takes account of the way the population is composed.

Quota sampling

Quota sampling specifies how many of various kinds of people are to be questioned. For example, you might decide to interview 20 managers in a company. On the basis of the whole population of managers, you might specify:

    7 from among junior managers and supervisors

   13 from middle managers

    9 aged under 45

  11 aged 45 or over.

This would give a sample which was roughly representative of the composition of these groups in the company for each variable – age and status – considered separately. However, it would not necessarily be the case for the variables taken together. To some extent, this can be overcome by 'interlocking'. For example, by ensuring that some of the middle managers were under 45 and some junior managers were over 45, there would be an overlap or interlocking of variables. However, this increases the degree of complexity in sampling and may even allow biases to creep in (junior managers over 45 may be rare, for example). Care must be taken to balance representativeness with interlocking.

Sample size

See Selecting your sample, p. 142.

The degree of precision in any set of results is a function of not only how representative a sample is but the *size* of the sample. In general, the larger the sample, the greater the likelihood of obtaining results that represent an average cross-section of the population under study, with any chance deviations tending to cancel each other out. A common question you might ask is therefore: 'How large does my sample need to be?'. Unfortunately, there is no straightforward answer to this question. Normally, a small representative sample of the population is drawn. For example, in opinion polls carried out by market research organisations a small sample of the population will usually be surveyed and then findings extrapolated to the rest of the population. However, the larger the sample you draw, the more accurate your findings are likely to be. A question you need to ask yourself is therefore: 'How accurate do my findings need to be?'. Often, a high degree of accuracy is less important than a quick snapshot of opinions.

If the sample is too small, however, it may not be typical or representative and you will not be able to generalise your findings to the population as a whole. As the sample becomes larger, there is a better chance of it representing the population on the variables of interest to you. The more you already know about the population and how the variables are distributed within it, the better.

Within a management research context, it is common to take the figure of 30 as a useful safe minimum size for the set of data on which you will conduct your statistical analyses. However, you will have to request and collect far more than 30 sets of data. There are two reasons for this.

First, non-response to questionnaires or interviews must always be built into your research design. Companies and shoppers become irritated by the number of surveys they are asked to complete, so be prepared to send several reminders and still receive a disappointing number of returns.

If you were contacting complete strangers by direct mail for their views on a potential product, you might have to write to well over 1,000 addresses to obtain 30 completed returns, because it is common to find that only around 2.5 per cent of people contacted will be willing to co-operate.

The second reason is statistical. If you are testing a hypothesis, you are likely to want to compare the replies of subgroups within your data set. If you are comparing the buying habits of Europeans with US citizens, or of small firms with medium-sized ones, you will need 30 responses in each category. Even for some of the simpler descriptive statistics you will need at least five cases in a category. So if you are analysing cat ownership against age group, and there are three categories of each (no cats, one cat, several cats; under 21, 21–59, 60 and over) you will need 45 responses, and each cell in your results matrix should contain some data. This is because there are nine cells and you need at least five cases in each (see Table 7.1).

Table 7.1 Sample grid for analysing cat ownership against age group			
	Number of cats owned		
Age	None	One	Several
Under 21	❏	❏	❏
21–59	❏	❏	❏
60 and over	❏	❏	❏

When we use sample data to draw conclusions about the larger population from which the sample is drawn, we must allow for the likelihood that the sample is not an absolutely accurate representative of the population.

Validity

It is important for researchers to demonstrate that their inquiry is free from bias and conforms to its declared purpose. This is the fundamental meaning of validity, although there are many types of validity that relate to different aspects of research, from methods to the drawing of conclusions.

See Using your data, p. 156.

Consider whether you would trust the findings of an investigation if, for example:

■ A test purported to measure the arithmetical ability of job candidates but in fact measured their verbal ability because of the way the questions were asked.

See Logical reasoning and critical thinking, p. 60.

■ The reasoning process used to draw conclusions did not conform to logical principles.

■ A survey on dress code sought responses only from staff under 30, despite half of the staff of the organisation being over 45.

See Selecting your sample, p. 142.

You would rightly protest that the conclusions drawn in each case were not valid.

Issues of validity arise at every stage in an investigation. The design and method must be appropriate to what you want to find out. The population sample from which you gather data must be appropriate. You must recognise that the data analysis techniques you use will have limitations and disadvantages. Biases may inadvertently creep into your interpretation of the findings – and at many other stages of the investigation.

Your background, class, gender, ethnicity and experience are all sources of bias.

Some methods of research are particularly problematical in terms of validity. For example, if you have decided to conduct a series of interviews to gather qualitative data, you will need to pay attention to some common sources of bias.

BOX 7.1   SOURCES OF BIAS IN INTERVIEWS

Respondent bias The respondent may lie, try to impress or they may have rehearsed their story in order to present consistency.

Interviewer bias The prejudices, background and assumptions of the researcher are likely to influence questions (and responses to them).

Setting of the interview The context or the setting of interviews can be too formal to encourage intimacy or too informal to encourage adequate response.

(Source: based on Plummer, 1983)

It is impossible to remove all sources of bias or error, but it is important to consider as many as possible when planning and conducting your research, to avoid your conclusions being invalidated by them. A means of improving validity is through the process of *triangulation*.

Triangulation

Triangulation is a term borrowed from navigation and surveying, where a minimum of three reference points are taken to check an object's location. In research, triangulation normally refers to studying one issue or theme using *more than one* method (or source, investigator or theory). It is crucial when looking at complex questions and issues. For example, the relationship of interview data with a wider population might be clarified using official statistics or other documents. Typically, triangulation involves this kind of combination of micro- and macro-level studies, each complementing and verifying the other. But there are four different forms of triangulation which are all designed to improve the validity and robustness of research.

BOX 7.2   FORMS OF TRIANGULATION

Triangulation of theories This involves using models and theories from different disciplines to explain situations in another discipline.

Data triangulation Data are collected at different times or from different sources.

Triangulation by investigators Different people collect data on the same situation and the results are then compared.

Methodological triangulation This uses a combination of different methods, both qualitative and quantitative.

(Source: Easterby-Smith *et al.*,1991)

Collecting data

An argument or case will be strengthened by the inclusion of appropriate data. There are many occasions when you will need to collect these data yourself, or instruct someone else to do so. Data need to be relevant to your case, and they also need to be *reliable*. Using appropriate techniques for the collection of data, and considering carefully who and where you collect data from, will provide the best basis for this – one from which you will be able to draw sound conclusions.

There are a number of methods of collecting data, both quantitative and qualitative. Many methods can produce either type of data. Some of the most well known are discussed in the following pages. Select the methods which best suit your purposes and are most appropriate to your research questions. It is important to comply with data protection laws (Data Protection Act 1998 in the UK). Details and free copies can be found on the internet. See References, p. 356.

Primary and secondary data

Primary data are data that you, or the investigator, have collected and which did not exist before. Primary data are 'first-time' data. Secondary data are data that already exist. Once you collect and use your primary data, then the data will be secondary data for someone else.

Using primary and secondary data

When you want to find out about something, first look for the data that already exist, the secondary data. Existing data may be sufficient for your purposes. When they are not, you will have to identify what information you need, and collect new or additional data. Suppose you wanted to discover the views of your staff and customers on the adoption of casual dress at work. It is safe to say that you would have to question staff and customers. In other words, you would gather primary or 'first-time' data. Yet some secondary data, if they were available and if you knew about them, could be helpful. A report of a similar investigation somewhere else might be good enough for your purposes. If not, it might still help you to think about the issues and to frame your questions. An existing report might contain a copy of the investigator's questionnaire. Make a point of looking for secondary data before you collect primary data.

Public sources of information

There is a wide variety of sources of public information available to you as a manager which can provide useful contextual information for any research you undertake. Much of this information can be found either through libraries or on the internet. Such public information can be used to provide data about social trends, or about what organisations similar to your own are doing.

The following sources of information are usually available:

- libraries
- printed information
- computer databases
- internet sources of information on organisations (e.g. on their home pages).

The main problem is how to navigate through all the information you do not want in order to find the information you do want!

BOX 7.3   A CHECKLIST FOR CONDUCTING INFORMATION SEARCHES

Clarify your aims What do you need to know?

Set limits How much time do you have? How precise an answer do you need? How current does the information need to be? How comprehensive an answer do you want?

Explore the topic Do some background reading. Note down useful sounding references and the names of relevant organisations. Look at some abstracts and indexes in printed form and note down the keywords that emerge.

Choose your information sources What kind of information do you require? What sort of source is likely to have what you want? Which sources will you use and in what order? Which sources are easily accessible, for example in public libraries, on your bookshelf or on the internet? Consider visiting a more specialised library with a clear idea of what you are looking for.

Use sources systematically If you are using printed sources (even via the internet) start with the most recent volume and work backwards. Work out the subject headings and appropriate keywords you want to search; check synonyms or similar words, check broader terms and check related fields.

Obtain material and use it effectively Obtain the material you need from the library or the internet. Then decide whether the articles suggest new approaches, give you useful further references, reveal any important organisations, or suggest any key journals. Do you need to change your search strategy? Do you need to go any further?

Uses and advantages

- Public sources of information may provide much of the information you need (often free through libraries and the internet)

- Their use can contextualise your research.

- They can enable comparisons with other organisations to be made (good and bad).

Problems and limitations

- Using public sources of information can be time-consuming and costly.

- Searches can be fruitless.

- It can be difficult to assess what the information actually means for your organisation.

Internal documents

Internal documents can provide useful information which can assist in tracking the history of a project or organisation. They can consist of original project proposals, letters, minutes of meetings, costings and so on. Such documents are particularly useful when seeking to establish baseline information for an evaluation, such as the original objectives of an activity and why these were set out in the manner they are.

Uses and advantages

- They are usually cheap and easy to obtain.

- They help you to understand why the activities or project have developed as they have.

- They counteract any tendency to evaluate activities against your own expectations rather than against those which were originally agreed.

Problems and limitations

- Internal documents can be difficult and time-consuming to analyse.

- They can be limited in their capacity to give a rounded picture.

- The quality of the minutes of meetings can vary according to the ability of the minute taker.

- Deficient filing systems and archiving can leave significant gaps in the records.

Records or statistics

Keeping records or statistics is a routine way of monitoring activities and performance. It is a way of recording in a standard and systematic fashion what is happening. You may not have considered these to be research tools at all, but records can be a source of information about trends in things as diverse as sales, patterns of demand for services, the effectiveness of job advertisements, as well as actual spending compared to budget forecasts.

In order to keep records which can be useful for research, you need to consider:

- what you need information about

- how you will collect this information

- who will collect it

- how it will be used

- how it will be maintained and kept up to date

- who will have access to it.

It is really important that any records you intend to use to support a case, or as evidence of performance, are collected and maintained in a consistent manner, otherwise you will find it difficult to compare trends over time.

Uses and advantages

- Records can be reliable.

- They are controllable and implementable in-house.

- They make it easy to extract comparisons over time and between events and activities.

Problems and limitations

- Record keeping can escalate into a resource-costly and bureaucratic obsession.

■ Records may not reveal what really matters.

■ Changes to the methods of keeping records can undermine comparison.

Some organisations are bad at keeping records. They start out devising all kinds of information systems only to find that a key factor has been omitted or neglected. It can also be hard to persuade others of the importance of keeping good records, especially if they are very busy. But well thought-out records can be invaluable in reviewing activities of all kinds.

Surveys and questionnaires

Surveys are a technique in which a sample of the population is asked questions about the issue or issues the investigator is interested in. As far as possible the sample should be representative of the wider population. A knowledge of sampling techniques and related statistics is needed for this purpose. The greater your confidence in your sampling techniques, the greater will be your confidence in generalising your survey findings to the wider population.

See Selecting your sample, p. 142, and Sample size, p. 144.

Questionnaires are the main instrument by which surveys are conducted. Questions asked in surveys are most commonly in the form of closed questions. That is, there is some predefined range of possible answers such as 'Yes' or 'No' or some kind of scale, often from 1 to 5. The predefined answers mean that responses can be analysed using appropriate statistical techniques. It is possible to include open-ended questions in surveys, that is, questions where individuals are completely free to generate their own answers. This means, however, that to be statistically useful, the resulting answers have to be grouped into categories that make some sense. This requires someone to go through the questionnaires and interpret the respondents' often cryptic comments. This may introduce an additional source of error and is time-consuming and costly.

Any survey is only as good as the questions asked. Questions need to be skilfully and carefully developed. There are three important points to bear in mind when designing survey questions.

BOX 7.4   SURVEYS: THREE QUESTIONS FOR DESIGNERS

1 **Do the questions allow people to respond in a way which meaningfully reflects their opinions and behaviour?** In other words, do your questions allow people to express their views, or are they being unduly influenced by your preconceived ideas of what is important? You may need to carry out some preliminary research, perhaps individual interviews or group discussions, to establish what are relevant questions and appropriate response categories.

---

2 **Will respondents understand the questions in the way that was intended?** The use of jargon, unusual vocabulary or complex sentence construction can all lead respondents to misunderstand questions and so give inappropriate answers.

3 **Do the questions lead respondents to answer in a particular way?** It is possible to let our own biases influence the way we construct questions so that the respondents give the answer *we* want rather than their own opinion. Pre-testing questions with a small group of people similar to those you are going to survey can help to identify problems with language and to reduce bias.

Surveys can be conducted using self-completion questionnaires sent electronically or by post, or by using interviewers to ask questions by telephone or in personal interviews.

Uses and advantages

■ Surveys are more likely to give results that are representative of the population as a whole than other interview or observation techniques.

■ Data can be compared against expectations and targets.

■ When professionally administered – using short, clear questions and piloted first – surveys can add credibility to your research.

■ Postal surveys have a low cost per person.

■ Telephone surveys usually get a good response rate and are quicker than postal surveys.

■ Telephone and personal interviews are a good way to handle complex questions.

Problems and limitations

■ Response rates to postal questionnaires are nearly always low and therefore probably unrepresentative.

■ You get answers only to the questions you have asked. The responses may not be appropriate, clear or revealing of people's real opinions.

■ Survey results often lack the richness and subtlety it is possible to uncover using other methods.

■ Statistical knowledge (and a computer) are often needed to analyse the data.

Interviews

Interviews are generally face-to-face encounters between two or more people for the purpose of asking questions about satisfaction with products or services, establishing views, or suitability for employment. Interviews may be formal or informal. The terms 'structured', 'semi-structured' and 'unstructured' are commonly used to refer to levels of formality or informality.

See Selecting your sample, p. 142, and Sample size, p. 144.

Formal interviews use a structured questionnaire with set questions. These may use closed questions inviting a 'Yes' or 'No' response or brief answers. There may be pre-coded answers so that the interviewer ticks the appropriate box according to the respondent's answer. Often these will have been piloted or tested with a small sample of people to ensure that questions are understood, are not biased and do not lead to particular kinds of answers.

Informal interviews allow more freedom to the interviewer over the questions which are asked and to the interviewee over the manner in which they answer. Informal interviews can be unstructured but are more usually semi-structured. There is a *schedule* of issues or topics to be explored in the interview and the interviewer will ask an open question to start the interviewee talking, and then probe or ask linked questions, depending on the response of the interviewee.

The art of asking questions in ways which do not lead the interviewees to answer in the way they think you want them to answer can be difficult. You need skills to *frame the questions* so that you talk for a minimum amount of time and the interviewee talks for longer.

Questions should always be clear and succinct. There are a number of types of question which can be used in interviews. These include:

- **Open questions** These begin with phrases such as 'How did you...?' 'Tell me about...?'. These give the interviewee time to respond fully and prevent the interviewer from revealing their own views and opinions.

- **Closed questions** These demand very short answers, often 'Yes' or 'No'. For example, 'Did you do x before y?' 'Do you have a driving licence?'. They are useful for checking facts. Inappropriate use, though, can lead to important information not being revealed because the interviewee is not given the opportunity to mention it.

- **Hypothetical questions** These ask 'What would you do if ... ?'. They are used to try to uncover attitudes and views about something and may be indicative of future behaviour. However, these should be used with care because the best predictor of future behaviour is actual past behaviour. Future behaviour may be more effectively explored with questions which ask 'Tell me about a time when you had to do y? How did you handle it?'.

- **Probing questions** These ask, for example, 'When you ran the project and concentrated on a, did b happen then or later?'. These are used for exploring statements or facts in greater detail.

There are several types of question to avoid. These include:

- **Leading questions** These impress the views of the interviewer on the interviewee and try to influence them into agreeing or disagreeing. For example, 'I usually think... don't you agree?'.

- **Trick questions** These are bad practice and generally unethical.

- **Complex questions** If you add too many factors into your question, the interviewee will simply get lost in a web of queries and not know where to start. Important factors may be overlooked in answering such questions.

Uses and advantages

- There is usually a good response rate – people are less likely to refuse a face-to-face interview.

- They are good for handling complex issues.

- They can reveal what really happened and why.

- They can provide a cross-section of relevant stakeholder perspectives.

- They can be informative, yielding much qualitative data.

Problems and limitations

- The average cost of an interview is high compared with the cost of other research methods.

- They are time consuming and costly to analyse.

- They are difficult to analyse without some bias.

- It can be hard to get honest answers from some categories of respondent, for example, when you ask people questions about *your own* work. Fears about confidentiality can also inhibit responses.

Observing

Observation, or 'naturalistic observation', is a way of collecting information without any form of intervention or manipulation. An example of this would be making a video recording of customers visiting a retail store layout to see how they moved around the displays. 'Participant observation' is a particular method commonly employed in social research. It means entering a social situation of some kind and acting as if the researcher were one of the group being researched. The researcher then records all they can recollect about the group activities, together with their impressions. Stated in this way the method sounds simple and straightforward. However, it raises some complex issues concerning bias and ethics.

To what extent can the researcher be part of the group if they do not share the same values? If they are known to be a researcher, will that affect the group's behaviour?

If they enter the group in a covert manner, how ethical is this? Consider for example, the employer who recruits a researcher to an office, ostensibly as another employee, but in reality to find out what staff really think of a new proposal, or a retailer who employs researchers to pose as difficult customers to test staff's ability to handle such situations. This is not to say that such methods are unethical, but rather that the ethics of such issues should be considered very carefully.

Uses and advantages

- Observing may be the only way to see things as they are, and not as other people wish to portray them.

- It can reveal realities and ways forward that are not evident to those intimately involved on a day-to-day basis.

Problems and limitations

- Observing is time-consuming.

- It can be potentially intrusive and ethically problematic.

- It can be stressful for both the subject being observed and for the researcher.

- It can be subjective.

- Unless many observations are taken, judgements can be formed from one instance of observation or hearsay.

- The observer can influence events.

Focus groups

Focus groups are small groups, usually between five and twelve people, whose opinions are sought. They may be asked about their responses to an organisation and its work, or their views about a specific product, campaign or project. It is usual to run a number of groups concerned with different aspects of the topic under investigation. Note that issues of sampling are as relevant to focus groups as they are to other methods. Issues of sampling are as relevant to focus groups as they are to other methods. Focus groups often require facilitation by a trained person. A moderator or facilitator leads each group in a discussion of the topics about which you want to discover the group's views and opinions. The moderator's main job is to facilitate the discussion, ensuring that it is not dominated by particular individuals. The discussions

See Selecting your sample p. 142.

are recorded, usually on audio or videotape. A transcript of each discussion may be made. What people said in discussion is analysed by the moderator and key points are drawn out, which then serve as the basis for a report.

Uses and advantages

- Focus groups are useful for getting reactions to new policies or communications. For example, you might want to get reactions to a new brand, logo or advertising material.

- They are commonly used for seeking the views of a random selection of customers unknown to each other.

- They are relatively quick to organise and often cheaper than large-scale surveys.

- People's motives and thoughts emerge through interaction.

- Consensual ways forward can emerge.

- The researcher can watch the group or replay tapes to get a better feel for what different stakeholders are saying.

- People often like being asked for their views on an organisation they favour or support.

Problems and limitations

- If sampling methods are not used, it is difficult to know how representative the group is of the particular stakeholder group they are drawn from. So it is hard to know the validity of any conclusions drawn.

- Care needs to be taken that the moderator's own views do not bias the group – the moderator does not need to justify the work of the organisation or express their own views.

- Group dynamics can affect people's views so that members express views they don't usually hold.

- Focus groups usually require expert facilitation.

CHAPTER 8 WORKING WITH DATA

Using your data

This chapter covers basic techniques for understanding and analysing data. However reliable and relevant are the data you have gathered, data do not speak for themselves. You must analyse and interpret them; you must draw meaning from them (and remember, of course, that different people can take different meanings from the same data). Sometimes you may be able to draw what you regard as conclusive lessons from the data. You may be able to say: 'The data show beyond reasonable doubt that...'. At other times, the data may be indicative rather than conclusive, so that you will be able to say no more than: 'The data *suggest* that...'. Either way, you will be confident that you have drawn the maximum value from your data. You will have studied the information you have gathered, analysed it and interpreted the results using logic, good judgement, and where necessary, statistical techniques. You may first need to refresh your memory on number representation, arithmetical operations, percentages and other fundamentals. If so, you will find these in Chapter 5 'Working with numbers'.

Qualitative data

Qualitative data are information that cannot be quantified and expressed as a number. Such data are usually in text form – in the form of opinions expressed during interviews or focus groups, or the open-ended comments on a completed survey questionnaire. Some qualitative data can be converted to numerical data, such as categories, which can be analysed using statistical techniques. More often, however, qualitative data require qualitative analysis involving classification and coding.

Analysing qualitative data

There are a number of stages involved in analysing qualitative data. These can be set out as seven steps.

Step 1 Convert any rough field notes you have made into some form of written record which you and your colleagues will still be able to understand in later months. When writing your field notes you may wish to add your own thoughts and reflections. This will be the start of your tentative analysis. You should distinguish your speculation from your factual field notes.

Step 2 Ensure that any material you have collected from interviews, observations or original documents is properly referenced. The reference should indicate what was involved, the date and time, the context, the circumstances leading to the data collection and the possible implications for the research. You may find it useful to record your references on a proforma summary sheet, which you can then keep in an indexed system for ease of retrieval.

Step 3 Start coding the data as early as possible. This will involve allocating a specific code to each variable, concept or theme that you wish to identify. The code may be allocated to a specific word or phrase. The use of exemplars is helpful in applying the code and explaining its significance in your research report. The code will allow you to store the data in an organised set, retrieve the set and reorganise it in a variety of ways. You will find it easier if you start with as many codes as you feel necessary and later condense them into a smaller number.

Step 4 When your data are coded, you can start grouping the codes into smaller categories according to the patterns or themes which emerge. This is not a mechanical task, but will require considerable effort and thought. If you are not using a strong theoretical framework, do not attempt to impose categories, but allow them to emerge from the data. Compare new data as they are collected with your existing codes and categories, and modify them as required.

Step 5 At various stages write summaries of your findings. The discipline of putting your thoughts on paper will help your analysis and highlight any deficiencies to be remedied.

Step 6 Use your summaries to construct generalisations with which you can confront existing theories, or which you can use to construct a new theory.

Step 7 Continue working on Step 6 until you are satisfied that the generalisations arising from your data are sufficiently robust to support or challenge existing theories or to construct a new theory.

(Source: Hussey and Hussey, 1997)

Quantitative data

Quantitative data are numerical. When data are numerical, mathematical and statistical, operations can be performed on them so that we can summarise and interpret them. This is one way in which we create knowledge.

Data types and frequency

Statistical techniques are useful to managers, but there are some key concepts in data analysis which you will need to understand before you can make use of them. The most basic of these concepts is the *type* of data you are dealing with. The most basic distinction is between discrete and continuous data.

Discrete data are measurements or observations whose units of measurement cannot be split up in a meaningful way, such as the number of stores a company has, the number of staff, shoes sizes and the number of eggs in a carton. Saying that a company has 3.5 stores or 4.3 people makes no sense. Conversely, continuous data are measurements or observations whose units of measurement can be split into smaller parts, such as time, weight, and height (1.5 hours makes sense as do 8.3 kilos and 2.1 metres). When you present discrete and continuous data, there are conventions about how you deal with each, in particular in terms of frequency.

Frequency refers to the number of times a particular observation or measurement is made. For example, if you were counting the number of branch stores (discrete data) that retail companies have in a particular geographical region, you might create a table that looks like the one below. The categories or class boundaries used constitute the number of branches (from 2 to 7, the maximum number found in that region); the observed frequency is the number of companies falling into each category:

Number of branches	2	3	4	5	6	7
Number of companies (observed frequency)	27	18	14	10	5	5

Discrete data are easy to set out this way. If you wanted to display continuous data, such as the body mass indices (a measure of obesity) of patients seen at a weight clinic, you need to establish some sensible groupings. You might create a table like this using weight categories and the number of people falling into each category:

Weight category	Overweight	Obese	Morbidly obese
	Body mass index of 25-29.9	Body mass index of 30-34.9	Body mass index of 35+
Number of patients	179	103	68

Note that category or class boundaries must not overlap. If they do, some observations could fall into two categories. If the body mass index had been 25–30 and 30–35 in which weight category would you have placed a client with a body mass index of exactly 30?

Data scales

There are a number of different types of quantitative data which result from different methods of collection. These, in turn, depend on what it is that is being measured or counted. Each can be useful depending on what you are trying to find out. When we talk about different types of data, we usually refer to what are known as *scales*. It is important to note that data scales can produce discrete or continuous data depending on the scale type, and some scales can produce either.

Nominal (categorical) scales

Nominal or categorical scales are the most basic. Individual items of data are grouped into qualitative classes or categories. There is no quantitative difference between classes. Examples of data categories relating to people include religion, gender, job title and country of birth.

Ratio and interval scales

Ratio scales and interval scales are the simplest true quantitative scales. The ratio scale is used where the intervals between data points are identical, as when we measure height in centimetres. The scale begins at zero and moves upward in centimetre intervals. It is meaningful to say that an object which is six centimetres tall is twice the height of one which is three centimetres tall.

Interval scaling often looks as precise as ratio scaling in that the measurements move upwards in regular intervals, but is a little deceptive. This is because, on an interval scale, the zero point is arbitrary, perhaps because we don't know what or where zero is. In such cases the zero on the scale will not be a true zero. This is the case, for example, when we measure temperature in Celsius and Fahrenheit. The problem with interval scaling is that we cannot say, for example, that something is twice as hot as something else. To do that we would have to measure temperature in Kelvin, a ratio scale where the zero is *not* arbitrary. Then it would be appropriate to say that one temperature is twice as hot as another.

This is important for physicists and chemists, but, in terms of the data you are likely to collect as a manager, data from interval and ratio scales can be treated in the same way. When we are working with data about the length of time people have spent in a job, their wage levels, or ages, it makes sense to say that one person has been in a job twice as long as another, is paid a third as much again, and is half their age. We don't have to worry about the fact that many types of measurement do not conform to ratio scaling.

Ordinal scaling (ranked data)

Ordinal scaling ranks observations along a dimension. An example of an ordinal scale would be a manager's ranking of staff performance. For example, the manager may think staff member A outperforms staff members B and C. So staff member A is ranked first, followed by B and then C. We can attach some degree of difference between the rankings, but we do not know by how much someone ranked first differs from the person ranked second. That is, we cannot say that the gap between employees A and B is the same as between B and C. We know only the order in which they are placed in terms of quality of performance as perceived by their manager. When summarising and analysing these data, we need to take care. For example, we cannot use the same methods as when we are dealing with interval and ratio scales where we can calculate the arithmetic mean (or average) of a set of data.

See Understanding averages: the three Ms, p. 161.

Ordered metric scale

The ordered metric scale lies somewhere between ordinal and interval measures. Ordered metric scaling was developed as a means of representing the strength of a person's attitudes in some quantitative form. An attitude scale is built up from responses to a series of associated questions. It consists of a series of items that tend to go together. An example of an ordered metric scale is the 'Approaches to Learning and Studying Inventory' in Appendix 1 of this book. Because of the amount of work carried out to develop an instrument that measures an attitude, the intervals (the difference between scale points) in ordered metric scaling can be ranked by order of magnitude, unlike ordinal scaling.

Understanding averages: the three Ms

The average is a familiar concept. We talk about 'the average number of days it takes to complete an order' and 'the average length of time that patients wait for an operation', for example. But the term average in fact refers to any one of *three* measures of the *central tendency* of a set of numbers. The three measures are: the arithmetic mean, the median and the mode. These three Ms – mean, median, mode – are all calculated differently and are suited to different purposes. You will need to be able to use all of them – and be ready to explain your choice!

The arithmetic mean

The *arithmetic mean* (usually called the mean) is the most frequently used average. It is the common meaning of the average.

Suppose an ice cream vendor sold the number of ice creams during one week in the summer as shown in Table 8.1.

Table 8.1	Ice cream sales					
Monday	Tuesday	Wednesday	Thursday	Friday	Saturday	Sunday
753	846	929	114	752	1,057	2,412

The mean is calculated by adding together all of the numbers, and then dividing the result by the number of observations (the number of days, in this example).

753 + 846 + 929 + 114 + 752 + 1,057 + 2,412 = 6,863

6,863 ÷ 7 = 980.43

The mean is 980.43

See Rounding,
p. 110, and
Significant figures,
p. 111.

The result (980.43) is the point of balance, as it were, of the whole set of sales. The word 'mean' comes from the Latin for 'middle'.

Using the mean

The mean is the most commonly-used average. It is easy to calculate and it takes account of all the observations in the series. But it has some drawbacks. The mean can be a number that is not among the observations: on no day did the ice cream vendor sell 980.43 ice creams and no one bought 0.43 of an ice cream. Also, it does not tell you the way in which the observations are distributed around the mean. In our example, ice cream sales were particularly poor on one day and particularly good on another. While the mean does identify the point of balance of the observations, it is also useful to know something about the way the observations are distributed.

The median

The median is another average. It is the *middle value* when the values are arranged in rank order.

Suppose that a teacher marked 11 assignments and gave the marks shown in Table 8.2.

Table 8.2	Assignment marks									
Marks awarded										
20	40	50	60	65	70	70	70	75	75	95

Then the median is the middle mark – the sixth mark when all the eleven marks are ranked. The median mark is 70. The median is particularly easy to discover when there is an odd number of values. It will be the middle value.

When there is an even number, as shown in Table 8.3, there is no single middle value. Instead, you must add the two middle values and divide by two.

Table 8.3	An even number of observations								
Marks awarded									
20	40	60	65	70	70	70	75	75	95

The two middle values are the fifth and the sixth. So the median is $(70 + 70) \div 2 = 70$. When the two middle values are the same, as in this case, then the median is the same as the two values. If the two middle values had been 65 and 70, then the median would be the mid-point between them, $(65 + 70) \div 2 = 67.5$. In this instance, the median would be a value that does not appear in the table of observations.

Using the median

The median value divides the whole distribution into two halves. Half of the distribution lies below the median, and half lies above. Note that the median value is not affected by the extreme values in the way that the mean is. If the lowest values in Tables 8.2 and 8.3 were 10, and the highest values were 100, the median would be unaffected. The median is useful when extreme values would make an arithmetic mean very misleading.

The mode

The third type of average is the mode. It is the value that occurs *most frequently*. Table 8.4 shows the number of purchases of a particular monthly magazine by 20 customers at a newsagent's shop over a period of one year.

Table 8.4	Purchases of a monthly magazine over one year																			
Customer	1	2	3	4	5	6	7	8	9	10	11	12	13	14	15	16	17	18	19	20
Purchases	0	0	0	0	1	1	1	1	2	2	8	9	10	10	10	10	10	11	12	12

The mode is 10 because it is the value that occurs most often. If customer 5 had not bought a copy of the magazine, there would be two modes – 0 and 10. The distribution of purchases of the magazine would be bimodal.

Using the mode

The modal value is important for anyone who wants to know 'What is the most frequent occurrence?' It is particularly useful when values are not evenly distributed. For example, a college library wants to know the use students are making of the current periodicals in its reference-only section, and asks a random sample of 25 students each week for a month. At the end of the first week, the results are as shown in Table 8.5:

Table 8.5	Use of periodicals by students over one week																								
Student	1	2	3	4	5	6	7	8	9	10	11	12	13	14	15	16	17	18	19	20	21	22	23	24	25
Periodicals	0	0	0	1	1	1	1	1	1	1	1	1	2	2	2	3	3	3	4	5	7	8	11	11	15

The mode is 1, the value that occurs most frequently in the range of data. Note that the mean of these data is 3.44 periodicals and the median is 2. It is usual to set out data such as these as a frequency bar chart because the mode can be identified easily.

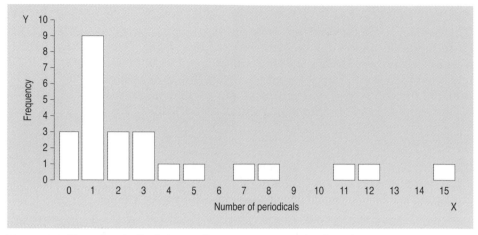

Figure 8.1 **Use of periodicals by students over one week – bar chart**

The relationship between the mean, median and mode

When creating bar charts, the shape of the bar chart will depend on how frequently values occur. When collecting data on, for example, women's shoe sizes, we would find that a few women need very small shoe sizes and some need very large sizes; the shoes sizes that the remainder need would fall between the two extremes. The bar chart would have a peak in the middle and the bars to either side of the middle would be symmetrical, like the idealised one in Figure 8.2. The mean, median and mode would be the same (shoe size 6 in this case). Whenever a bar chart is symmetrical, the mean, median and mode will be identical or at least very similar (perfectly symmetry is rare). In such cases the mean is normally used as the measure of central tendency.

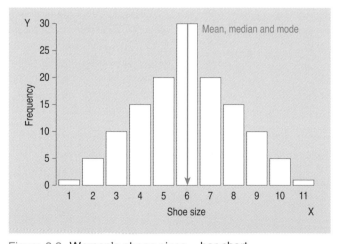

Figure 8.2 **Women's shoes sizes – bar chart**

Bar charts can be very asymmetrical. They can be skewed to the left or right, or they may even have two peaks or none. If we look at Figure 8.1 *Use of periodicals by students*, we can see that it is skewed to the left.

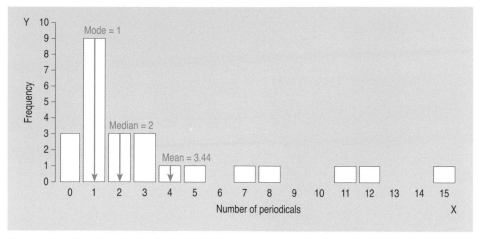

Figure 8.3 **Use of periodicals by students over one week – bar chart with mean, median and mode**

In such cases, the user must decide whether the mean, median or mode is the most useful when interpreting the data. Note that it is easy to make an inappropriate choice and inadvertently mislead people! When considering salaries, for example, it may not be useful to know the average salary of staff at a company: there may be a few very highly-paid people whose salaries make a large contribution to the mean. In such a case, the mode (the highest peak of a frequency bar chart) may be the most useful. In yet other cases, the median may be most useful. Note how important it is to know the *distribution* of values.

Understanding correlation

Suppose that you looked at two sets of data: (i) the sales of ice cream on the seafront of a popular resort, and (ii) the daily rainfall on the seafront. It is safe to say that the data would show that sales were higher on dry days than on wet ones and vice versa. An ice cream manufacturer could say: 'There is a strong correlation between sales and rainfall', meaning there is a strong relationship between them.

Suppose, secondly, that you looked at two other sets of data: (i) admissions to an exhibition in the resort, and (ii) the daily rainfall. In that instance, you would be likely to find that there were more admissions on wet days than on dry ones. The exhibition manager would also be able to say: 'There is a strong correlation between admissions and rainfall', meaning that admissions to the exhibition were higher on wet days than on dry ones and vice versa.

The correlation between two variables (ice cream sales and rainfall, or admissions and rainfall) tells you about the strength of the relationship between them. The two likely relationships, and a third one, are shown in Figure 8.4.

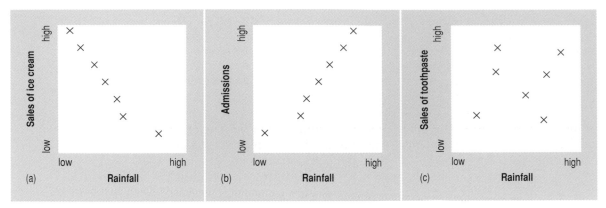

Figure 8.4 Correlation between variables: (a) Ice cream and rainfall; (b) Admissions and rainfall; (c) Toothpaste and rainfall

In Figure 8.4 (a) you can see that high sales are associated with low rainfall and vice versa; Figure 8.4 (b) shows high admissions are associated with high rainfall and vice versa; Figure 8.4 (c) shows no clear relationship between sales of toothpaste and rainfall. The correlation in Figure 8.4 (a) is a negative one because high values of one variable (ice cream sales) are associated with low values of the other (rainfall), or low with high. When high values of one variable are associated with high values of the other, or low with low (as in Figure 8.4 (b)) then the correlation is said to be positive.

When you calculate (on a spreadsheet) the correlation between two sets of data, the strength of the correlation will be expressed by a number between 0 and 1. The number is referred to as the correlation coefficient (or correlation number). The closer the number (the coefficient) is to 1 (or −1), the stronger the correlation; the closer the number is to 0, the weaker the correlation. A positive number shows a positive correlation; a negative number shows a negative correlation.

Using correlation

The discovery of a strong correlation between two variables may be helpful to a manager's planning. Suppose that an exhibitions manager discovered a strong correlation between rainfall and admissions or a hotel manager discovered a strong correlation between rainfall and the number of lunches that were sold. As a result, both managers would take account of the local weather forecast as they planned their staffing for the following day or for the next few days. If the data were sufficient, then it might be possible for the exhibitions manager to say something like 'For every 1 mm of rain I expect the admissions to rise by 50' and for the hotel manager to say something like 'For every 1 mm of rain before 11am I expect to sell 20 more lunches'. When a correlation (a relationship) between two variables is stable and when the strength of the relationship has been calculated, then it will be possible to use a knowledge of the likely value of one variable to predict the likely value of the other one.

In the two examples, it is easy to see that the change in the rainfall will cause a change in the number of admissions or in the number of lunches that are sold. One event (one variable) causes the other. When there is a strong correlation between two variables, it may be easy to assume that one is the cause of the other. You need to be on your guard, however. Suppose that a bus manager noticed that there was a strong correlation between the late running of buses on a particular route and the number of young students on the buses. The manager's first thought might be 'The lateness is due in some way to the students'. And it might be true that the students' boisterous behaviour did make it more difficult for the driver to keep to time. Or it might be that the students were travelling at times, in the morning and afternoon, when traffic was generally heavy, and that their presence on the buses had nothing to do with the late running. Always remember that a strong correlation tells you something about the strength of the relationship between two variables; it does not tell you that one of the variables causes the other. Correlation does not imply causation.

Understanding the range of a set of data

You can make more sense of an average when you know something about the spread or the range of a set of values.

Suppose that two selection panels have assessed the performance of candidates during a series of tests. Each panel has seen eight candidates and has awarded marks out of 100 to each candidate. The panels set out the marks they awarded in ascending order. This way it is easier to see the *range*, or *distribution* of the marks awarded by each panel. Table 8.6 shows how the marks are spread.

See Understanding averages: the three Ms, p. 161.

Table 8.6	The spread of marks						
Selection panel assessment							
Panel A	20	45	55	65	65	70	70	90
Panel B	45	50	60	60	60	65	65	75

The mean of both distributions is 60 (480 ÷ 8).

Though both distributions have the same mean, 60, the range of Panel A's marks – the gap between the lowest mark and the highest – is wider than the range of Panel B's marks. In a report on the quality of candidates, it would be sensible to include both the mean and the range.

The two boundary posts of a range are the lowest and the highest values. If there is something atypical or misleading about one or both of these values, then the range will also be misleading. The gap, or range, between Panel A's lowest and highest mark is 70 (90 – 20), compared with a gap of 30 (75 – 45) for Panel B's. However, Panel A's two boundary marks (20 and 90) could be said to be extreme when you compare them with the other six marks. Sometimes, it may be sensible to give the range, not from the two boundary values, but from the values that are one above the lowest and one below the highest. In this instance, Panel A's *adjusted range* would be 25 (70 – 45) compared with 15 for Panel B's (65 – 50). You will have to use your judgement. Of course, always make clear what you have done.

Quartiles and the interquartile range

Extreme values or *outliers* in a data set can be a problem because they provide a misleading picture. One way of overcoming this is to divide up the distribution and look only at the distribution of the more 'normal' scores. This has to be done in a very systematic way, however. There are two steps in the process.

Step 1: Quartiles

First, split the distribution into four quarters or quartiles. To do this, first calculate the median. This will separate the distribution in two.

Take Panel A's distribution again (make sure they are ranked in ascending order) shown in Table 8.7.

Table 8.7	Panel A's scores						
20	45	55	65	65	70	70	90

The median value is 65 because the two central values, the fourth and the fifth, are both 65. The median value has split the distribution into two halves as shown in Table 8.7.

Now work out the median values of the four marks in the lower half of the distribution and then in the upper half. In the lower half the median is 50 (45 + 55 ÷ 2). That value has split the lower half into two. The median value of the upper half is 70 (because the sixth and seventh marks are both 70). That value splits the upper half into two. The medians of the lower and upper quartiles are shown in Table 8.8.

Table 8.8	Quartile medians							
Quartile medians	**Scores**							
	20	45	55	65	65	70	70	90
Median = 65								
Median of lower half = 50								
Median of upper half = 70								

Step 2: The interquartile range

The interquartile range is the distribution of data between the lower quartile line and the upper quartile line. It is a useful statistic because it shows the extent to which the scores are clustered around the middle of the distribution. To calculate the interquartile range we leave out the lowest and highest quartiles of the data – the bottom 25 per cent and the top 25 per cent. This leaves the middle 50 per cent shown in Table 8.9.

Table 8.9	The interquartile range							
Scores	20	45	55	65	65	70	70	90
Interquartile range								

If we look again at Table 8.7 and the quartile medians (50 and 70), we can see that the interquartile range of values is from 50 to 70. Without the extreme values, we now have a better idea of the distribution of the data around the middle.

Standard deviation

The normal distribution and standard deviation

When you record a large number of randomly occurring events or features and then plot your data on a bar chart, *the general* shape of the curve will look like the one in Figure 8.5. The distribution of your data will be a 'normal' one.

See Data types and frequency, p. 158, Data scales, p. 159, and Bar charts, p. 123.

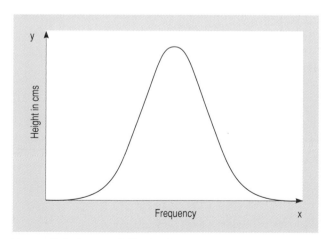

Figure 8.5 **A normal distribution**

Suppose, for example, that you select 100 adults at random and measure their heights. To create a bar chart of the results, you draw the vertical axis (the *y* axis), marking intervals in centimetres starting at the bottom at 90 cm and ending at the top at 180 cm (or whatever the least and greatest heights you measured). You mark the horizontal axis (the *x* axis) from 0 to 100 to represent *frequency* – the number of people of a particular height. You then plot the 100 results on the bar chart. The dot you make on the 90 cm line would show the number of people who were 90 cm high, the dot on the 180 cm line would show the number who were 180 cm high, and so on. As you would expect, most of the heights will be close to the mean height. There will be just a few people who are extremely short and just a few who are extremely tall. The general shape will look like Figure 8.5.

This general shape is an important one. It will approximate the shape of a normal distribution curve – a symmetrical, bell-shaped curve which has some mathematical properties of great interest. It tells you about the distribution of values, in this case heights, around the mean. This distribution is described by what is known as the *standard deviation*.

The useful attribute of a normal distribution curve is that it doesn't matter whether the curve is tall and thin or short and fat: the relationship between known points remains the same. We can mark these points. Let's call the highest point of the curve, the flattest point, 0 (zero). This corresponds to the mean and cuts the curve in half. On either size of the mean there are three other points whose relationship to the mean and each other remains the same. To the left of zero, we will call these −1, −2 and −3. To the right, we will call them +1, +2 and +3. Beyond −3 is the negative tail of the curve and beyond +3 is the positive tail. Because of the mathematical properties of the curve, we know the proportion of values (in this case heights) that will fall between −1 and +1 (that is, within one standard deviation from the mean), between −2 and +2 (within two standard deviations from the mean), between −3 and +3 (within three standard deviations from the mean), and the proportion that will fall under each 'tail' of the curve. The proportions are shown in Fig 8.6 as percentages. Our marks represent, respectively, one, two and three standard deviations from the mean.

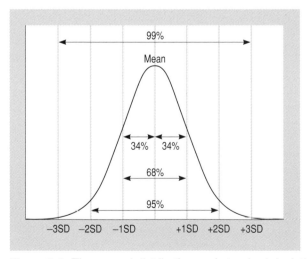

Figure 8.6 **The normal distribution and standard deviations**

BOX 8.1 IMPORTANT FEATURES OF A NORMAL DISTRIBUTION

1 The mean value will be in the middle of the distribution; it will be the value at the top of the curve.

2 68% of the values will lie within one standard deviation from the mean.

3 95% of the values will lie within two standard deviations from the mean.

4 99.7% of the values will lie within three standard deviations from the mean.

5 The percentages reflect the proportion of the total area under the curve, that is, within one, two or three standard deviations from the mean.

6 The standard deviation tells you about the range of a set of observations.

Whenever you collect data using ratio or interval scales, plot your data on a graph. If the graph *looks* like a normal curve, that is, if it *approximates* a normal distribution curve, you can treat the data as normally distributed. Because the properties of a normal distribution curve are fixed, you will be able to draw conclusions from it.

How to use the standard deviation

The standard deviation tells you about the way that the different values are distributed around the mean. Suppose you recorded the times that 100 customers have waited for service in a store during a busy time of the day. You have plotted the data on a bar chart and found that they approximate a normal distribution curve. You then calculate both the mean and the standard deviation (SD). The mean waiting time is 5 minutes. One standard deviation is 2 minutes. You can now use the mean (5 minutes) and the standard deviation (2 minutes) to draw the following conclusions:

See Standard deviation, p. 169, and Deciding whether data are normally distributed, p. 172.

- About 68 per cent of the customers are likely to wait between 3 and 7 minutes, that is, between the **mean −1SD** and the **mean +1SD**.

- Nearly all customers (95 per cent) are likely to be served between 1 and 9 minutes, that is between the **mean −2SD** and the **mean +2SD**.

You can draw general conclusions like these from the data as long as: (i) there are 30 or more values, and (ii) there is nothing special or odd about the distribution of the values. With insufficient data or with a distribution that does not approximate a normal distribution curve it would be unsafe to draw the two conclusions.

Calculating a standard deviation

The standard deviation (SD or STDEV) is one of the functions on a computer spreadsheet or calculator. When you want to calculate a standard deviation, input your set of values (e.g. the time each customer waited to be served) and follow the instructions on how to obtain the standard deviation. Alternatively, calculate it yourself using the instructions in one of the many books available on statistical analysis.

Mean and standard deviation

Use both the mean and standard deviation together whenever you can. Instead of thinking about the mean, think about the mean *and* standard deviation. It is a more accurate and more meaningful way of describing data.

Deciding whether data are normally distributed

Always check to see if your data approximate to a normal distribution before you draw conclusions and make inferences from them. An alternative to plotting a bar chart is set out below.

See Standard deviation, p. 169, and How to use the standard deviation, p. 171.

BOX 8.2   HOW TO CHECK THE DISTRIBUTION OF YOUR DATA

Here are some figures representing the number of breakdowns each month in a manufacturing plant:

5, 8, 2, 4, 4, 6, 5, 3, 7, 6, 9, 7, 4, 2, 6, 5, 3, 5, 5, 4.

We can group these 20 values as follows:

Value	0	1	2	3	4	5	6	7	8	9
Frequency	–	–	2	2	4	5	3	2	1	1

The arithmetic mean is 5.0 and the standard deviation (SD) is 1.9. What is theoretically expected from a normal distribution with this mean and SD is that 68% of the observations will lie between 5.0 ± 1.9 and 95% between 5.0 ± 3.8 (and so on). If we now calculate the actual percentage of observations lying within ± 1SD of the mean, and within ± 2SD of the mean, we can compare them with the theoretical percentages, 68% and 95%:

	Observed %	Theoretical %
Mean ± 1 SD: **3.1 to 6.9**	60 (calculation: 12 ÷ 20 × 100)	68
Mean ± 2 SD: **1.2 to 8.8**	95 (calculation: 19 ÷ 20 × 100)	95

Mean ± 3 SD:
–0.7 to 10.7   100 (calculation: 20 ÷ 20 × 100)   99.7

We can use our judgement here to say that the match is acceptable, but sometimes we need to resort to statistical techniques to compare our data with what is theoretically expected under an assumption of normality.

(Source: based on Targett, 1983)

Standard error and confidence intervals

When we generalise research findings from a sample to the wider population from which the sample was drawn, we must allow for the likelihood that the sample is not an absolutely accurate representation of the population. We need to see if our sample relates to the population, or whether our results apply only to our sample. The *standard error* of the mean and *confidence intervals* are important concepts to grasp before drawing general conclusions from data. Both are based on the concepts of the normal distribution, the mean and the standard deviation. Their description and the formulae needed to calculate them are beyond the scope of this book. However, you are advised to check your sample and work out your margin of error. The concepts are well-covered in many books on statistical analysis, and spreadsheets can be used for calculation.

Index numbers

An index (or index number) will enable you to use one value (the base value) to measure or express other values.

Constructing an index

Suppose that the number of staff in an organisation over three years was as shown in Table 8.10.

Table 8.10 Staff in the organisation	
Year	**Number of staff**
(i)	(ii)
1	10
2	12
3	15

The manager could say: 'By the end of Year 2, the number of staff was 120% of the number at the end of Year 1, and by the end of Year 3 the number of staff was 150% of the number at the end of Year 1'. Table 8.11 shows this way of describing the changes in the number of staff.

Table 8.11	An index (Base Year = Year 1)	
Year	Number of staff	Number of staff as % of staff in Y1
(i)	(ii)	(iii)
1	10	100
2	12	120
3	15	150

The values in column (iii) express exactly the relationships between the original values in column (ii). For instance, the relationship (or ratio) between 120 and 100 is exactly the same as that between the original 12 and 10.

Suppose now that the manager said: 'I want to take Year 2 as my reference year, as my Base Year'. In that case, the table would look like Table 8.12.

Table 8.12	An index (Base Year = Year 2)	
Year	Number of staff	Number of staff as % of staff in Y2
(i)	(ii)	(iii)
1	10	83
2	12	100
3	15	125

The number of staff in Year 1 (10) is now expressed as a percentage of the number in Year 2 (12). Also, the number of staff in Year 3 (15) is expressed as a percentage of the number in Year 2 (12). The number in Year 2 has become the base for the entries in column (iii). The ratio of 83 to 100 is exactly the same as the ratio of 100 to 120 shown in Table 8.10. And the ratio of 100 to 125 is exactly the same as the ratio of 120 to 150 shown in Table 8.10.

The manager could also have chosen Year 3 as the Base Year. See Table 8.13.

Table 8.13	Three different indices			
Year	Number of staff	Number of staff as % of staff in		
		Y1	Y2	Y3
(i)	(ii)	(iii)	(iv)	(v)
1	10	100	83	67
2	12	120	100	80
3	15	150	125	100

Each of the three columns, (iii), (iv) and (v), presents an index of staff numbers in the organisation. Each of the three sets of index numbers has a different base. The index number for the value in the Base Year is presented as 100. No one base value or year is mathematically preferable to another.

Using an index as a general measure

An index number is a general measure of the increase or decrease in the value of a variable. The particular units of measurement (money, weight, number, etc.) are transformed into a simple index number. Every index number is calculated by comparing the current value of the variable with the value in the base period.

The Retail Prices Index in the UK

The Retail Prices Index is one of the measures used in the UK to calculate inflations. It expresses the change in the general price level from one month to another (and, with the annual series, from one year to another). All the individual changes in prices are the inputs to a process (a complex calculation) which leads to a number, the Retail Prices Index for the period.

The current Retail Prices Index in the UK is calculated by reference to the prices for a representative collection of goods and services in January 1987.

This index is perhaps the most familiar one in the UK. It shows what has happened to the general level of prices in the UK. See Table 8.14.

Table 8.14	The UK Retail Prices Index, 1996-2005 (Jan 1987 = 100)		
Year	**Index**	**Year**	**Index**
1996	153	2001	173
1997	158	2002	176
1998	163	2003	181
1999	165	2004	187
2000	170	2005	192

The base values are the prices that were charged in January 1987 for the various goods and services that were selected as representative of general retail spending. The total cost of the selection was calculated. That sum became the base sum and was given the index 100. In every month since then, the total cost of that same collection of goods and services has been calculated, and the sum has been converted into an index. For instance, by 2005 the index had risen to 192, showing that the total cost of the representative collection of goods and services was 92 per cent higher (192 compared with 100) than it had been when it was first costed in January 1987. We can put this point another way by saying that in 2005 a person would have to spend £192 in order to buy what the person could have bought for £100 in 1987.

Probability

Probability is about quantifying the likelihood that something will happen or will not happen.

The probability that something will happen is expressed as a number between 0 and 1. An event that is certain to happen has a probability of 1; an event which has no chance of happening has a probability of 0. Events that might or might not happen have probabilities somewhere in between. If something is just as likely to happen as not to happen, for example, then it has a probability of 0.5. Probabilities are also expressed as percentages, so we can say 'There is a 50 per cent chance of it [whatever it is] happening'. Or we could talk about 'a 10 per cent probability' (where the probability is 0.1) or 'a 90 per cent probability' (where the probability is 0.9) and so on.

If the probability that an event will happen is assessed to be 0.6, then the probability that the event will not happen will be 0.4. Notice that the two probabilities add up to 1, as it is certain that the event will occur or will not occur.

Estimating probabilities

There are different ways of finding out or estimating the probability that an event will occur. Sometimes, it will be possible to be entirely confident about the probability. Suppose that 60 women and 40 men work in an organisation. In this case, there will be a 60 per cent probability that a randomly chosen member of staff will be a woman. At other times, a manager may have to take a representative sample of the relevant population. If, for example, 20 per cent of the sample remember a particular advertisement that was shown on television the previous day, generally speaking there is a 20 per cent probability that any one member of the population will remember the advertisement. On other occasions, though, a manager must be prepared to settle the probability of an event by the application of a personal, subjective judgement. Judgements of this kind are inevitable when hard data are not available.

Calculating probabilities

Suppose that a manager looked ahead and allocated probabilities to two unconnected events as shown in Table 8.15.

Table 8.15	The probability of two unconnected events
Outcome	**Probability**
I will be promoted	0.2
I will win a prize in the annual vegetable competition at the village fête	0.4

The probability that both events will occur is 0.08, that is, the probability of promotion (0.2) multiplied by the probability of the win (0.4). When we talk of 'the probability of [Event A] and [Event B] happening', we calculate the overall probability by multiplying the probability of each of the events occurring separately.

We can also calculate the probability of at least one of the events occurring, as follows:

The probability of the manager not being promoted is 0.8 (i.e. 1 – 0.2).

The probability of the manager not winning a prize is 0.6 (i.e. 1 – 0.4).

The probability of the manager not being promoted and not winning a prize is therefore 0.48 (i.e. 0.8 × 0.6).

So the probability that the manager will achieve at least one success (either a promotion or a win) is 0.52 (i.e. 1 – 0.48).

Inferential statistics

Inferential statistics go beyond descriptive statistics which are concerned with summarising data and organising them in a meaningful way. Inferential statistics are used to enable investigators to interpret patterns in the data, for example, to answer such questions as whether two or more groups differ on a given attribute, or whether a relationship exists between two variables. Their purpose is to enable inferences to be made about the population from which the particular samples have been drawn.

Three commonly employed statistical testing procedures are: the chi-squared (χ^2) test of association, Pearson's product moment correlation (Pearson's r) and the t-test. These statistical tests can be carried out using specialist computer software packages. Worked examples can be found in most books on statistical analysis, along with explanations of how the tests work and when it is appropriate to use them. Thus, we have not included them in this book.

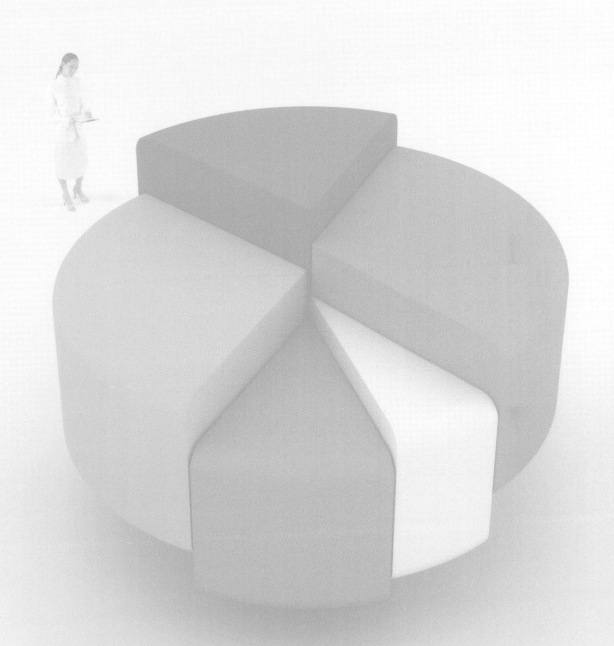

SECTION 3 YOUR CAREER

Work takes up a large part of our lives, so it's important that we are doing what we enjoy and that it brings out the best in us. Whatever stage you are at in your career, there will be times when it is necessary to plan, review and sometimes to make changes. Have you ever asked yourself any of the following questions and found it difficult to work out the answers?

- Where am I now?

- Where do I want to go?

- How will I get there?

If so, this section of *The Manager's Good Study Guide* will help you to manage your career and progress along your chosen path. It leads you through the logical and sequential steps that you will need to take to identify your career goals, what you need to do to achieve them, and how to plan a timescale for implementation. In doing so it will help you to:

- identify the skills you have – and any deficiencies

- decide what career path you want to follow

- plan a systematic approach to job hunting

- learn how to be successful at interviews.

See Planning, p. 102.

CHAPTER 9 MANAGING YOUR CAREER

Your personal marketing plan

One way of considering career development is to think of it in terms of a personal marketing plan. This doesn't mean you are about to sell your soul! Rather it means adopting a realistic view of yourself as the supplier of a service for which you need to find customers. These customers may be internal – within your own organisation, or external – in other organisations.

Creating your own individual marketing plan will take time, of course, and as you work through it you may discover aspects of yourself about which you feel uncomfortable! This is because an important part of planning will be the learning you do as a result of the process. The plan you arrive at will not – and should not – be set in stone. You may need to modify it from time to time, or even change it substantially to accommodate life events, changes in your priorities, and unexpected opportunities.

See Assessing the competitive position, p. 206, and Developing a Marketing plan, p. 243.

Evaluating your abilities

The first step in creating your personal marketing plan is to conduct a career audit. This will allow you to evaluate your own abilities, identify any gaps in your education and experience that need to be addressed, and help you to make decisions about your future aspirations.

Gathering information

Start by thinking about all the sources of information that you have about yourself. You may be able to use:

- your last report
- a recent performance appraisal
- any academic or professional qualifications you have
- 360-degree feedback (also called multi-rater, multi-source feedback) reports
- project or assignment feedback.

See 360-degree feedback, p. 305.

If you are looking for richer sources of information than these, or if these sources are not available to you, there are some others:

- analytical interviews
- personality tests.

Analytical interviews provide a valuable source of information. The idea is that you interview friends, family and colleagues to find out how they perceive you. You have to be courageous and able to take constructive criticism, but most people who complete this exercise find it valuable.

Personality tests are also useful, although you will need to make sure that you make a sensible choice of instruments, and have sufficient information about interpreting the results of those you use. Many internet websites offer free self-assessment tests. However, if you are unsure, many careers-advisory services and career consultants also offer appropriate tests. The results of such tests should not be taken as immutable facts, but as useful prompts for you to think about yourself.

Non-work experiences

Now you can supplement the information from all of these sources with data from your non-work experiences. Think about your social life, for example. Do you belong to any clubs or societies? Do you play sports? Do you have any hobbies? What skills, knowledge or attributes do you use for them?

Identify your strengths and weaknesses

Using all these sources of information, work and non-work, make a list of all your strengths and weaknesses. Turn this list into a short questionnaire to give to a sample of friends, family and colleagues and ask them to rate which of the listed strengths and weaknesses apply to you. In drawing up your list you may want to group your skills under similar headings to those shown in Table 9.1.

Table 9.1 Topics for your questionnaire	
Information technology	Do you have basic office IT skills?
Technical	Do you have any specialised technical skills?
People	Are you good with people? Are you a good team player? Can you motivate people? Are you a good listener? Are you good at persuading people to do things?
Creativity	Can you draw or design? Are you an ideas person? Do you think about new ways of doing things?
Leadership and teaching	Can you lead a group? Are you good at teaching others new skills?
Reliability	Are you a good timekeeper? Do you deliver? Do you respond to others who need help? Are you a problem solver?

The main purpose of the questionnaire is to discover if your own view of yourself is realistic. You may underplay your strengths, for example, or underplay weaknesses that you might want to remedy. The results of your questionnaire will provide constructive feedback – and you will probably be surprised at how positively others perceive you.

What do you enjoy?

Another part of this first step – identifying what you have to offer – is finding out what you enjoy and what draws out the best in you. So now you need to reflect on all your successes to date, work and non-work. Complete the statements in Table 9.2 by writing down the most important or significant experience.

Table 9.2 Positive experiences checklist
I did well and am proud of
I valued most
I became absorbed in
I handled well
I felt passionate about, or was very interested in
I learned quickly
I felt I had achieved something
I contributed
I felt I belonged – it felt 'natural'

Your completed statements will provide you with practical examples of what you have achieved. They should also tally with many of your strengths that you identified earlier.

Talents, knowledge and skills

Once you have completed this research you should be able to identify:

Your talents These are the so-called 'natural' abilities which you have, that you enjoy and are good at. Examples include drawing, singing or being able to empathise with other people. You may be a 'born' leader or good with numbers. If you are not sure what your talents are, try to take a step back and observe yourself. Identify those activities that you quickly pick up and become absorbed in.

Your knowledge This may include bookkeeping or computing, for example. It doesn't matter if you are not currently using this knowledge or do not use it very often. You could be a fluent French speaker, for example, but only get a chance to speak the language on your annual holiday.

Your skills These are abilities or expertise that you have acquired by training or experience. The key here is transferability. For example, when you bring up a family you learn to negotiate, manage money, manage your own and other people's time, motivate people, teach, use the internet, and so on. All these skills are transferable and so are valuable in a wide range of organisational settings.

Putting it in context

Finally, you need to think about what is happening in your own life right now. It doesn't matter where you are on the career ladder. Take a long hard look at what you are doing at the moment. Make a list of the good and bad points about your work and home situation. At this stage don't try to make judgements, just note down as many points as you can under the headings 'Positive' and 'Negative'. The items in each column will not be equal either in number or weight – one good point may compensate for several bad ones!

You have now completed your personal survey. You will have lists of:

- your talents, knowledge and skills
- your strengths and weaknesses
- examples of your positive experiences
- positive work and domestic factors
- negative work and domestic factors.

Now you must build a bridge between where you are now and where you want to be. But do you know where you want to be? The next step is deciding on your career goals and the path to them.

Identifying your career goals

There may be a particular reason why you are reading this chapter of *The Manager's Good Study Guide*. Perhaps you are being made redundant or you are bored at work. Maybe you need to earn more money or perhaps you simply feel restless and have no idea what to do next. Whatever your reasons for thinking about planning a career path, you will need to identify them and take them into consideration as you build a vision of your future.

What is it that you really want? Can you answer the following questions?

BOX 9.1 WHAT DO YOU WANT?

■ Do you have or want a family? How important is family life to you?

■ Where do you want to live/work? Is relocating a possibility? How far are you willing to commute?

■ What kind of lifestyle do you aspire to?

■ Could you continue with your current career? What are your future prospects with your present company?

■ Do you have enough income to support your lifestyle and family aspirations?

■ Would a job providing more income still be in keeping with your current value system?

■ What sort of trade-off are you prepared to make between your family life and your career?

■ Are you prepared to retrain if necessary? Could you live on the reduced income this might entail?

Using a drawing or picture is a good way to help you refine your aspirations. Draw or, if you prefer, visualise a picture of your ideal life. Where would you live? Who is with you? What would you do? What does your house look like? Is it in a town or in the country? Using pictures instead of words, you may be able to identify aspirations and desires you didn't know you had.

What are your values?

Next you need to consider the values that are important to you. One way of identifying them is to think about all the different roles you play in your everyday life. What are the values that are consistent across these roles? What is important to you? These values will have a marked influence on the career path you choose.

The interpersonal values set out in Box 9.2 may help you to identify your own.

BOX 9.2   SIX CRITICAL PERSONAL RELATIONSHIP VALUES

1 **Benevolence** Doing things for others.

2 **Conformity** Being accepted, doing what's socially correct.

3 **Independence** Making decisions, getting your own way.

4 **Leadership** Being in charge, having power and authority.

5 **Recognition** Being highly regarded and admired, having status, being important.

6 **Support** Being treated with understanding and consideration.

(Source: Coomber et al., 2002)

By considering how important each of these elements is to you, you can put together your own personal mission statement. An example of a mission statement is: 'To live with integrity and to make a difference in the lives of my family and other people'.

You will need to make sure, of course, that your mission statement is consistent with the talents, knowledge and skills you have to offer! Now you can begin to think about personal and career objectives with the aim of fulfilling your mission.

Identifying career opportunities and sectors

The next step is to find a match between what you want – your aspirations and your mission – and what you can realistically achieve with what you have to offer, or could offer with some more training or education. This step will first involve seeking information about types of work and job opportunities. It is important to keep an open mind while you do this, so don't discard any idea unless you really dislike it. There are several ways you can go about your search, and some are listed in Box 9.3. Remember that the internet is a good source of information for your research.

BOX 9.3 SEEKING INFORMATION

On your own

- Seek information from books on sectors that interest you, for example, banking, health and social care, the media.

- Use the internet to find out about opportunities in those sectors and the personal qualities and qualifications required.

- Link information about yourself to the requirements.

- Talk to people already working in the sector. But remember that their values and aspirations may be different from yours.

- Find out whether there are any suitable opportunities within your current organisation.

Careers advisers

- In some countries careers advice is free to people in particular circumstances. Find out whether you are eligible for free careers advice.

- Use the services of a private careers counsellor. Check that they are suitably qualified to provide careers advice.

Professional organisations

- Professional organisations are usually able to provide information regarding the education and experience required to join a profession, and how the profession is structured.

- They may have a recruitment agency or be able to supply literature on how to join the profession.

- Many have their own journals or magazines which will give you a good idea of how competitive the job market is, and what the salary levels are.

Putting it all together

Earlier in this chapter you looked at your strengths and weaknesses in terms of your talents, knowledge and skills; your positive work and non-work experiences; your positive and negative domestic and work factors; your personal values and your mission statement. You also identified a possible career sector in which you might work. Figure 9.1 shows how you can bring these elements together to identify what might be your ideal job and who might be an ideal employer. Note that 'threats' are what our weaknesses expose us to.

See Ansoff matrix, p. 210.

Your work is not yet over, however. You may need new qualifications. You may need to change jobs and you may need to change employers.

Figure 9.1 Identifying your ideal job and ideal employer

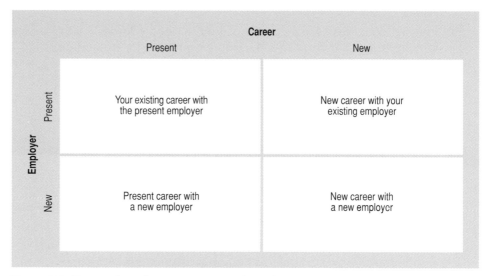

Figure 9.2 **Your options for your career and employer**

(Source: based on the Ansoff matrix, 1988)

The choices you have can be analysed using an Ansoff matrix, a tool used in marketing.

Exploring the options

As you can see from Figure 9.2, your four career options are:

1   To pursue your present career with your present employer.

2   To begin a new career with your present employer.

3   To follow your present career but with a new employer.

4   To start a new career with a new employer.

Your present career with your present employer

If this is the option that you have chosen, then you will need to think about how you are going to market yourself to your colleagues. Identify their needs, then set about trying to satisfy them. Your aim is to create your own individual brand, based on your values and your mission statement. If you do this people will know what you stand for and will be able to match you with future opportunities in the company.

A new career with your present employer

If you have chosen this option you will already have identified opportunities for you to change the direction of your career within your organisation. If you have a proven track record, your present employer may be willing to give you an opportunity in a new field, whereas a new employer would probably not be willing to take you on unless you had some relevant experience.

Your present career with a new employer

This is the most common form of career change and is an appropriate choice if you enjoy your present job. You will need to do further research to identify the kind of employer you want to work for – the industry, the sector, the size of the company and the location.

A new career with a new employer

If this is your preferred option, you may be intending to transfer your existing skills to a different setting, or you may need to learn a set of completely new skills to work in a different sector. If you need to retrain you may choose to do so through part-time study or you may decide to study full time.

Two special cases of a new career with a new employer are freelancing and starting your own business. You should seek specialist advice if you choose either of these options.

Getting a new job

Writing your CV

Whichever career option you choose, it is likely that you will need a really good curriculum vitae (CV). When drafting a CV first think about your prospective employers. Your aim is to encourage recruiters to put your CV on the 'interview' pile, not the 'reject' pile.

> ### BOX 9.4   AN IDEAL CV
> - highlights your experience
> - indicates the relevance of your experience to your job application
> - includes all relevant specialist skills
> - conveys the breadth of your experience
> - shows the depth of your experience.

There are two basic forms of CV. The first is *historical*, taking the reader through your career, job by job, in chronological order. Start with your current job and work backwards. Remember that job titles mean different things in different organisations, so explain what your responsibilities were. Don't include reasons for leaving but do focus on your strengths and key achievements.

The second form of CV is a *functional* one. This format suits people who have had a number of different job experiences. It emphasises the nature of the work done. Names of employers, dates and positions held are listed at the end.

The job search

Searching through job advertisements is the most common way to find vacancies but there are other ways such as networking and making speculative approaches.

Networking

Networking is a useful tool in getting a job, and even more useful for keeping your career path on track. A significant proportion of all new positions are identified through networking. Friends, friends of friends, and family, are all potential contacts. Those who are in work may know of job vacancies in their area.

Make contact with people who have influence in the field that you hope to work in and ask for an informal meeting. Before you go to the meeting, research the industry or organisation the person works for. Dress appropriately and prepare questions in advance. The purpose of the meeting is not to ask the person for a job but to find out more. Ask for the advice that they would give to someone who wants to enter the sector or organisation. Finally, ask if they know anyone else who might be able to help you.

After the meeting write notes to remind you about the conversation and the person you met. Most importantly, follow up any useful leads. Send the person you met an email or note thanking them for their time. If they forget to send you any of the information they promised, gently remind them after a week or so.

Speculative approaches

You need to apply for as many jobs as you can without compromising the quality of your applications. Consider writing to companies with your details asking if they have any suitable vacancies. To avoid the appearance of a mass mail shot, personalise your letters making sure you have a specific name to write to. Expect only a one per cent response rate to your speculative approaches – so use this tactic as one of several.

Making a job application

When you have prepared a 'standard' CV, you must tailor it for each job you apply for. There will be a different job specification for each vacant post and you will need to make your CV match the specification as closely as possible.

You will probably also be asked to complete a job application form.

BOX 9.5 TIPS ON FILLING IN JOB APPLICATION FORMS

- Make copies of the form and practise filling in the copies before you attempt the real thing.

- Use your CV only as supplementary material to include with your application, write essential information out again.

- Answer all the questions on the form.

- Include a covering letter. This provides another opportunity for you to sell yourself to the recruiter. Pick out one or two points that highlight your suitability for the job, and link them to the job advertisement and specification.

- Take care with your spelling and punctuation or all your efforts may be wasted.

The interview

Preparation is the key to a good interview. If your application results in an interview, gather as much information about the employer and the sector as you can. The internet is usually a good source. You should be able to find annual reports, company accounts and details of product ranges as well as information about competitors.

Some organisations offer you the opportunity to visit their premises before your interview. Make the most of this opportunity to start to build a relationship with the interviewer before the formal interview. Turning down such an offer would make you seem uninterested.

Before your interview, make sure you know the name of the person who is going to interview you. Work out your travel arrangements and times. Make a list of all the interview questions you can think of and prepare answers to them all. If you're stuck for inspiration, try the internet. A number of websites offer advice on interview technique and list the kinds of questions you may be asked. Also identify some appropriate questions to ask at the end of the interview.

In some cases the first interview will be with an agency or the human resources department. You may not see the person who hires you until the second round of interviews. Remember that interviewers are also human and may also be nervous. Your task is to form a relationship with them as quickly as possible (using their names once or twice is a way of doing this). Answer their questions in such a way as to convey as much relevant information about yourself as possible, giving examples from your previous experience. The interviewer is trying to find out if you can do the job – your task is to help them do this.

If you aren't offered the job, a follow-up phone call or letter asking for interview feedback may give you some useful pointers for future interviews. You may feel reluctant to do this, but it helps to remember two things. The first is that you may have been a very strong candidate, it's just that there happened to be an even stronger one on the day. The second is that the feedback is likely to be honest and constructive if you ask in the same way as you would when seeking information.

If you are left with a positive impression of the company, you should view the unsuccessful interview as a first step. Now you know more about the interview process and the company, you will be even better prepared next time. Employers are looking for persistence, and for people who really want to work for them. So if you like the company always try again when another post becomes vacant.

If you are offered the new job, do try to leave your current job on good terms. There might be a company takeover, your manager may be recruited into your new company or your old company may become a customer of your new firm. You never know when you might meet people again!

Taking stock – again

Once you have been in your new job for a while you might wish to rate your job satisfaction.

Table 9.3 shows one way of doing this.

Table 9.3 Job satisfaction checklist		
Compared with your last job, are you more or less:	**More**	**Less**
Energetic		
Stressed-out		
Enthusiastic about going to work		
Interested in what you are doing		
Inclined to think positively about your job outside of working hours		
Happy with your lot		
Relaxed		
Even-tempered		
Irritable		
In control of your life		
Able to find time for interests outside of work		
Confident in yourself		
Keen to set further goals		
Able to achieve a good life/work balance		

Ask your friends and family to assess you on these questions too – they may see things differently. The exercise will enable you to judge whether, on balance, your last job move was beneficial and it will give you pointers for when you consider any future move.

Lifelong learning

You may want to think about expanding your knowledge base. You might need further training to help you acquire or improve some specific skill or technique that your present job requires or a future job will need. Alternatively, you may want to explore education to help you build a body of knowledge, with the goal of becoming a specialist in your field. Whatever training or education you believe you need, make sure your educational goals match your career aspirations.

Don't give up!

Finally, don't give up. If you actively try to manage your career, opportunities will arise – and some of them may be in areas you might not have considered. Good luck – you deserve the job you have made so much effort for.

Useful books and websites for careers advice

Books

The following books provide useful advice on careers:

Bennett, S. (2001) *The Which? Guide To Changing Careers*, Which? Books.

Coomber, S., Crainer, S. and Dearlove, D. (2002) *The Career Adventurer's Fieldbook: Your guide to career success*, Capstone Publishing Ltd.

Grout, J. and Perrin, S. (2001) *Kickstart Your Career: The complete insider's guide to landing your ideal job*, John Wiley and Sons Ltd.

Longson, S. (2001) *Changing Your Career (Creating Success)*, Kogan Page.

Nelson Bolles, R. (2003) *What Color Is Your Parachute?: A practical manual for job-hunters and career changers: 2003*, Ten Speed Press.

Pyke, G. and Neath, S. (2002) *Be Your Own Career Consultant: How to unlock your career potential: Help yourself to your future*, Pearson Education Ltd.

Spillane, M. (2000) *Branding Yourself: How to look, sound and behave your way to success*, Pan.

Websites

The internet is a good source of information and help. There are a number of useful websites, including an official careers website in the UK. There is also an Open University careers website.

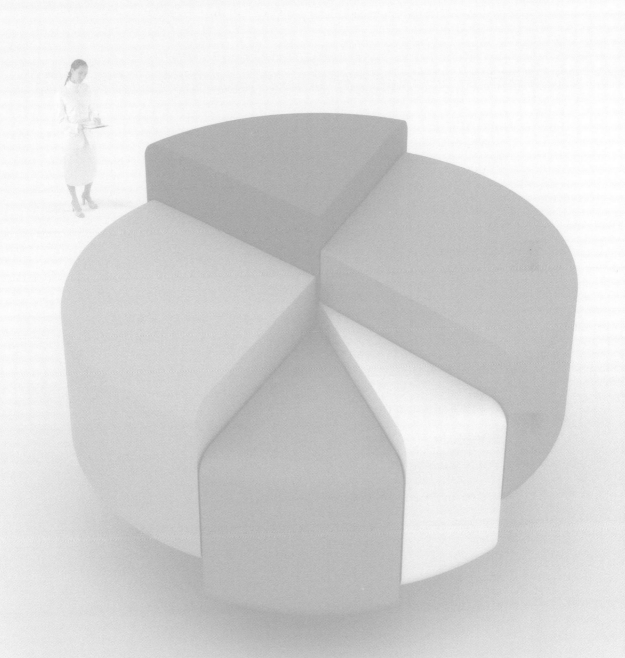

SECTION 4 COMPENDIUM OF KEY MANAGEMENT IDEAS

This section contains a compendium of key management ideas – the essential concepts that you will need as a manager. It has been organised into six chapters. The first three chapters cover topics concerning the organisation: strategy and the organisation; marketing; and finance. The final three chapters cover topics which relate to the manager's job: leadership, management and motivation; managing people; and monitoring and evaluation.

The placing of strategy and the organisation first may puzzle you if your main focus is on learning techniques to become a better manager in just one part of a large organisation. The purpose of placing this topic first is:

- to remind managers of their organisation's 'reason for being'

- to stress that the organisation operates in a wider environment which is not under managerial control

- to emphasise that the organisation is an environment itself (but one that is subject to the control and influence of managers).

The mission of any organisation will be linked to the wider environment, while the internal environment of the organisation needs to be managed in a way that supports the mission. This sets the context for other topics – the means by which managers help to ensure that an organisation achieves what it sets out to. These topics include:

- marketing and how to put the customer at the centre of the organisation

- understanding finance, including budgets and budgeting

- leading, managing and motivating

- managing people sensitively and effectively in order to achieve organisational objectives

- management control – the all-important monitoring and evaluation of people, operations and systems to ensure the link between the activities in the organisation and the overarching set of organisational goals – the ultimate connection.

Each key management idea may be referred to independently of the others. Margin notes guide you to related concepts which may aid understanding.

CHAPTER 10 STRATEGY AND THE ORGANISATION

The organisational context

Our lives, whether we are managers or not, are lived in organisations. These range from micro- to macro-organisations, that is, from systems as small as the smallest family unit to those as large as the government or state. We can think of these organisations as embedded or nested sets of systems, with influence flowing in both directions, but not in equal amounts. Clearly, a government will have more influence on an individual than the individual will have on a government, except in exceptional cases. Influence takes place through the interaction of systems and individuals. We can easily adapt this idea to the situation of an individual manager, the employing organisation and the wider community. This is shown in Figure 10.1.

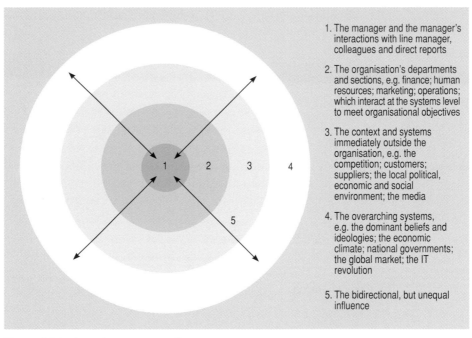

1. The manager and the manager's interactions with line manager, colleagues and direct reports

2. The organisation's departments and sections, e.g. finance; human resources; marketing; operations; which interact at the systems level to meet organisational objectives

3. The context and systems immediately outside the organisation, e.g. the competition; customers; suppliers; the local political, economic and social environment; the media

4. The overarching systems, e.g. the dominant beliefs and ideologies; the economic climate; national governments; the global market; the IT revolution

5. The bidirectional, but unequal influence

Figure 10.1 **A systems perspective**

(Source: based on Bronfenbrenner, 1979)

Just as individuals are influenced by systems which are shaped by culture, politics and economics, so managers and organisations are influenced by the wider environment. This external or far environment needs to be understood if organisations are to be successful. It is not under the control of the manager or organisation. Managers need to analyse it, understand what its implications are, and make appropriate plans. The near environment of suppliers, buyers, customers, competitors and other stakeholders can be influenced by managerial action. Only the internal environment of the organisation itself can be controlled directly – although, as many managers will agree, even this has its challenges!

The fundamental principle of strategic management is a Western cultural one – that we are controllers of our own destiny and can make things happen. In the quest for improving an organisation, current practices are constantly scrutinised along with what is happening in the far environment where both threats and opportunities may exist. This necessarily involves scrutiny of the near environment too.

Importantly, the near and far environment can also be viewed from the perspective of time, as shown in Figure 10.2. This is particularly vital in planning: identifying trends over time and ascertaining whether these trends constitute threats or opportunities which might indicate the need for organisational change.

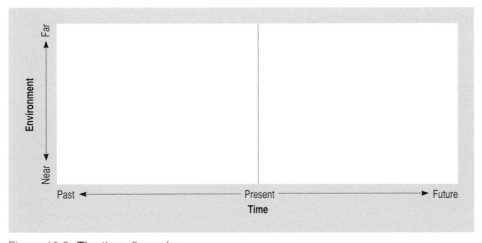

Figure 10.2 **The time dimension**

This chapter covers key management ideas that focus on: analysing the far and near environment; organisations and different types of organisation; and assessing the need for change. Its aim is to provide you with a sense of managerial purpose for managing operations, functions and people.

An organisation's mission

An organisation's mission statement sets out what the organisation wants to be. It should be the starting point for setting objectives and making strategic decisions. It contains the organisation's value proposition – its reason for being – and therefore influences the entire organisation's thinking.

Typical format of a mission statement

Good mission statements are concise and to the point, and capture the essence of the organisation by stating: its purposes (why the organisation exists, for example, to meet a specified need); its business statement (for example, to build homes); and its values (for example, a commitment to affordability and quality). There is no strict format, however. Mission statements typically contain one or more of the following four components:

1   the organisation's philosophy

2   specification of the product/market domain

3   the organisation's key values

4   critical factors for success in the marketplace.

Developing an organisational vision

The terms 'mission' and 'vision' are often used interchangeably, although 'mission' is usually focused on the tangible goals of the organisation, while 'vision' may include quite abstract elements. An organisational vision is a framework that includes the guiding philosophy, core values, beliefs and purposes from which the mission statement is developed.

The purpose of developing an organisational vision is to encourage management teams at the corporate level, the business unit or the brand level, to think in detail about what they are trying to create.

An effective vision, whether for the organisation as a whole or for a specific unit within it, holds various dimensions in balance. There will be a reference to an idealistic future but it will be based in the present. It will have an outward focus but be cognisant of inner strengths and weaknesses, and it will be broad enough to inspire yet specific enough to differentiate the particular product or service of the organisation from any other.

The six F test

The following questions will help you to identify how well a vision is likely to be embraced. Because there are six questions, each playing on a keyword beginning with the letter 'F', the questions are known as the six F test.

1   Is it *fantastic?* Does it grab attention? Will it stretch everyone involved to the limit?

2   Is it *feasible?* Can it be achieved with the resources and people available, and in the time specified?

3   Is it *focused?* Could it describe the outcome of a number of other projects currently being undertaken, or just one?

4   Is it *flexible?* Is there room for manoeuvre if key players, corporate goalposts or circumstances change (which they will)?

5   Is it *faxable?* Can it be remembered easily and communicated succinctly?

6   Is it *fun?* Is it positive and playful rather than dull and restrictive?

An example of the power of a vision statement can be seen at the car manufacturer Toyota. Their vision was to create a car that would allow them to undercut the prices of German luxury cars while at the same time beating them on quality. The result was the Lexus.

The future environment

Organisations do not operate in isolation, but in a wider context or environment. This influences not only what a manager does, but what a manager will be thinking about and planning for: the conditions in which a unit or organisation operates, or will be operating in a few years' time. One of the first things that a manager needs to do is to identify features of the far environment that are significant to the organisation. By identifying trends and paying particular attention to those trends which will help or hinder the organisation, the manager hopes to place the organisation in a position of competitive advantage. For not-for-profit organisations, the focus may be on sustainability and improving or widening the provision of services.

The STEEP model

The STEEP model will help you to construct a long-term forecast for your unit, your organisation, and for yourself. It will direct you to think about the five broad features of the future environment. First, it directs you to think about the **S**ocial conditions that will apply; then it prompts you to think about the **T**echnological, the **E**conomic, the **E**nvironmental, and, lastly, the likely **P**olitical conditions.

The STEEP model helps you think about the environment in which your organisation will be operating in (say) five years' time.

Table 10.1	The conditions in which your organisation will be operating in five years' time	
STEEP factor	**Major features**	**Consequences for the organisation**
Social	Consumers' habits and preferences; general and particular attitudes and behaviour	
Technological	The relevant technology that will be available to customers and to competitors	
Economic	The general state of the economy; salaries, disposable income, interest rates, taxation, and so on	
Environmental	Likely thinking on environmental matters	
Political	The likely political regimes, the laws	

Of course, there will be connections between the categories. For example, the answer to the question 'What do I think will be the likely political regime?' might prompt the inclusion of 'Higher taxes' in the economic box and maybe 'More emphasis on environmental matters' in the environmental box. A first entry in one of the right-hand boxes could well prompt entries in others. The model emphasises the connections between the different categories.

Scanning the environment

The STEEP model provides a checklist for scanning the far environment to see what it is like now or will be like. As you identify the broad features of that environment, you need to ask yourself the question: 'What is the significance to the organisation of what I can see?'. If your STEEP analysis has focused on the future, there are likely to be a number of features of the environment that you cannot be certain of. Then, you might want to ask 'What if...?'. STEEP analyses naturally lead to what is known as scenario planning.

The kind of information you are likely to need for your analyses and scenarios include:

■ changes in government policy which may affect regulations or money supply and economic growth

■ social trends such as the aging population in most industrialised countries and the effects of this on new markets or services

■ technological changes which can result in rapid developments in computers and communications which affect the content of goods and services and how they are delivered.

The PEST and PESTLE models

An alternative to the STEEP model is the PEST model. This is useful for forecasting demand by studying current and past patterns, and how these are likely to be affected by possible future changes in the organisation's environment, including **P**olitical, **E**conomic, **S**ocial and **T**echnological changes. Sources of information are identical to those listed earlier. Note that in a PEST analysis, environmental factors are included but as subsets of factors under the main headings.

Yet another variation is the PESTLE model, which includes **L**egal and **E**nvironmental factors separately. All the models are very similar and include the factors most likely to have an impact on an organisation. The important issue here is not the particular model you use, but that your environmental scanning includes all the relevant factors.

Analysing the competition

Porter's five forces of competition helps managers to analyse the near environment. This analytical tool is widely-used as a means of understanding the structure of an industry or sector, and as a framework within which to identify possible structural changes.

Porter's five forces model

Much strategy (particularly in the private sector) is concerned with establishing and maintaining competitive advantage. Porter's model identifies five types of competitive pressure within a sector: established competitors, new entrants to the market, substitute products, the bargaining power of suppliers and that of customers. These are summarised in Figure 10.3.

Porter argues that rivalry among existing firms is not the only competitive force. The degree of competitiveness or rivalry within an industry depends, too, on the availability of substitutes, the strength of suppliers and buyers (customers), and the threat of new entrants (which in turn depends on the ease of entry).

Suppliers are important because their relative power can determine what proportion of the price of the final product they capture. In the automotive component business, for example, many makers of components vie with each other to supply a small number of car manufacturers, allowing the car manufacturers to put pressure on suppliers to reduce their prices and thus their profit margins too. (The profit margin is the difference between a company's total revenues and the costs incurred in creating its products or services.)

Organisations need to consider not only the behaviour of current competitors but also the potential for other organisations to enter the market. The important issue here is the level of barriers to entry. A barrier to

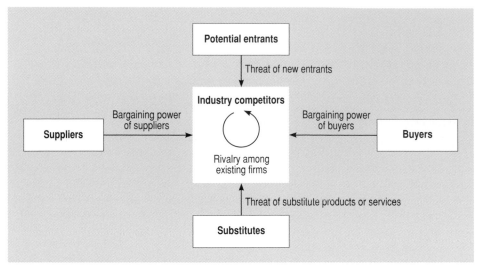

Figure 10.3   The five forces of competition

(Source: Porter, 1980)

entry is something that increases the expense or difficulty of breaking into a market. For example, in sectors where brand recognition is important (like confectionery) new entrants need to spend heavily to build a brand. In other sectors (such as car manufacturing) the minimum economic scale of operations may be high, so requiring heavy capital investment by new entrants.

See Branding, p. 231.

An organisation needs to consider not only those competitors offering similar products or services, but also those offering products or services that may act as substitutes. For example, cheaper restaurants may suffer considerable competition from supermarkets selling high-quality, easily prepared ready-meals to eat at home as a substitute for dining out.

The value chain

A value chain shows the activities or functions within an organisation that contribute to the creation of the product or service that is delivered to external customers. By identifying these different activities, the manager will be better able to assess whether any of them can be completed more cheaply or better.

Porter's value chain model

In Porter's value chain model, there are five primary activities that are strategically important for the organisation. See Figure 10.4.

The first three activities by themselves comprise an input/transformations/ output model. 'Inbound logistics' refers to the management of the flow of

Inbound logistics	Operations	Outbound logistics	Marketing and sales	Aftersales service

Figure 10.4 **The five primary activities in the value chain**
(Source: Porter, 1980)

inputs to the organisation. The 'operations' are what the organisation does to the inputs in order to transform them into the goods and services (the outputs) that the organisation intends to sell to customers. So the 'outbound logistics' are those activities that deal with the initial storage and then the distribution of the outputs to the customers.

However, along with these three activities, Porter regards two further ones as being primary activities. Both of them are concerned with the disposal of the outputs. First, 'marketing and sales' comprises those activities that are intended to achieve the sale of the outputs while 'aftersales service' is directed towards people who have bought the output.

The primary activities are supported by others which result in the fuller model shown in Figure 10.5. This includes four support activities. 'Procurement' deals with the purchasing of the inputs All activities will reflect the current state of 'technology development' within the organisation. 'Human resource management' deals with the management of the organisation's staff, and the 'firm infrastructure' covers the other supporting activities.

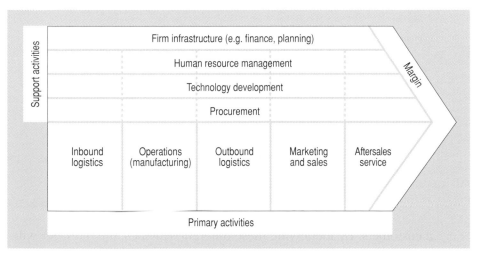

Figure 10.5 **The value chain**
(Source: Porter, 1980)

Using the value chain

Value dictates what the market is prepared to pay for what an organisation produces. This sets the level of the organisation's total revenues. The margin is the difference between total value (the total revenues) and the costs that have been incurred in the creation of that total value. The function then of the value chain model is to expose the components of that total value, so that managers can analyse and improve their processes. The more that an organisation knows about these components, the better equipped it will be to find opportunities to reduce the cost of an activity or to improve the way it completes an activity.

Assessing the competitive position

The SWOT model is used to assess the competitive position of a product or service. As Figure 10.6 shows, it comprises four cells set out in two rows and two columns. The two cells in the top row are labelled **S**trengths and **W**eaknesses, and the two in the bottom row are labelled **O**pportunities and **T**hreats. Note that opportunities are listed under strengths, and threats under weaknesses.

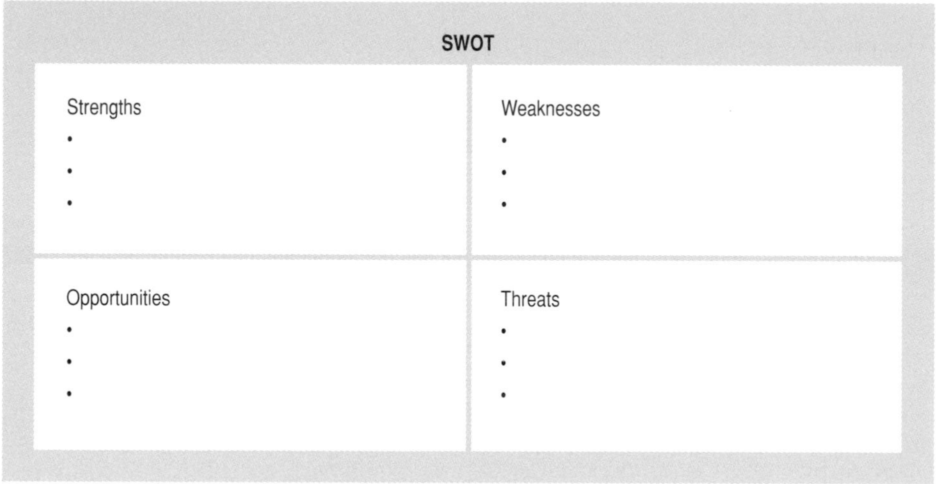

Figure 10.6   **The SWOT framework**

An organisational SWOT analysis

When reviewing your organisation's position in the market, first set out the organisation's competitive strengths, that is, its strengths in relation to its competitors. Then make an honest assessment of the weaknesses. The strengths and weaknesses (the contents of the top row) provide an internal picture of the organisation as it is now. This can help you to answer the question 'Where are we now?'. Once that question has been answered, two further questions can be addressed: 'What opportunities exist because of our strengths?' and 'To what threats do our weaknesses expose us?'. Completing the bottom row brings in the external perspective, describing two possible future pictures, one positive but the other threatening.

See The future environment, p. 201, Analysing the competition, p. 203.

Note that the components identified when you use Porter's value chain aid the strengths and weaknesses analysis within SWOT, while STEEP and

Porter's five forces of competition inform the opportunities and threats analysis.

Overall the SWOT model contributes to a long-term, strategic review of the organisation's position in the market.

Approaches to strategy

A useful definition of strategy is: the pattern of activities of an organisation in pursuit of its long-term purposes. We can understand strategy in three ways. First, strategy is concerned with the broad pattern of an organisation's activities, not the day-to-day detail. Second, strategy is concerned with the long-term. Finally, strategy is concerned with organisational purposes. These may have a commercial focus such as market penetration, profitability and growth or, for some organisations, they may concern political or social goals.

Strategy – planned or emergent?

A planned strategy involves a formal, rational, process of strategic choices. An emergent strategy is less deliberate – it's what the situation brings forth from the organisation rather than an agreed plan. Unexpected crises and opportunities, and quickly changing environments, may produce a significant gap between intended and realised strategy. Consequently the quality of an organisation's emergent strategy is as much determined by its systems and routines for responding to crises and opportunities as it is by the quality of its formal strategic planning process.

A market-based approach

A market-based approach to strategy starts by analysing the environment outside the organisation – the customers, suppliers and competitors – and then seeks to fit the organisation and its resources to its environment through a process of further analysis and planning.

A resource-based approach

A resource-based view of strategy shifts the emphasis from the external to the internal context: the focus is placed on the resources that an organisation possesses, or needs to possess, as the basis for a sound strategy.

All organisations possess unique bundles of resources, and it is how these resources are used that determines differences in performance between organisations. Resources are not productive in themselves – they need to be converted into capabilities by being managed and co-ordinated. By capabilities we mean an organisation's capacity to engage in a range of productive activities.

It is the capabilities based on the resources that, if hard to imitate, give the main source of competitive advantage. Strategy, from the resource perspective, is therefore about *choosing from and committing to long-term paths of capability development.*

Strategic planning

In many organisations, strategic choices are made through a strategic planning process. A typical strategic planning process, as shown in Figure 10.7, draws on both market- and resource-based perspectives.

The market-based approach to planning starts by analysing the near environment and the organisation's resources. The resource-based approach starts with an account of the organisation's capabilities and seeks to find synergy with opportunities occurring in the external environment.

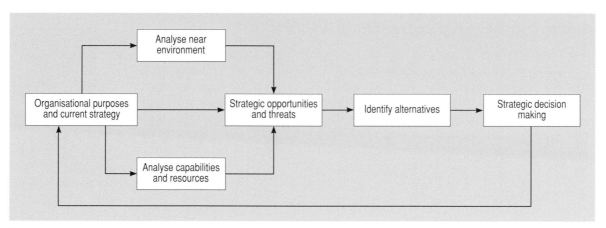

Figure 10.7 A strategic planning process

The planning process

This strategic planning process may be the preserve of a management team or a specialist strategic planning department. In smaller organisations the whole process may go on in the mind of one individual. In some organisations managers throughout the organisation will be involved in the strategic planning cycle, with the results from one set of planned activities influencing a new cycle of objective setting and tactical implementation.

Strategic choices

Porter's model of generic strategies, shown in Figure 10.8, is a useful framework for understanding sources of competitive advantage. It provides the basis for a structured analysis of your own organisation.

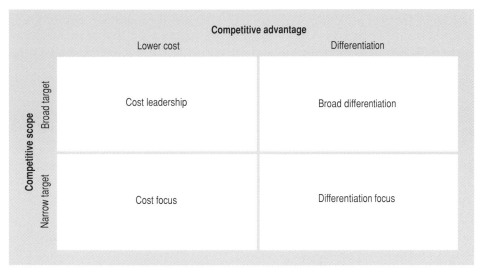

Figure 10.8 Porter's generic strategies (1985)

The model is based on two key measures: competitive scope and competitive advantage.

Competitive scope This defines the range of products or markets over which an organisation chooses to compete – the range can be narrow or broad. To some extent an organisation can choose whether to compete on a narrow front or on a broad front. In the motor industry, the major companies have moved to a broad scope but there are still specialised car manufacturers.

Competitive advantage This refers to the edge that an organisation has over its competitors – the edge that persuades customers to bring their business to the organisation. The search for competitive advantage is at the heart of organisational strategy.

Sources of competitive advantage

Porter contends that there are two fundamental sources of competitive advantage: cost leadership and differentiation.

Cost leadership Here the organisation sets out to be *the* low-cost producer in its sector, exploiting all possible sources of cost advantage. Low-cost production should not be confused with low pricing, although low production costs are usually reflected in prices to the consumer. If an organisation can achieve and sustain cost leadership by producing goods or services at a lower cost than its competitors, then it will be an above-average performer in its sector, provided it can command prices at or near the sector average. Of course the low-cost producer must still offer a level of functionality and quality that is acceptable to its market.

Differentiation In contrast to cost leadership, an organisation following a differentiation strategy seeks to offer extra advantages to its customers. It identifies particular elements that are important to its customers and offers them increased benefits in this area. If it gets this right, it is able to charge a premium price for its product or service, allowing it to recover its higher costs and increase its margin and profit.

Ansoff matrix

The Ansoff matrix is a way of presenting the strategic options that are open to an organisation in relation to its products or services, together with the risks associated with those options. The matrix, shown in Figure 10.9, allows four options to be generated depending on whether present or new markets or products are involved.

Product / Mission	Present	New
Present	MARKET PENETRATION	PRODUCT DEVELOPMENT
New	MARKET DEVELOPMENT	DIVERSIFICATION

Figure 10.9 **The Ansoff matrix**

(Source: Ansoff, 1988)

The four options

Market penetration (present/present)

The first option is to seek extra sales for the product in the present market, to penetrate the market more and so increase the market share. The sales can come from present customers or from new customers in the present market. This is the least risky option because it uses the organisation's existing capabilities and resources, but it is not necessarily the best option if a market has reached saturation point and no further growth is possible.

Market development (present/new)

Alternatively, the organisation can seek to find new markets for the current product. Those new markets may be at home or in other regions or countries. This option is riskier than the first, market penetration, because it involves expansion into a new market. But it is a good strategy for an organisation whose core competencies relate primarily to its products rather than to a particular segment of the market.

Product development (new/present)

Rather than seek new markets, the organisation may modify the product and seek customers for it in the present market. This strategy carries a similar risk to that of market development, but it is an appropriate one for organisations whose strengths lie in their existing customer base and marketing rather than their specific products.

Diversification (new/new)

The fourth option requires a new product to be marketed in new markets. This option may be appropriate for an organisation which has relied heavily on a product but where the market for the product is now subject to long-term decline. This option is the most high risk of the four because it requires the development of both product and market, and the organisation's core competencies may be inadequate for such an undertaking. But it may be an appropriate option if the rates of return are attractive, or if the organisation needs to enter a new or more attractive industry, or if it means the organisation can reduce its overall business risk. Perhaps the most basic and typical example of this in Europe is the diversification of rural industries (e.g. farming, fishery, forestry, mineral and slate mining) to embrace tourism.

New product development process

An organisation which opts for developing a new product will first test the viability of a new product or service, in preparation for full-scale development. Any new product development contains creative elements. As these creative elements can be unpredictable, much of the product development process comprises a series of steps designed to minimise risk. Indeed, the first stage is a review of the concept, the initial screening of the ideas put forward for development. The contexts for this screening process are the organisation's corporate and marketing strategies.

The key stages of the new product development process are:

- concept test
- product development
- product and service testing
- test marketing.

Identifying gaps in the market

Some new products and services are developed from idiosyncratic ideas and are launched without much investigation of the market. However gap

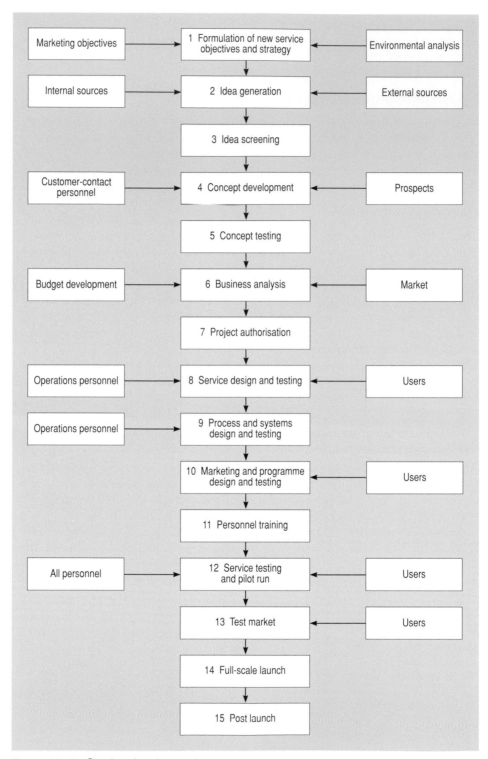

Figure 10.10 **Service development**

(Source: Scheung and Johnson, 1989)

analysis is a technique that can help analyse, in consumer-oriented terms, where market gaps may exist. Gaps come from four main causes.

Usage gap This is the gap between the total potential for the market and the actual current usage by all customers in the market.

Access gap This is the gap caused by limits to the availability of the product or service. The remedy for this is to maximise distribution.

Product/service gap This is the part of the market from which the individual organisation is excluded because of product or service characteristics. This may be because parts of the market have different needs and the organisation does not have an offering for each of these groups or segments.

Competitive gap This gap relates to the organisation's competitive performance. How does your organisation compare with other similar providers?

Once these gaps are identified, it is most likely that some kind of new product development process will be followed successfully.

Developing a new product or service

The stages of new product development are shown in Figure 10.10. This depicts the development of a new service, focusing on the service-delivery process and the involvement of customers and of staff who are in contact with them.

Understanding your own organisation

An important consideration in strategic planning and implementation is the nature of an organisation itself.

Organisational structure

The structure of an organisation reveals how the organisation has been built. The organisation may have a flat structure with only a few managerial levels, or the structure may be tall with many levels in the managerial hierarchy. The structure will also show how the total organisational task is divided among the staff and how all the different jobs that contribute to the overall task are co-ordinated. The structure of the organisation provides a framework for understanding people's relationships to each other in the organisation and their responsibilities.

The formal structure

The formal structure is the one that is portrayed in an organisational chart and in the various staff job descriptions. The chart and the job descriptions describe the way that each post in the organisation is related to the others.

The reporting and the command lines are made clear, as are the content of the different jobs. From these charts and descriptions, it is then possible to see:

- the number of managerial levels in the organisation

- the extent to which important decisions are taken at the centre or by the different operating units

- the extent to which the jobs in the organisation are specialised or more general

- the lines of communication between people.

Informal structures

In addition to the formal structure, there will be other relevant relationships within the organisation. There will be networks of different kinds, such as the alliances that a manager forms with other managers.

When two organisations merge, the loyalties to the two original organisations will remain in place, at least for a time. The members will feel they are still part of one network or the other. A manager who wants to be effective within the organisation needs to be sensitive to these informal structures or relationships as well as the formal ones.

The network or virtual organisation

A network or virtual organisation consists of a partnership of several organisations instead of differentiated functional departments bound together in one organisation. The principles underpinning this approach are described as follows:

> Networks seem most likely to form when organisations face rapid technological change, shortened product cycles, and fragmented specialised markets. In a network, necessary assets are distributed among several network partners in such a way that it is not a single organisation that produces products or services, but rather the network at large that is the producer or provider.

> A network can be the result of massive outsourcing, or collaboration between small firms whose scale of operations would not allow them to compete in international markets by themselves.

> Outsourcing means that many of the activities of a once complex organisation are moved outside the organisation's boundary. Sometimes the suppliers will be spin-off units, with the original organisation retaining only those activities for which it has a particular competence. All other necessary activities are purchased from other organisations. When all the task activities are outsourced, you have a virtual organisation.

(Source: Hatch, 1997)

The Benetton organisation

The worldwide clothing company, Benetton, has subcontracted most of its operations. Freelance designers do the styling and design largely outside the company, although creation of, and responsibility for, the overriding look remains in-house. Most of Benetton's manufacturing is subcontracted and most of its shops operate on an exclusive franchise. So Benetton is very much a network organisation. However, it keeps the capabilities that it sees as giving it competitive advantage – such as responsibility for the overall look and feel of Benetton – within the core organisation.

Culture

Culture is hard to define, but there is a consensus that it consists of patterns of behaviour, beliefs, ideas, values and knowledge embedded in practices, systems, artefacts and symbols. To belong to a culture is to share, often unconsciously, the beliefs and values of that culture – a shared understanding and shared meanings. Culture operates at many levels from ethnic culture to the family unit – from culture with a capital 'C' to culture with a very small 'c'. Organisations have a culture too. The organisational culture refers to 'the way that things are done around here'. It refers to the atmosphere or climate within the organisation and to the values that influence the way that people work and are managed. The culture of an organisation will be an important part of the whole experience of working there.

Organisational culture

Each organisation will have its own collection of values and attitudes. The culture will be expressed publicly in the mission statement, in the organisational logo and in the way that the financial accounts are presented. All these expressions will have been chosen deliberately to present a particular image of the organisation. But the culture will also be expressed in other ways; in the rites and the rituals within the organisation; in language; in the way that workplaces are set out; and in the stories (such as those told at ceremonies) which seem to express the nature of the organisation. Along with the organisational culture, there can be local cultures (subcultures) within the different departments or establishments.

Some examples of organisational culture

Organisational culture is something that is felt as well as being something that is expressed in more concrete ways. In a market-oriented organisation the staff will be imbued with the view that customers are really important and will work in a way that expresses that view. Any activity on behalf of a customer, or on behalf of customers in general, will be applauded and celebrated. There will be an atmosphere of 'customer first'. In another organisation there might be a strong sense that 'You're as good as your last job'. You will know more-or-less straightaway whether you are meeting your targets, and you know that if you fail to meet them you are liable to lose your job. We could describe this as a 'tough guy' culture. Or you may work in an organisation where there is an organisation-wide commitment to high-quality outputs. Then, we could talk about the 'quality culture' of the organisation. The term 'culture' is being used to describe a widely-shared understanding of what is important.

Organisational change

Organisational approaches to change

Organisational approaches to change focus on changing what the organisation is like. Examples of this include change following privatisation or deregulation, or following the establishment of a joint venture or strategic alliance. Change might also be intended to shift the business emphasis of an organisation, for example, away from a geographical structure based on grouping activities by physical location, to one that emphasises product or service categories.

Restructuring

Many organisations have restructured themselves in an attempt to operate more efficiently in the face of globalisation, technological advances and increased competition. Public sector organisations have also restructured, to try to improve their performance as they have come under increasing government pressure to do so. Traditional organisational structures were based on the bureaucratic model, constructed around a management hierarchy which could contain as many as twenty levels. In general the intention of restructuring has been to eliminate many of these levels, one aim being to improve efficiency by speeding up communication and decision making. In some large organisations there are now as few as three layers between the most junior and most senior staff. Restructuring of this kind is often referred to as 'delayering' or 'downsizing' because, inevitably, removing layers in a management hierarchy means that fewer managers need to be employed.

Focusing on core competencies

As well as delayering and downsizing, organisations have restructured the way in which they operate in order to focus better on their core competencies – that is, the things they do very well. These competencies are an organisation's source of competitive advantage. This type of restructuring manifests itself as:

- an increasing number of mergers, alliances and joint ventures
- the establishment of closer links with suppliers and customers
- moves to outsource non-core activities.

Culture change

Managing the culture of an organisation ('the way we do things around here') is seen as an important way of responding to a need for change, since the culture of an organisation and its performance are said to be inextricably linked. The aim is to shape the organisational culture to help align employees' values and behaviour with the organisation's goals and priorities. This will increase employees' commitment to the organisation, it is suggested, and thereby improve loyalty, productivity and dedication to the organisation's purpose.

See Culture, p. 215.

Overcoming barriers

There are barriers to culture change. Some of the factors that are central to overcoming such barriers and bringing about culture change in organisations are:

- the strength of leadership at the top of the organisation

- an effective means of cascading the initiative down through the organisation

- the involvement of employees at all levels in the organisation

- a focus on behaviour rather than values

- manipulation of important cultural symbols, for example, company logos, advertising campaigns, the working environment, and even dress codes.

Assessing the feasibility of a change

The present situation of an organisation needs to be analysed in order to decide how feasible a change might be. A useful technique for this is a force-field analysis. The concept is shown in Figure 10.11, and its application to the reorganisation of an IT unit in Figure 10.12.

An organisation or group can be thought of as being held in balance, or equilibrium, between driving forces that are seeking to change it, and restraining forces that are preventing movement and change.

See Force-field diagrams, p. 127.

A force-field analysis helps us to assess the prospects for change. In conducting one, we should be able to:

- see how likely the restraining forces are to strengthen or weaken

- identify ways of promoting change, that is, shifting the balance of forces in favour of change.

Equilibrium may not exist, of course, and in any organisation changes happen at different rates and in different directions.

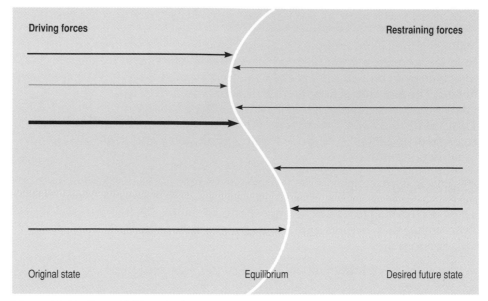

Figure 10.11 **Force-field analysis**

(Source: based on Lewin, 1951)

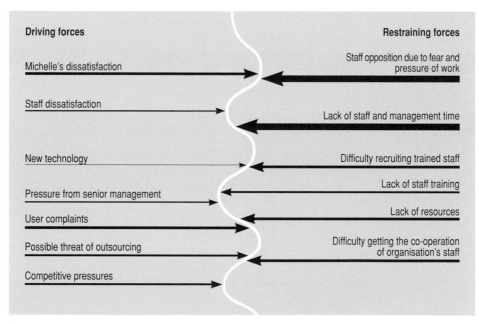

Figure 10.12 **Force-field analysis of the reorganisation of an IT unit**

Common problems

Some of the common problems associated with change are:

■ people may not see the need for it

■ people may think the reason is mistaken

■ it may threaten practices that people value highly

■ it may have unintended consequences

■ it may threaten the interests of some staff.

Roles in the change process

Three different roles have been identified in the change process:

■ change strategists or initiators, who initiate and set the direction of change

■ change implementers, who are responsible for the co-ordination and implementation of the change

■ change recipients, who are strongly affected by the change and its implementation.

Six-step model of change

Figure 10.13 shows a six-step model of change that draws together a number of key components of successful change management and proposes a sequence of activities.

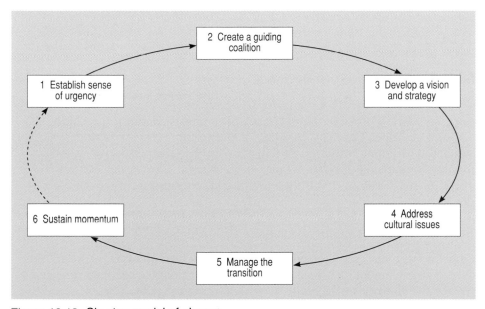

Figure 10.13 Six-step model of change

Step 1 – Establish a sense of urgency

While there is often an intuitive awareness of the current problems and the need for change, this is often matched by an overwhelming sense of complacency and/or inertia within the organisation. The urgency and energy for change are dependent on a range of external and internal triggers. Some common triggers are shown in Table 10.2.

Table 10.2 Triggers for change	
External triggers	**Internal triggers**
Economy (e.g. collapse of currency)	New staff
Suppliers	Conflict
Government policies (e.g. cuts in funding)	Lost sales
Competitors	Drop in profits
Funders	Demotivation
Customers	Overstocks
Shareholders (e.g. drop in share prices)	Skills gaps
Financial community franchises	Loss of key staff
The media	A fire
The public	
Technology	

Step 2 – Create a guiding coalition

An obvious next step is to target senior managers who are already sympathetic towards or convinced of the need for change. These individuals can then champion the cause in their departments or functional areas. They can be seen as the senior sponsors of the change initiative and they can lobby more widely in the organisation.

Step 3 – Develop a vision and a strategy

The real value of defining the purpose of any major change project lies in the consultation process: the purpose of the project needs to be clarified through genuine consensus building. It is one thing to have a clear statement of intent (which should mesh with the organisation's overall mission and strategy), but it is quite another for this to express a future vision or set of values that is meaningful and energising for the staff concerned.

Step 4 – Address cultural issues

One way to try to change a culture is through a comprehensive programme of staff involvement, in which groups of staff are encouraged and assisted to retrace for themselves the steps by which top management first realised the need for a change programme. A second way is through the propagation of a corporate vision. Here, the new culture is 'sold' to the company staff through a combination of charismatic leadership, symbolic action and powerful advertising. Both methods depend heavily on effective communications but the first relies mainly on rational argument, and the second on emotive response.

Step 5 – Manage the transition

Following all the above preparatory work there then comes the difficult task of implementing, managing and consolidating the actual change process.

Step 6 – Sustain momentum

At some point it becomes necessary to assess the impact of the various change activities that have been set in motion. When change initiatives are focused on a single system (a project) rather than many interrelated substructures, management is relatively straightforward. This is because the criteria of success are likely to be predetermined and quantifiable.

Stakeholders

A stakeholder is someone who has a share or an interest in an enterprise. For example shareholders are stakeholders in a public limited company, and patients are stakeholders in their local hospital. Managers in the not-for-profit sector sometimes describe these stakeholders as constituencies.

Meeting multiple stakeholder needs

Organisations need to serve the interests of multiple stakeholder groups simultaneously. Failure to serve the needs of one is likely to prevent them from effectively serving the needs of others. For example, failing to serve the needs of customers will damage a firm's ability to serve the financial needs of shareholders.

Most organisations have a wide range of stakeholders to consider. Figure 10.14 shows a typical set of stakeholders. While failure to serve the needs of each set of stakeholders is likely to cause problems, there may also

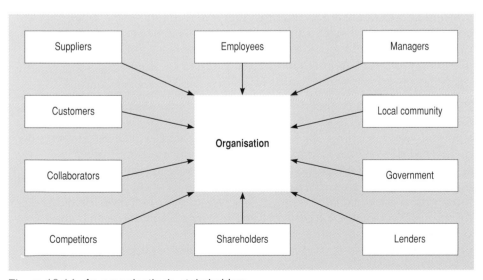

Figure 10.14 **An organisation's stakeholders**

be conflicts between their interests. Organisations often have to make trade-offs between conflicting objectives: for example, disposal of toxic waste products versus environmental concerns.

Stakeholders and change

For every change initiative an organisation undertakes, there will be a range of individuals or groups who have an interest in its conception, execution and outcome. They could be the end users of an IT system, the line managers who will be expected to lead a restructuring initiative throughout the organisation, or the marketing department which will promote a new product. The support of these stakeholders is essential if the project is to succeed. Therefore a key responsibility of managers involved in change initiatives or projects will be to identify these stakeholders at an early stage, anticipate their responses, and gain and maintain their support. Their involvement is an important determinant of the success or failure of a change.

CHAPTER 11 MARKETING

What is marketing?

Marketing is concerned with exchange relationships. In commercial (for-profit) organisations, products and services are exchanged for money and resources from customers. In not-for-profit organisations the exchange can involve non-financial resources from either side. For example, charities or public-sector organisations are involved in marketing exchanges with customers, where what is being exchanged can include ideas, time, commitment to particular beliefs, and so on. When you buy your Christmas cards from an international development charity such as Oxfam, you are investing in more than just stationery. Examples of other exchange relationships are shown in Figure 11.1.

Exchange relationships need to be managed. The term 'relationship marketing' emerged as common terminology in the 1990s. It has evolved from the vast expansion of customer profiling data (lifestyle data) and financial data available to organisations, and the increasing power and speed of data processing and transmission. However, relationship marketing is much more than this. The concept focuses on creating and managing long-term customer relationships. It involves moving activities away from those designed to create a series of one-off transactions, to managing a complex network of relationships involved in the production of the whole offering to the customer. Table 11.1 contrasts these two types of marketing.

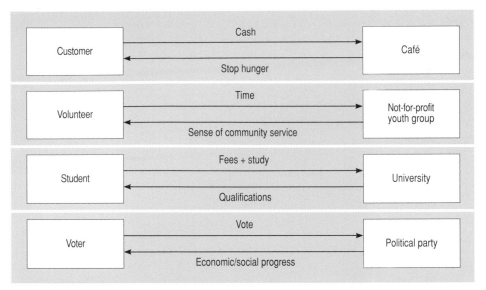

Figure 11.1 Exchange relationships

Table 11.1 Transaction marketing versus relationship marketing	
Transaction marketing	**Relationship marketing**
Orientation towards single purchase	Orientation towards repeat sales
Limited direct customer/supplier contact	Close, frequent customer/supplier contact
Focus on product benefits	Focus on value to customer
Emphasis on short-term performance	Emphasis on long-term performance
Limited level of customer service	High level of customer service
Goal of customer satisfaction	Goal of delighting the customer
Quality is a manufacturing responsibility	Quality is the responsibility of the whole organisation

The key relationships in relationship marketing

To become a market leader, an organisation has to progress from a culture in which marketing is the preserve of the marketing department, to one in which there is a market orientation throughout the business. This is known as a value-driven market culture. It involves managing relationships that are beyond the control of the marketing department – relationships which are crucial to adding value to the organisation's product or service offering and, ultimately, adding to the success of the company. Figure 11.2 shows the four key relationships. They occur in most business organisations, within the network of business systems, supply chains and virtual networks. Suppliers, shareholders, customers and employees are not rivals in a battle for profits, they are partners. Organisations will be more successful once they learn to work together with these partners. Relationship marketing is a concept that focuses on managing this series of network interactions.

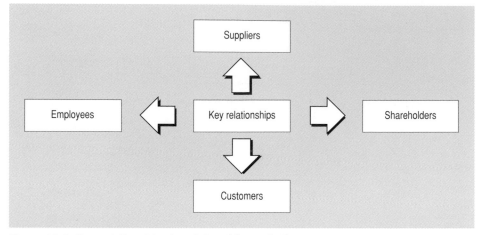

Figure 11.2 **Key relationships in relationship marketing**

(Source: based on Piercy, 1997)

Understanding customer behaviour

Most models of customer buying behaviour describe the series of actions that customers go through before, during and after making a purchase.

The traditional model

The traditional model of buying behaviour has the usual stages of any decision-making process, but also includes a final post-purchase stage:

■ need recognition

■ information search

■ evaluation of alternatives

■ buying decision

■ post-purchase evaluation.

Figure 11.3 shows the roles that external and internal stimuli play. It also gives scope for a non-linear progression through the decision-making stages, which may be more appropriate for service purchase decisions.

For the most part we make buying decisions every day, without even thinking about them. It is only when the product is complicated or new to us that we become aware of the decision processes involved. Consider the last time you bought a high-risk item – such as a holiday, a car or even a house. You will probably be able to identify the five stages described.

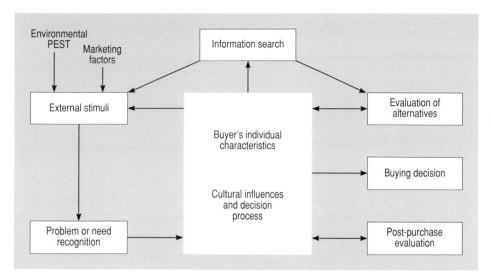

Figure 11.3 Factors involved in the decision-making process

For PEST see The future environment, p. 201.

Dimensions of decision making

The more complex a buying decision the more we rely on people around us for help – either in a formal decision-making unit at work, or informally as a member of a family or group. If a purchase is complicated, it is not uncommon for people to take advice from others in their family or group. There are two dimensions to these purchase decisions: the extent of the decision making, and the degree of involvement in the purchase. Four categories of customer decision making emerge from these two dimensions as shown in Figure 11.4.

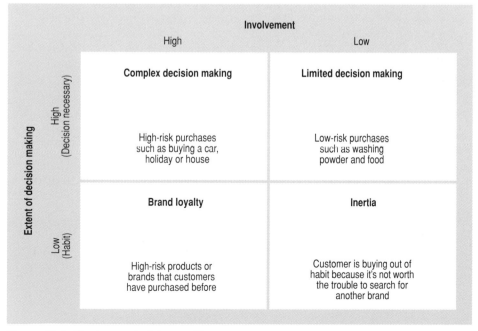

Figure 11.4 Customer decision making

Segmentation

Segmentation is the process of breaking down a total market into smaller, more distinct segments that have similar characteristics. Individual segments must be large enough to be practicable but small enough to allow the use of a distinct marketing approach for each.

Two phases of segmentation

There are two phases involved in market segmentation.

Phase 1 Understanding the customers and the market The organisation's products and services and those of its competitors are scrutinised. This will identify customers' buying behaviour and the key features that they use to decide between alternative products and services.

Phase 2 Identifying customer characteristics The key features of customers' buying behaviour are identified. Particular features are combined to form segments and to develop profiles that describe the resulting segments.

Features of a viable segment are size, identity, relevance and accessibility. Segments need to be large enough to be viable but not too large to make them impossible to manage. The segments should be different enough to have their own 'personalities' and yet need to be compatible within the organisation. In most markets there are normally between five and ten segments.

Segmentation in practice

Marketers describe segments in terms of how customers use products and services (e.g. frequency of use, loyalty, reason for purchase, attitude towards purchase). This is called behavioural segmentation. Other ways of describing segments include demographic (e.g. age, gender, income, social class), geographical (e.g. urban, rural) and psychographic (e.g. aspirations, self-image). These categories are frequently used in combination, for example, wealthy urban women are an important segment for fashion marketing. Figure 11.5 shows the segment variables used to define how customers view healthcare provision.

From subsequent analysis of the variables shown in Figure 11.5, nine healthcare segments were identified. These are listed in Box 11.1.

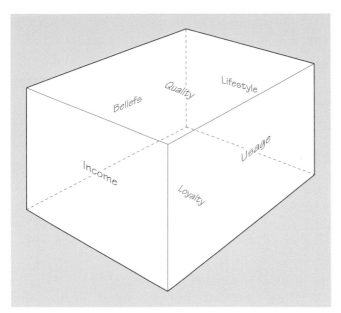

Figure 11.5 Segment variables in healthcare

BOX 11.1 HEALTHCARE SEGMENTS

1 Quality-minded users who look for the best healthcare at any cost.

2 Ready users who are very receptive to healthcare and will readily accept whatever is available.

3 Healthy people who participate in sports, are concerned about nutrition, and will pay more for healthcare.

4 Avoiders who stay away from healthcare.

5 Naturalists who seek alternatives to modern medical healthcare.

6 Family-orientated users who believe their children's health to be paramount, and are interested in nutrition, wellness and family.

7 Clinic cynics who are sceptical about all forms of organised healthcare.

8 People who see no difference between healthcare providers.

9 Loyalists who find one institution and stay with it.

(Source: Sargeant, 1999)

The marketing mix

How can organisations design products to satisfy their customers' needs? The marketing mix is a framework developed to help managers to consider all the relevant factors (the mix) when designing and marketing their products to attract particular segments. It is used to position an organisation's offering in the minds of the target segment – segmentation is what sets off an appropriate marketing mix.

The four (or seven) Ps

Four main factors are considered in the marketing mix. Referred to as the four Ps, they represent **P**roduct, **P**rice, **P**lace and **P**romotion. Sometimes the four Ps are extended to seven to include **P**eople, **P**rocesses and **P**hysical evidence. All seven are listed below.

1 **Product** This is the tangible product or the intangible service offered for sale.

2 **Price** This is the sum of money and/or other valuable resources such as time and attention that the customer must exchange for the product or service.

3 **Place** This is where the product or service will be available. Consideration of this factor provides the opportunity for an organisation to arrange its distribution system to make its products or services conveniently available to customers.

4 **Promotion** This is the part of the marketing mix that relates to all communications, both persuasive and informative, with prospective and existing customers.

5 **People** Apart from the sales of commodities, many products are now combined with services when they are offered to customers. Managing the people who are involved with delivering a service becomes important because they are responsible for fulfilling the promises made by the organisation's marketing and promotional activities. Services can be divided into back- and front-office activities. Front-office activities such as customer care are concerned with managing the customer/ supplier interface, back-office activities (such as invoicing) are out of sight but support the visible processes.

6 **Processes** These are the processes of service delivery that can be described as back-office activities. For example, the IT systems involved in getting your bank statement to you each month, with the correct information in the right format, would be considered a back-office service process.

7 **Physical evidence** Because services are intangible, customers use physical evidence to help them make judgements about quality. The physical environment of a fast-food outlet, for example, will have an important part to play in your perception of the overall service. If the outlet is grubby and in need of repair you may think that the food will not be of an acceptable standard and you may decide to eat elsewhere.

All the Ps are interrelated; a change in one can be expected to lead to consequential changes in one or more of the others.

The four Cs

The marketing mix concentrates on an organisation's operations rather than on its customers' requirements. For this reason a number of alternative mixes have been proposed. One of these is the four Cs, which concentrates on the customers' perspective. The four Cs represent **C**ustomer needs and wants, **C**ost, **C**onvenience and **C**ommunication.

1 **Customer needs and wants** All the elements of a product or service must be designed to ensure that what is finally offered will satisfy the customer. The product must be a partial or complete answer to customer needs and wants.

2 **Cost to the customer** The customer will consider many factors when deciding if a product is value for money. For example, the time taken to purchase the product, the psychological cost of owning it, and other resources which may be needed.

3 **Convenience** The delivery of products and services to customers involves factors such as quality, access, availability, reliability and the need to develop good customer relationships. The place of delivery must be convenient.

4 **Communication** Organisations need to ensure that customers know about the benefits of their products and where to obtain them. They need to communicate with customers and let customers communicate with them.

The four Ps unpacked

The four main elements of the marketing mix described as the four Ps – product, price, place and promotion – are themselves bundles of components which require individual analysis. A number of management concepts and tools have been developed to help managers to understand and scrutinise them. These are grouped under the headings of the four Ps.

See The marketing mix, p. 227.

Product

Three-level product analysis

Three-level product analysis provides a way of looking at products, and/or services, to analyse key features and benefits. Figure 11.6 shows the three different levels of a product and/or service.

Features of the three levels

1 **Core product and/or service** This describes customers' fundamental reason for wanting to buy the item. This will be a generic description of the core benefit that will apply to a number of competing offerings. For

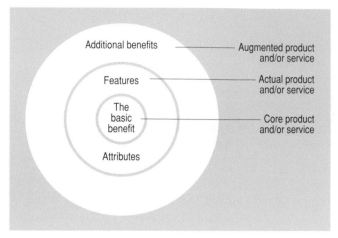

Figure 11.6 The three-level product and/or service analysis

example, the basic benefit of a savings account is that it is a safe place to keep extra money, or money that is not needed immediately. The basic benefit to, or need of, the customer identifies the core product or service.

2 **Actual product and/or service** This describes the key features a customer expects. As a minimum, customers expect from a savings account certain access conditions, a rate of interest and a number of branches at which to do business.

3 **Augmented product and/or service** This features additional benefits and customer services that have been built around the actual product. These often differentiate it from other offerings and provide reasons for choosing one product over another. One savings account may offer transactions via the internet and telephone as additional features that will benefit customers.

Benefits of three-level analysis

The analysis helps an organisation to identify the features, benefits and additional offerings of its products or services. It helps a marketer to create effective marketing messages which stress the benefit, not just the product or service. For example, marketers will promote 'the ability to manage your own account exactly when you want to' not 'a savings account on the internet'. Another way of putting this is to talk about 'selling the sizzle not the steak' or 'selling the va va voom not the car'. Three-level product analysis also helps organisations compare their product or service offerings with those of competitors.

Branding

Branding means creating an identity for a product, associating it with buying not just a product but 'buying into' a lifestyle and certain values. Beans are not just beans. For a consumer, buying a tin of beans may be buying into ideas about nature, wholesomeness and the family. Brands have emotional appeals as well as physical, rational ones. A brand can be a product, service, person, organisation or place. It can be represented by a sign, name, symbol, colour or design – or any combination of these – which create a distinct, individual and clear identity that differentiates products and services from the competition.

The components of a brand

Figure 11.7 illustrates the different components of a brand in the form of an iceberg. This framework shows how branding goes well beyond naming and advertising a product. Some components of a brand are hidden from view, much as the bulk of an iceberg is out of sight.

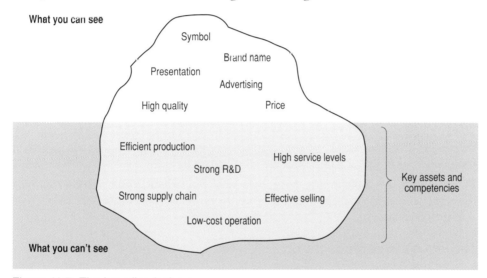

Figure 11.7 **The branding iceberg**

(Source: Davidson, 1997)

To provide their brand with an effective foundation, organisations need to consider all the elements that fall in the area below the waterline.

The benefits of branding

■ Brand names can be a good way of differentiating products.

■ Well-known and trusted brands can serve as a shortcut for consumers trying to choose between competing offers.

■ Customers can immediately identify specific products or services they do and do not like.

- Companies can benefit from a brand image when launching new products, because customers may attach their perception of the brand value to the new product.

- Sellers benefit because branding encourages repeat purchasing, leading to brand loyalty.

- Brand loyalty can enable companies to charge a premium price, leading to higher profit margins.

- Top brands present an image of quality to such an extent that superior brand position is linked with market leadership.

Successful brands

Successful brands do the following:

- deliver functional benefits to meet the market need at least as well as the competition does

- offer intangible benefits over and above the basic benefit of the core product

- comprise various benefits that are consistent with each other and present a unified character or identity

- offer special features that customers want, value and believe that no one else can offer.

Product life-cycle

The product life-cycle charts the progress of a product in the market from its introduction to its decline. The idea is derived from the natural life of a living organism.

The stages in a product's growth

Figure 11.8 shows time on the horizontal axis and sales income on the vertical axis. The graph shows the sales of a product, or service, over its life. The different stages are easy to recognise.

Introduction When the product is launched, the organisation's purpose is to create an awareness of the product in the market. If the product then appeals to consumers, sales will rise. They may rise sufficiently to take the product into the next stage, the growth stage.

Growth This stage is characterised by a much faster rate of increase of sales – the slope of the line becomes steeper. The organisation will still be promoting the product and substantial investment may be needed.

Maturity As the rate of increase of sales falls, the line will begin to flatten. The product has reached the maturity stage. The organisation will try to manage this steady state by forming a body of loyal customers, and

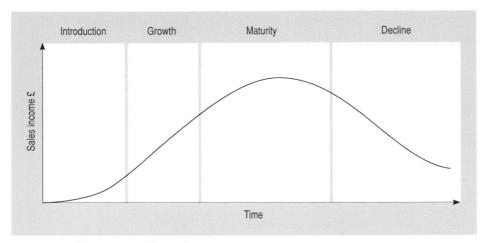

Figure 11.8 **The product life-cycle**

defending its customers against competing products which will now have entered the market.

Decline Beyond maturity lies a decline in sales. The product may become overshadowed by competing products in much the same way that the product, when launched, began to overshadow existing products. Or the whole market may decline.

Instead of sales, profits can be plotted on the vertical axis of the graph. For some time after the product is launched, profits will be negative. As sales rise – and the product moves towards the growth stage – the profits will become positive.

The Boston matrix

The Boston matrix, originally devised in the 1960s by the US management consultancy the Boston Consulting Group, is still a very powerful model intended to contribute to the management of an organisation's cash flow.

Earnings and investment

The Boston matrix is shown in Figure 11.9, and concerns the flow of cash in an organisation. The horizontal axis of the matrix shows the relative market share. The assumption is that the higher a brand's share of the market relative to the strongest competitors, the higher the earnings a brand will produce. The vertical axis shows the market growth rate, the assumption being that the higher the growth rate, the higher will be the call for investment in a brand.

Using the matrix

Each of the four cells describes a particular combination of market growth rate and relative market share.

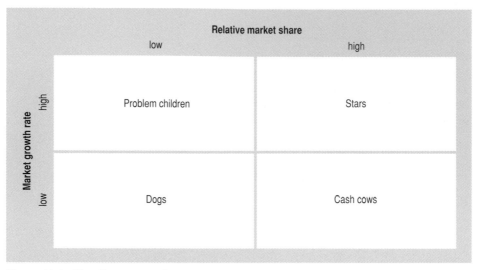

Figure 11.9 **The Boston matrix**

■ **Problem children** This term describes products that occupy the low share/high growth cell of the matrix. A typical example is a recently-launched product. The market is growing, but the product has not built its market share. As a result, the product is likely to require more cash than it generates. However, the organisation hopes that the product will turn out to be a good investment.

■ **Stars** This term describes products that occupy the high share/high growth cell of the matrix. The market is growing; the product has a high share of the market relative to the strongest competitors. The products may well be generating enough cash to cover the investment.

■ **Cash cows** This term describes products that occupy the high share/low growth cell of the matrix. The cash cow product will be a cash generator. The product has a high market share, and so is generating cash, whilst the need for investment in the product is low because the market is growing slowly, if at all.

■ **Dogs** This term describes products that occupy the low share/low growth cell of the matrix. Such a product has few prospects. It may not yet be making a loss, but the next step may well be the withdrawal of the product from the market.

A product may begin as a problem child, will move – all being well – to being a star, and will then become a cash cow. Eventually, the product may become a dog, and will finally be withdrawn from the market.

Managers can use the Boston matrix to analyse the position of their own organisation's products, and also to analyse competitors' products as a means of assessing their competitive position.

Price

Demand

The demand for a product or service will depend on different variables. In open markets, the demand for a product or service is the extent to which people are able and willing to buy the product or service at different prices.

The determinants of demand

The demand for a product depends on the following four elements:

1   the price of the product

2   the prices of competing products

3   the consumer's income

4   the consumer's preferences.

It is not so much the absolute price of a product that matters but the relative price, that is, the price relative to other, competing prices and relative as well to the consumer's income. The price of the product is something that the seller can control, in the sense that the seller chooses the price to attach to the product. The prices of competing products are outside the seller's control, as is the consumer's income.

The first three determinants of demand are objective ones, and they also relate to the consumer's ability to buy the product. The fourth determinant, the consumer's preferences, is the consumer's general estimation of what the product is worth. This relates to the consumer's willingness to buy.

These four elements help to clarify how a person's demand for a product or service will vary. They also determine the market demand as a whole. Consider what would happen if one variable changed but the others did not.

Pricing strategies

Pricing policy may well have a powerful effect on an organisation's financial viability in the short term, but it is a key element of long-term marketing and corporate strategy. Prices need to be set at a level that provides a return on the resources consumed in producing the product or service. But they also need to be acceptable to the potential customer and to be consistent with the objectives and direction of the organisation.

Organisations need to set their pricing levels to meet all of the following four criteria. The price must:

1   provide the customer with value for money

2   cover the costs of the product or service

3   be competitive

4   be consistent with corporate objectives.

Some pricing policies

The optimum pricing policy will vary according to a number of factors.

Penetration pricing If the objective for a new product is to establish high-volume sales and low production costs, it may be attractive to price the product at its long-term equilibrium price from the start, even though this will result in losses in the early stages. This will have the advantage of expanding the market more rapidly, and may deter potential competitors.

Marginal pricing If a company can boost its volume and reduce overall costs through economies of scale, it may be attractive for it to price a product below full cost but above variable cost in selected markets. This is called marginal pricing. For marginal pricing to be successful, it is essential that the low-price markets are insulated in some way from the full-price markets. Simple examples include 'happy hours' in pubs or bars and 'early bird' discounts in stores. Decisions about marginal pricing are usually made on the basis of whether the extra business is worth it in a particular situation.

Market-based pricing A product is worth what someone will pay for it. A product or service can be priced at the maximum that the market will bear at, or just below, the level at which it is beginning to encounter price resistance.

Loss leading This policy entails offering products or services at below cost. It describes a deliberate pricing policy aimed at attracting initial customers, in the hope of repeat or future business.

Skimming Here pricing policies skim the cream off the market by charging a high price for a short time. Such policies are relatively unusual and are attractive only in price-inelastic markets and where the product life-cycle is short. Price skimming is most common in high-technology products, where the differentiation based on the technological edge is likely to be short-lived. Profits need to be taken quickly before competition increases and reduces the product to commodity status.

Price elasticity of demand

Price elasticity of demand (PED) describes the way in which the demand for a product responds to a change in its price. If a small change in price leads to a large change in demand, a product is said to be highly *price elastic*. Many consumer goods such as calculators, DVD players and washing machines are price elastic. If the demand for a product shows little response to changes in price, the product is said to be *price inelastic*. Essential goods such as basic foods (e.g. bread, potatoes) and fuel tend to be price inelastic, as do cigarettes.

PED is important because it helps organisations to predict the effect of a price change. Managers therefore need to be able to calculate the PED.

BOX 11.2 CALCULATING THE PED

PED is expressed as a number and can be calculated as follows:

$$PED = \frac{\text{percentage change in demand for the product}}{\text{percentage change in price of the product}}$$

Three steps to calculating the PED

1   Work out the percentage change in price.

    If the original price of the product was £32 and the new price of the product is £28, the percentage change in the price is therefore −12.5%.

2   Work out the percentage change in demand.

    If original quantity of the product sold (the demand) was 80 units and the new quantity of the product sold (the demand) is 100 units, the percentage change in the demand is therefore 25%

3   Calculate the PED.

    The PED for the product can therefore be calculated as follows:

$$PED = \frac{25}{-12.5} = -2.0$$

In this case the PED for the product is −2.0. However, because PED values are usually negative, it is customary to drop the minus sign and give the PED value as simply 2.0.

What do the PED values mean?

■   A PED of 0 means that the product is *perfectly price inelastic* – demand does not change at all when the price changes. This case is shown in Figure 11.10 (a).

■   A PED between 0 and 1 means the product is *price inelastic*, but not perfectly so. This case is shown in Figure 11.10 (b).

■   A PED of 1 means the product has *unit elasticity*, the demand changes by the same percentage as the price change. This case is shown in Figure 11.10 (c).

■   A PED of more than 1 means that the product is *price elastic*. The higher the value the more price elastic the product is, that is, the demand for the product changes by a larger percentage than the price change. This case is shown in Figure 11.10 (d).

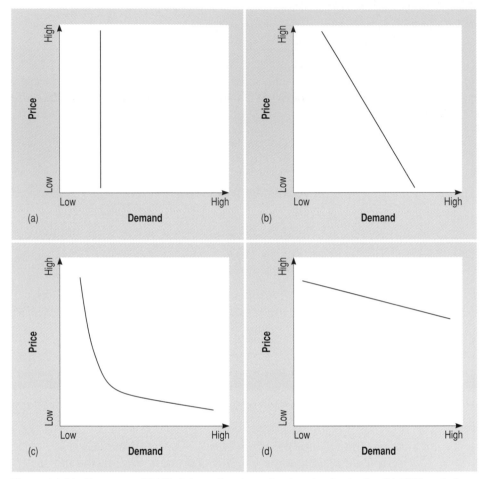

Figure 11.10 Degrees of PED: (a) product is perfectly price inelastic; (b) PED = 0–1, product is price inelastic; (c) PED = 1, product has unit price elasticity; (d) PED > 1, product is price elastic.

Using the PED

Once the PED is known, it is possible to work out how the demand for a product will be affected by a price change. Suppose that the manager of a food retail outlet learns that the PED for a product is 2. This tells the manager that a price increase of 10 per cent would lead to a reduction in sales of 20 per cent (and conversely, that a price reduction of 10 per cent would lead to an increase in sales of 20 per cent).

So, if the PED of the products sold in a bakery were 2, cutting prices in the bakery at the end of the day by 10 per cent would result in a 20 per cent increase in sales.

PED values – a simple rule

■ If the PED is less than 1 – an increase in price will result in an increase in revenue (because the demand changes in proportion to the price change).

■ If the PED is more than 1 – an increase in price will result in a decrease in revenue (because the demand changes by a larger proportion than the change in price).

Place

Distribution channels

Distribution is concerned with transporting goods and services in the most cost effective and efficient way, from where they are to where they need to be.

Although this topic may appear less exciting than other aspects of the marketing mix such as advertising and promotion policy, the choice and management of distribution channels can be a crucial element of marketing strategy. A distribution channel is a route between the supplier and the customer. It includes a range of functions: physical receipt, storage and delivery of the product or service and customer service, and provides a conduit for information to and from the customer. It is the face of the supplier as far as the customer is concerned. For this reason it is of key strategic importance for organisations to decide how they want this interface to be structured and managed.

A choice of channels

Suppliers have a range of choices in reaching the customer:

■ directly, through mail order (e.g. clothing catalogues), the internet (e.g. Amazon.com) or face to face (e.g. hairdressers)

■ through a sales force (e.g. many industrial goods)

■ through a retailer (e.g. food)

■ through an agent or facilitator as in many business-to-business sales (e.g. computers, photocopiers).

Issues to consider in distribution

The choice of a distribution channel will depend partly on the nature of a business and partly on the strategic direction of the organisation. There are five main issues to be considered.

1 **Cost** Distribution and storage incur costs. These will include the cost of the physical facilities in which to hold the product, operating costs (such

as heating, refrigeration, security and storage), losses or deterioration of quality during storage, and the working capital tied up in the stock. In many businesses, distributors will incur these costs, which will then be reflected in the margin taken by the distributor and will reduce the control exercised by the supplier.

2 **Coverage** In some businesses, access to the product or service is all-important. In these cases, marketing decisions will focus on distribution as a means of achieving strategic advantage. Whereas storage costs are likely to be important primarily in product-based industries, the importance of access is likely to be critical for service businesses.

3 **Communication** The form of distribution chosen will determine the interface with the customer and so provides an opportunity – or even a requirement – for the organisation to communicate a consistent message to customers. An organisation therefore needs to be clear about what messages it wishes to give to and receive from the customer, and it must ensure that its choice of channel delivers this message.

4 **Control** An issue related to communication is that of control: how important is it for the supplier to control the customer interface? For some products or services there is little value to be gained from control of the purchasing transaction, but for others it is critical to the supplier's competitive advantage. In general, control is less important for commodity products or services than it is for high value-added products. For example, food suppliers (selling commodity products) generally do not own supermarkets. Conversely, car dealers (selling high value-added products), although not owned by the manufacturers, operate within the strictly-defined guidelines set by them.

5 **Competitive advantage** In competitive markets it is necessary to seek advantage in all stages of the value chain. Distribution, with its contact with the customer, is often an important source of advantage.

Promotion

Customer decisions and marketing communications

Marketing communications can be seen as a process of persuasion – seeking to convince potential customers to purchase specific goods or services. The AIUAPR model is fairly typical of a range of models used to identify the steps in the customer decision-making process and the role of communication at each step. The model takes its name from the steps to be considered: **A**wareness, **I**nterest, **U**nderstanding, **A**ttitude, **P**urchase and **R**epeat purchase.

■ **Awareness** The potential customer must be aware that the product or service exists.

- **Interest** The prospective customer must receive a message that interests him or her.

- **Understanding** The prospective customer needs to understand how well the offering meets his or her needs.

- **Attitude** The prospective customer must be persuaded to adopt a positive attitude to the offering.

- **Purchase** The customer carries out the transaction, facilitated by personal selling or a sales promotion such as a reduced price offer.

- **Repeat purchase** If satisfied, the customer will make repeat purchases. Advertising contributes to this by reassuring existing customers of the advantages of the brands they have chosen.

The customer is assisted in this decision-making process by two sets of influences:

- **Peer group influence** The influence of family, friends and workplace colleagues.

- **Supplier influence** The influence of the provider of the product or service.

These influences can be exerted at varying stages of the process.

The AIUAPR model is useful but the process of communication often begins earlier, and is more complex than the AIUAPR model indicates. Organisations are now looking at their relationships with their customers over a much longer timescale. As a result, they are moving away from the transaction-based approach that underpins the AIUAPR model.

The communication loop

Effective communication is a continuing activity which is best regarded as a loop, as shown in Figure 11.11, rather than as a chain. The loop reflects the long-term relationship between providers and users of goods and services. The stages in this loop are:

- understanding user needs – as delivered by the product or service features

- identifying appropriate groups of potential users – the target audience

- providing information on product or service benefits to the target audience

- collecting information on user satisfaction

- using this information to evaluate the quality of delivery of the product or service

- similarly, evaluating the effectiveness of the communication programme

- modifying the product or service on the basis of this feedback
- informing users of these modifications and of any new products or services being offered.

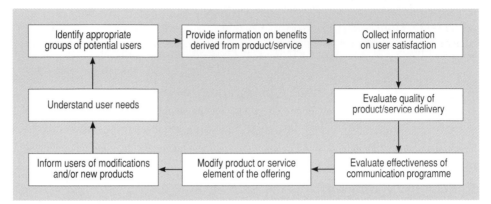

Figure 11.11 **The communication loop**

The communication mix

A number of tools are used by organisations to communicate with their audiences. Together, these tools are known as the communication mix. Some examples are: advertising, direct sales, personal sales, direct mail, public relations, trade fairs and sponsorships. These are illustrated in Figure 11.12.

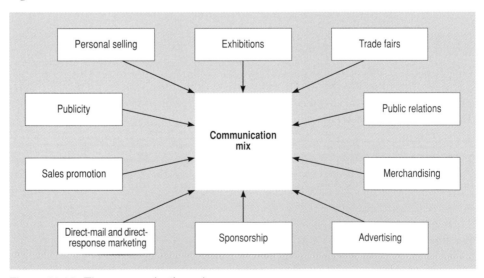

Figure 11.12 **The communication mix**

(Source: Murray and O'Driscoll, 1996)

Push or pull strategies

The emphasis that is given to different communication activities will vary according to the characteristics of the product or service, and the objectives of the organisation. Companies selling branded products with a high level of consumer recognition are likely to focus their communications on advertising to increase consumer awareness, and to create a *pull* for the product that distributors will have to respond to. Good examples of this are The Coca-Cola Company and Levi Strauss & Co.

See Branding, p. 231.

Companies that are not market leaders, or are not selling branded products, are more likely to adopt a *push* strategy. This involves an emphasis on promotional activities aimed at the distributors (typically retailers) with the objective of encouraging them to push the product to the consumers. This tends to happen with goods such as washing machines and freezers. These promotional activities are commonly referred to as 'below the line' activities, in contrast to advertising, which is referred to as an 'above the line' activity. Consumers are not normally aware of 'below the line' activities.

The marketing plan

A marketing plan is a set of activities that details a company's marketing effort.

The plan may be designed for a particular product or segment, or for an entire company and all its products. In each case the plan will specify the marketing goals and objectives to be achieved over a specific time period, and will detail specific strategies and tactics to be followed to achieve them. It may also contain a timetable of events and detailed responsibilities for carrying out the plan.

A marketing plan can be seen as a subset of the corporate plan. The corporate plan sets out objectives and strategies for the entire organisation. These requirements are given to individual functional directors (for example, human resources, marketing, production) who are required to create their own plans designed to accomplish these organisational goals.

Developing a marketing plan

Marketing plans should answer the following questions:

- Where are we now?
- Where do we want to go?
- How will we get there?
- How will we ensure arrival?

The stages of a marketing plan

Answering the four questions involves a number of stages. These are:

- complete a situation analysis
- set objectives
- choose a strategy to help you achieve your objectives
- segment, target and position your offer so it is differentiated in the mind of your customers
- create an action plan
- design control and evaluation measures to close the planning loop.

The overall planning process should be seen as cyclical. Marketers should be able to amend the plan where necessary. The planning process will involve a number of the concepts, tools and techniques covered in *The Manager's Good Study Guide*, in particular those set out in this chapter.

CHAPTER 12 FINANCE

The financial perspective

Talk of 'fixed assets', 'income and expenditure', 'value for money', 'the accounts' or 'the bottom line' can be puzzling or seem irrelevant to achieving a management task in which money seems an incidental if unavoidable aspect. Requests from the finance department or accountant about spending forecasts, or variances from budgets which may have been inaccurate to begin with, may be similarly regarded. Part of the reason for this probably lies in the organisational reality that securing, managing and accounting for financial resources have often been largely the preserve of finance and accounting specialists. These experts tend to surround themselves with complex professional concepts, documents and jargon, and tend to provide information in a form that is not readily understood. However, an organisation will rarely achieve its objectives unless all of its managers understand the relationship between what they do and the impact it can have on financial results. Thus, it is important for managers to understand how financial information is compiled and how it can be used.

Figure 12.1 sets out how financial information, frameworks, statements and budgets fit into the bigger picture, and links the tasks that managers perform with the ways in which financial information is put together, to make sense both within the organisation and to the outside world.

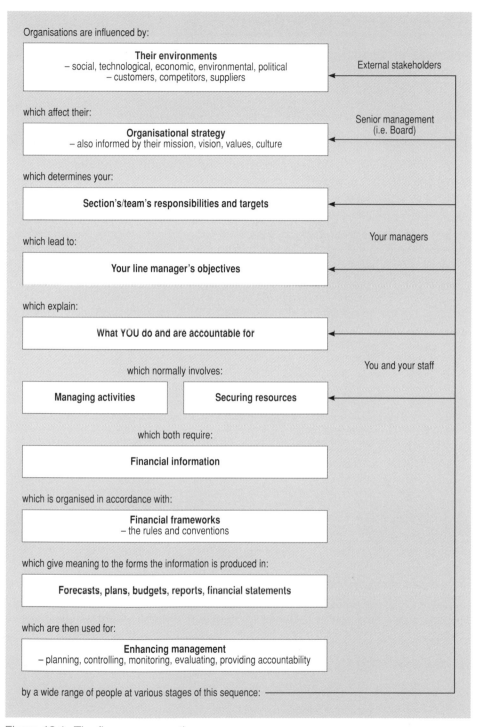

Figure 12.1 The finance connection

Accounting concepts and principles

Financial statements are prepared at the end of a period – usually a year – to present the results for the period and the period-end financial position to the organisation's internal and external stakeholders. The form and content of such financial statements are often regulated by statute (e.g. the Companies Act 1985, in the UK) or regulations produced by accounting bodies (e.g. the International Accounting Standards Board). There is often a general requirement that the financial statements should give a 'true and fair view' or should 'present fairly' the affairs of the organisation. Further guidance may be provided by, or based on, fundamental accounting concepts or principles. Some of the more important concepts and principles used internationally are summarised in Table 12.1.

Table 12.1   Fundamental accounting concepts and principles

Concept	Explanation
Consistency	Similar items should be treated in similar ways, both within an accounting period and from one period to the next. This is to prevent organisations using different methods to present a more favourable picture of the organisation.
Conservatism or prudence	Anticipate no profit and recognise all losses. This has traditionally been regarded as a counter to the optimism of some managers.
Accruals or matching	Revenues and costs are recognised in the period in which they are earned or incurred rather than when money is received or paid. This allows the users of financial statements to make sensible comparisons between income and expenditure because the two items match.
Going concern	There is a presumption that the organisation will continue with its activities for the foreseeable future. This is important for the valuation of the organisation's assets and liabilities on the balance sheet. If the organisation is to continue, then these valuations will differ from the break-up values – the values that would be obtained if the organisation were to be liquidated and all its assets sold on the open market.
Materiality, aggregation and offsetting	An item is material if it is significant to the understanding of the financial statements: the buildings owned by an organisation are usually material, but the calculator used by the accountant, the finance director's car and the potted plants in the offices are probably not. Each material item should be presented separately in the financial statements. The value of immaterial items need not be presented separately. The value of immaterial items of a similar nature or function should be aggregated (that is, combined) and presented in the financial statements. Assets and liabilities, and income and expenses, should not usually be offset (for example, liabilities cannot be used to cancel out assets): they must all be represented separately. This ensures that important items are highlighted in the financial statements.
Congruence	The opening balance sheet for a financial year must correspond to the closing balance sheet for the preceding financial year. This ensures all transactions are reflected in the financial statements.

Accounting periods are normally one year for external reporting, but often accounts are prepared for internal use on a quarterly, monthly or even weekly basis.

Profit or not-for-profit

Organisations are often differentiated in terms of the sector of the economy to which they belong: public or private. They are also classified according to whether or not their primary motive is profit – enhancement of their owners' or members' wealth. Thus, it is possible to allocate most organisations into one or other of the quadrants shown in Table 12.2.

Table 12.2	Public or private, for-profit or not-for-profit	
	Economic sector	
	Public	**Private**
Not-for-profit	Government and government departments, local authorities, armed forces, schools, hospitals.	Non-governmental organisations (e.g. aid agencies), charities, voluntary bodies, clubs and societies, professional bodies, employers' federations, trade unions, pressure groups, religious organisations.
For-profit	State-owned enterprises, which in some countries include public utilities, railways, airlines, nationalised industries.	Sole traders, partnerships, companies, producer and consumer co-operatives.

Not-for-profit financial survival

In not-for-profit (sometimes called non-profit) organisations the primary motives of the organisation are expressed in terms other than those of financial profitability. This does not mean that the intention is to make a loss! Nor does it mean that losses can be the normal or predominant financial outcome. Cash is as important to the wellbeing of not-for-profit organisations as it is to other organisations, individuals and households. Cash is used to acquire inputs (e.g. staff, expenditure items, fixed assets) and it is the form in which revenue (e.g. grants, donations) and long-term finance (e.g. endowments, bequests, loans) are received. For a not-for-profit organisation to survive and grow, revenues must equal or exceed expenditure and loan repayments, and long-term finance must be sufficient to finance fixed and net current assets.

See Assets and liabilities, p. 248.

Not-for-profit financial statements

Not-for-profit organisations prepare financial statements in which revenues (or incoming resources) for a financial period are matched against costs – as in a business's profit and loss account. In not-for-profit organisations these statements have various other names: statements of financial affairs, statements of financial performance, revenue and expenditure statements, vote accounts, appropriation accounts and operating statements.

Not-for-profit organisations usually also prepare balance sheets. These can help an organisation to evaluate whether the financial conditions for survival and growth are being met. Balance sheets are prepared on a variety of bases of accounting, ranging from a purely cash basis through modified-cash and modified-accruals bases to a full accruals basis. A cash basis means that only when cash is received or paid does an organisation record anything in its accounts. In contrast, a full accruals basis entails recording items in the accounts as soon as contractual obligations arise in a transaction, thus emulating commercial accounting where the accounts are prepared using financial values as opposed to cash values.

See Accounting concepts and principles, p. 246.

For internal purposes, many not-for-profit organisations use budgets to plan for expenditure. The actual expenditure is matched against the plans and any difference – or *variance* – is identified and has to be accounted for. Because of the length of time it takes for information to progress through the accounting system, the actual figures can often be out of date. Accordingly, managers will keep a record of the transactions – or *commitments* – they have just conducted or are just about to conduct, and will take these into account when making comparisons and identifying variance. These internal bases of accounting are very useful for budgetary control, which is critical in not-for-profit organisations.

Differences between businesses and not-for-profit organisations

There are some important differences between businesses and not-for-profit organisations:

- The prices charged by not-for-profit organisations to their recipients may be nominal rather than reflecting market forces (e.g. meals for the elderly in the community, prescription medicines, tertiary education).

- In public services the budget may have a special legal status, following the principle of no taxation without representation. Democracy also implies that government organisations should be publicly accountable.

Assets and liabilities

An asset is something which an organisation owns and which has a market value. A liability is a debt that the organisation owes to another person or organisation.

Assets

There are two kinds of asset. A *fixed* asset is part of the structure of the organisation. The organisation's buildings will be a fixed asset, as will the equipment that the organisation uses to carry out its operations. There is a sense of permanence about fixed assets. They constitute the organisation's operating capacity, so an increase or decrease in the fixed assets changes the productive capacity of the organisation. The value of the fixed assets will usually be the major part of the total value of the organisation's assets.

In contrast to fixed assets, a *current* asset is one that is short term. It is one that will be used or consumed in the organisation's operations within one year. The raw materials that the organisation has in stock are a current asset. So too, are the payments that the organisation's customers (debtors) are due to make (within the next accounting period, for example, one year) for the goods and services that the organisation has supplied to them. The cash that the organisation holds is also a current asset. During the organisation's operations, the composition of the current assets – the value of the stocks, the debts that are due, and the cash – will change.

Liabilities

There are also two categories of liability. A *long-term* liability (or debt) is one that is due for repayment in more than one year's time. A loan from a bank that is due for repayment in five years' time is an example of a long-term liability. A *current* liability is a debt that is due for repayment within one year. A bank overdraft is an example of a current liability. Payments due to creditors are usually current liabilities too.

Net worth

The net worth (or the net value) of an organisation is the value of the assets, less the value of the liabilities as recorded in the books of accounts. These accounts will show the net book value but this will almost certainly differ from the market value of the assets and liabilities.

Intangible assets

Assets are generally tangible, for example premises, equipment, stock, and so on. However, an asset can be intangible. The organisation's reputation – perhaps expressed in a brand – is an example. It can be difficult to put a value on an asset of this kind, and often no such value is included in the balance sheet.

See Branding, p. 231.

The balance sheet

An organisation's balance sheet is the financial account that shows the book value of the organisation's assets and its liabilities at a particular time, usually on a particular day. It provides a financial snapshot of the organisation.

A statement of assets and liabilities

Table 12.3 shows an example of a balance sheet for a small organisation.

Table 12.3 Balance sheet A	£000s	£000s
Fixed assets		
Premises		100
Current assets		
Stock	10	
Debtors	10	
Cash	5	—
Total, current assets	25	
Current liabilities		
Creditors	(15)	
Net current assets		10
Total net assets		110
Financed by		
Long-term borrowing		30
Owners' capital (see below)		80
		110
Note: Owners' capital		
Original share capital	40	
Accumulated profits from prior years	35	
Profit for the year	5	
	80	

There are variants on this layout but there are some general points that can be made.

■ Notice that the fixed assets are placed at the top of the column.

■ The net current assets are the value of the current assets less the amounts of the current liabilities, usually the amounts that are due to creditors. The net current assets are also known as the working capital.

■ The total net assets are the sum of the fixed assets and the net current assets.

The question then arises: how were these total net assets financed? There are two broad categories of finance: external sources and internal sources. In this illustration, the long-term borrowing has come from an external source, a bank or other financial institution. The other source has been the owners. They provided (i) the original capital, and (ii) the profits (that is, the increases in the organisation's wealth) that they have kept in the business to fund what is known as the organic growth of the organisation.

An alternative layout

You may also come across a two-column balance sheet, as shown in Table 12.4. This balance sheet displays the same information as is shown in Balance sheet A, but in a different way.

Table 12.4 Balance sheet B			
Liabilities	**£000s**	**Assets**	**£000s**
Long-term borrowing	30	Fixed assets	100
Current liabilities	15	Current assets	25
Total liabilities	45		
Owner's capital	80		
Total	125		125

Understanding the profit statement

The profit statement (sometimes called the income and expenditure account in a not-for-profit organisation) shows the income that the organisation has earned from its activities during a particular period and the expenditures it has incurred.

A simple profit statement is shown in Table 12.5.

Table 12.5 Profit statement		
	£000s	
Income from sales	200	(This will include cash and credit sales)
Direct costs	100	
Operating profit	100	
Indirect costs	40	
Net profit	60	

Earnings

The profit statement takes account of the organisation's earnings. The income shows the total money value of the sales contracts that have been made with customers. So the total – £200,000 in this instance – will include contracts for which the customers have paid and credit sales for which the customers have not paid. In the same way, the costs (direct and indirect) are all the costs that have been incurred, some of which will have been paid to the suppliers and some not. This is what is referred to as the accruals or matching process.

See Accounting concepts and principles, p. 246.

Operating profit and net profit

The operating profit is the difference between the income – the earnings – from sales, and the direct cost of those sales. When the indirect costs are taken from the operating profit, the result is the net profit.

The nature of profit

'Profit' is the term that is used to describe the increase in wealth of a for-profit organisation that has been brought about by the organisation's activities. A manager could say: 'As a result of our trading activities during the year our organisation has increased its wealth by £60,000'. The estimate of the increase in the organisation's wealth – the profit – assumes that the customers who have not yet paid for their products or services will do so. If a customer who owed £5,000 was unable to pay, then the organisation would have to revise the profit statement to show 'Bad debt £5,000' as a cost. As a result, the net profit would fall to £55,000.

Cash account

The cash account shows the cash that the organisation has received and the cash that the organisation has paid. As a result, it shows the cash that remains in the organisation.

When used in this way the term cash account includes not only banknotes and coins but also the balance – positive or negative – of the organisation's bank account.

The flow of cash

During a day, or week, or month, or during any particular trading period, the organisation will receive payments and will make them. These payments could be made in cash (banknotes or coins), by cheque, or by automatic payments such as direct debits or standing orders. The purpose of the cash account is to record each of these payments to, or from, the organisation. Sometimes people refer to the flow of cash into the organisation as the inflow of cash, and the flow from the organisation as the outflow of cash.

The stock of cash

Sometimes, the outflow of cash during a period will be greater than the inflow. As a result, the stock of cash in the organisation will fall and the organisation may become overdrawn at the bank. At other times, the inflow will be greater than the outflow, and the stock of cash will rise.

Managing the flows

The management of the organisation's cash should be an active process. The responsible manager should always know how much cash the organisation holds, what payments are expected (the inflows), and what payments must be made (the outflows). In this way, the manager can ensure that the organisation is holding a sufficiency of cash. The manager who monitors the cash account closely will be able to foresee a likely surplus of cash, or a likely insufficiency, and will be able to respond appropriately. A surplus, for instance, could be lent to a financial institution and interest received. Alternatively, when the manager foresees an insufficiency, it may be possible either to secure a short-term loan or to reschedule the cash flows to reduce or eliminate the shortage. The management of the cash calls for a continuing forecast of the likely inflows and outflows so that the organisation's cash needs are always met.

Budgeting

A budget is essentially a published forecast of how an organisation's resources are to be used in the best possible way to achieve its objectives. It states how these resources will be committed to the activities or projects to be carried out. At regular intervals (control periods), or when an unexpected event happens, the forecast will be revised and used internally to manage performance against the original budget.

Benefits of budgeting

A budget is a quantitative statement for a defined period of time, that may include planned revenues, expenses, assets, liabilities and cash flows. A budget:

- provides a framework for planning

- aids the co-ordination of activities – budgeting is an iterative and interactive process involving a number of people (or departments) who share in its creation and ownership

- provides the basis for monitoring progress and control and allows corrective action to be taken

- helps managers to justify their use of resources as well as sharing financial responsibility

- provides a steady pressure to improve performance, sometimes by innovation

- facilitates control – actual results can be compared with the targets set in the budget.

Phases of management control are shown in Figure 12.2 which sets out a cyclical process of designing and evaluating projects (programming), preparing budgets (budgeting), implementing the plans (operating and measurement), producing and interpreting reports and comparing the actual revenues and costs with those budgeted (reporting and analysis). Note the use of external information at each stage in the cycle, for example, that a supplier has raised its prices or a competitor has cut its prices.

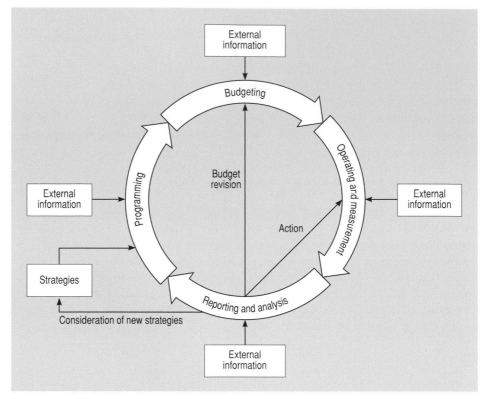

Figure 12.2 **Phases of management control**

(Source: Anthony and Herzlinger, 1980)

Table 12.6	Types of budget		
Type	**Method**	**Advantages**	**Disadvantages**
Incremental	Budget based on the previous year's actual or budgeted figures.	Simple and useful if the conditions are static.	Expenditure patterns might exhibit a 'hockey stick effect' with dips or surges in expenditure as the year-end approaches. New ideas might be ignored.
Zero-base	Targets, inputs, outputs and activities are planned and justified from first principles each time the budget is set.	Complacency and the 'hockey stick effect' can be overcome.	Time consuming.
Continuous (or rolling)	Budgets are updated at the end of each sub-period (e.g. monthly or quarterly).	The budget is always up to date. Future costs and revenues can be forecast more accurately.	There may be a sense that the goalposts are being moved.
Fixed	The budget is set envisaging only one level of activity.	Simple and useful when the activity level is known.	Monitoring actual performance against the budget is difficult, as the effect of differing levels of activity cannot be clearly identified.

Types of budget

There are different types of budget depending on the activity planned. For example, a manufacturing company will use flexible budgets so it can compare its actual costs with those budgeted for that level of activity. Types of budget are set out in Table 12.6.

Notice that the budget is a way of controlling the activity in an organisation. Managers set out what they intend. They register what is actually happening or what has happened. They compare the planned results with the actual. They seek the reasons for the variances. They take account of these reasons as they prepare or review the plan for the next period.

See Budgeting, p. 253, Different types of costs, p. 257.

Working capital

'Working capital' is the term used to describe how the day-to-day activities of an organisation are funded. It comprises current assets (stock + debtors + cash in the bank and in hand) minus current liabilities (creditors + accruals + any bank overdraft).

An organisation's working capital is constantly changing. For example, a wholesaler of vegetables will buy goods on credit from farmers. The wholesaler now has some *stock*, but he also owes money to his suppliers – his *creditors*. The wholesaler needs to sell the vegetables on to retailers while they are still fresh. The retailers will usually buy the goods on credit terms. After each sale, the quantity of goods in stock will be reduced, but the amounts owed to the wholesaler by his customers – his *debtors* – will increase. The balance of the wholesaler's bank account will change each time he pays one of his suppliers or receives money from one of his customers. The working capital cycle can be presented diagrammatically as shown in Figure 12.3.

Managing the working capital cycle

Management of the working capital cycle is essential to the successful management of an organisation. For example, the organisation must ensure it has adequate cash (or overdraft facilities) to pay its creditors when required. If it cannot do this, its supplies may dry up and it will be unable to continue with its activities. It must not have too much cash tied up in stock and it must receive payments regularly from its customers. It is important to

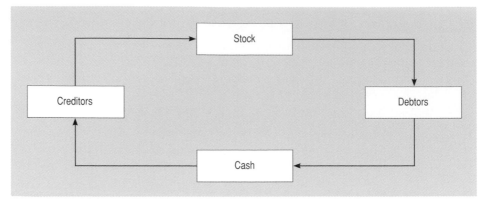

Figure 12.3 **The flow of finance – the impact of debtors, creditors and stock**

manage the quantity of stock being held. There must be sufficient goods available to meet customers' needs, but there are a number of costs associated with holding stock. Goods have to be stored, and during storage they may deteriorate, or go out of fashion. Nevertheless, it may be worthwhile buying in large quantities of some items to take advantage of bulk discounts. Many organisations have a department devoted to the management of debtors, often known as the credit control, or sales ledger, department. It is their responsibility to ensure that goods are sold on credit only to customers who can be relied on to pay, and to ensure that customers settle their bills on the agreed terms. The management of creditors is a balancing act. Organisations need to hold on to their cash, to pay as late as possible, but without adversely affecting their relationship with a particular supplier. Sometimes suppliers offer discounts to encourage prompt payments.

Understanding depreciation

Every organisation, for-profit and not-for-profit, charges (or records) the cost of the things it buys for its operations to a profit statement or to a statement of income and expenditure. When what is bought will be consumed within one year of its purchase, its cost is charged in full to the profit and loss account, or equivalent, in the year in which it was bought. When, however, an asset will have a working life of longer than one year, the total cost of the asset should be charged, bit by bit, over the expected working life of the asset. 'Depreciation' is the term that is used to describe this process of charging, over time, the cost of a long-life asset to a profit or income and expenditure statement.

An example of depreciation

Suppose a firm builds an extension to its premises at a cost of £20,000. The extension is expected to have a life of ten years. To begin with, the value of the premises on the balance sheet will rise by £20,000. After this, the cost – the £20,000 – will be charged to the profit statement (or to an income and expenditure statement) bit by bit, over the expected life of the asset. As this happens the figure on the balance sheet will reduce correspondingly.

Methods of depreciation

There are two well-known ways of depreciating a fixed asset (charging the cost of a fixed asset to the profit or equivalent statement). First, the cost could be charged in equal amounts each year. In the previous example, the appropriate annual charge would be £2,000 for ten years. The charges would be shown as 'depreciation'.

The second method is the reducing-balance one. A constant proportion (not amount) is charged each year. Suppose the proportion was set at 20 per cent. In that case, the charge for depreciation in the first year would be £4,000 (i.e. 20 per cent of £20,000). In the second year, the charge would be £3,200 (i.e. 20 per cent of £16,000), and in the third year it would be £2,560 (i.e. 20 per cent of £12,800). In this way, the early years of the asset carry a heavier charge for depreciation than the later ones. When the amount of the original cost that remains to be depreciated becomes sufficiently small, there can be a final charge to the profit (or other) statement.

Notice the following points:

■ The higher the charge for depreciation in a year, the lower the declared profit or surplus will be.

■ The cash account will show the outflow of cash at the time that the new asset is paid for.

■ The subsequent charges for depreciation will not represent cash outflows.

Different types of costs

Some costs vary with the level of activity while others do not; some costs can be attributed to certain activities and some cannot. We consider each of these types of costs.

Fixed costs

Some costs are not affected by changes in the level of an organisation's activity. For example, the rent that a law firm pays for its premises will not vary with the volume of the firm's business. The rent paid is independent of the level of the firm's activity.

Variable costs

Some costs increase or decrease as the level of activity rises or falls. In the law firm, for example, telephone charges would be expected to rise as the volume of business rises and to fall as the volume of business falls. So too, would stationery costs. Day to day, the variable costs are more likely to be within a manager's control than the fixed ones.

Direct costs

Sometimes it is possible to attach or attribute a cost to a particular activity. In the law firm, for example, it will be possible to say that a member of staff worked for so many hours or days on behalf of a particular client, and so that appropriate cost can be charged directly to the client.

Indirect costs

Not all costs can be attributed to particular tasks. Suppose the law firm has advertised its services in local newspapers. It will be impossible to allocate those costs to particular tasks in the way that it was possible to allocate the staff costs. Because the costs cannot be attributed directly to a particular client, they are regarded as indirect costs. Of course, these costs must be recovered. A share of these indirect costs will be attached to the costs of particular activities. Managers should make a point of knowing the rules that apply in order to understand the allocation of the indirect costs to their own activities.

The allocation of overhead costs

Overhead costs (also referred to as overheads or indirect costs) are those costs that cannot be directly attributed to an activity. Suppose a training manager was keen to know the cost of each training session in the department. It would be easy to allocate the cost of the trainer and the cost of any materials; such costs could be directly attributed to a particular session. But there are other costs that cannot be attributed as easily, including the cost of the training manager, and of any other members of staff who provide services to the training sessions in general rather than to particular sessions.

In principle, these overhead costs should be shared, or allocated, in a way that is recognised as reasonable. In a training department, it might be the practice to divide the expected indirect costs by the number of sessions, and to add the result to the direct costs of each session. Every session would then be charged the same amount. Or experience might have led the training manager to allocate the indirect costs according to the number of trainees per session, rather than the number of training sessions. Whichever way the indirect costs are to be allocated, they are charged to the different training sessions, each of which is treated as a separate activity with its own revenue and its own costs.

The impact of indirect costs

The addition of indirect costs can have a crucial effect on the financial results of an activity. A simple example is shown in Table 12.7.

Table 12.7	The effects of allocating the indirect costs	
	Activity A	**Activity B**
	£000s	**£000s**
Revenue	10	10
Direct costs	5	3
Surplus over direct costs	5	7
Indirect costs (a)	1	4
Overall surplus (a)	4	3
Indirect costs (b)	4	1
Overall surplus (b)	1	6

In the example, indirect costs of £5,000 must be shared between the two activities, A and B. Notice that Activity B produces the higher surplus over direct costs.

However, one allocation of the indirect costs (a) – leads to Activity A having the higher overall surplus. A different allocation of the indirect costs (b) – leads to Activity B having the higher overall surplus.

A manager who has financial responsibility for an activity (a cost centre) should know how the indirect costs have been allocated to it and should be ready to discuss the appropriateness of the rule that has been applied.

Break-even using numbers

A manager who is planning the sale of a product or service will be keen to know the volume of sales (the level of operation) at which the total costs of the operation will be matched by the sales income – the break-even level. Up to that particular volume, the operation will be making a loss; beyond that volume, the operation will be making a profit.

An example of break even

Suppose a wood carver rents a stall at a local arts and crafts exhibition to take orders for a toy train. Each buyer can specify the colour and the decoration, so that each train will be personalised, at least to some extent. The price of a train is £40. The carver reckons that the variable costs of the operation – materials and labour – for each train will be £20. Meanwhile, the fixed costs of the operation will be £600.

The break-even level of operation – the sales at which total costs will be matched by total income – can be calculated in different ways.

Table 12.8	Costs and revenue				
Sales volume	Fixed costs	Variable costs	Total costs	Sales revenue	Loss
	£000s	£000s	£000s	£000s	£000s
0	600	0	600	0	(600)
10	600	200	800	400	(400)
20	600	400	1,000	800	(200)
30	600	600	1,200	1,200	(0)

Table 12.8 shows what happens as the level of operation (the sales) rises. Each additional train that is made and sold adds £20 to the variable costs, but adds £40 to the sales revenue. So each sale closes the gap between total costs and total sales revenue by £20. By the time the wood carver has made and sold 30 trains, the gap has been eliminated.

Each train that is sold will bring in £20 more than the variable costs that were incurred in making it. That is, each train will contribute £20 towards the fixed costs. When 30 trains are sold, the contribution – £600 – will equal the fixed costs. So the break-even level of operation is 30 trains.

> When you know the fixed costs of the operation and the contribution that each sale makes to the fixed costs, then you can calculate the break-even as follows:
> Break-even = Fixed costs ÷ Contribution per unit sold
> So in this example:
> Break-even = 600 ÷ 20 = 30

Break-even using graphs

The break-even level of an operation can be calculated by drawing a graph, as shown in Figure 12.4. The data used are from the previous example.

See Break-even using numbers, p. 259.

As you look at the graph, notice that:

■ The fixed costs are represented by a horizontal line, showing that the fixed costs (of £600) do not change as the output changes.

■ The total costs line rises parallel with the variable costs line. The distance between them remains constant at £600, that is, the amount of the fixed costs.

■ The total revenue line rises faster – has a steeper slope – than the variable costs line. As a result, it also rises faster than the total cost line. As output rises, so the vertical gap between the total cost line and the total revenue line narrows. The gap is eliminated when output reaches 30. At that output, total cost and total revenue both equal £1,200.

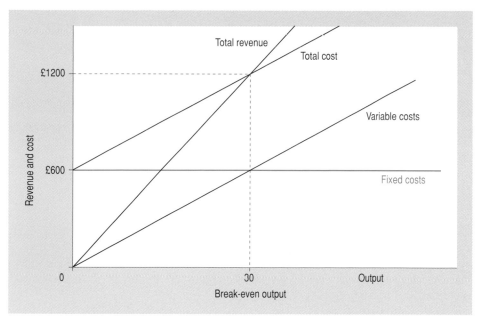

Figure 12.4 **Break-even analysis**

■ Up to an output of 30 units, the operation will be making a loss. When the output exceeds 30 units, the operation will be making a surplus.

The margin of safety

The margin of safety is the gap between the break-even output and the organisation's total capacity. Suppose that the wood carver could make 40 trains each week. Then the margin of safety would be 10 trains, a quarter of the total capacity. The wood carver has the capacity to produce 10 trains beyond the break-even output and so has the capacity to make a total profit of £200 a week. (Remember that each train sells for £20 more than the direct costs of production.) If the total capacity were 35 trains, then the scope for profit would be reduced to £100; if the total capacity were 50 trains, then the scope for profit would be increased to £400. If the total capacity were 30 units, then the present pricing and cost structure would not allow for any profit.

The margin of safety raises some issues:

■ the internal issues of pricing and costs and of capacity

■ the external issue of marketing.

Marginal analysis

The term 'marginal' is particularly associated with economic analysis. It directs our attention to small changes, in fact to changes of just one unit in a process or activity. 'Marginal analysis' can be used to ascertain an equilibrium level of activity and to identify the slight adjustments that may be needed to reach this level.

Marginal cost and marginal revenue

'Marginal cost' and 'marginal revenue' are common expressions of the concept of the margin. The marginal cost of a product or service is the additional cost of one extra unit of output. The marginal cost to a T-shirt manufacturer of supplying one more T-shirt is the additional cost of that one extra item, namely, the sum of the cost of the materials, the staff time, and any other cost that is brought about by the extra work. The marginal revenue from a sale is the additional revenue that results from the sale of one more item.

The significance of the two concepts begins to emerge. If we assume that, in the simple example, the T-shirt manufacturer is profit-orientated, then it is safe to assume that the manufacturer will continue to sell the T-shirts so long as the marginal cost of the most recently-produced T-shirt is not more than the marginal revenue received.

The equilibrium level of output

The concept of the margin helps us to think about, and to theorise about, the equilibrium level of output – the level at which the marginal costs equal the marginal revenue.

In general, the concept directs our attention to the edge, or to the margin, of a process or activity. The margin prompts us to look for this edge, to focus on the last event, the last unit of output, the last sum of money (price) that has been received. A manager will think about the adjustments to this edge – a pushing out of the edge or a pulling in – in order to reach the level of activity at which the manager's or the organisation's goals are maximised.

Ratio analysis

An organisation's financial performance and position can be interpreted from its financial statement. But more information can be gleaned by further analysis of the data contained in the statement. These data can be used to calculate financial ratios such as the return on capital employed (ROCE), return on investment (ROI), asset utilisation ratio (AUR), return on sales (ROS), stock turnover, and debtors' and creditors' turnover. The calculations shed light on an organisation's liquidity, financial structure and performance.

Such information is not only useful to managers within the organisation in order to assess financial performance and to compare it with that of competitors. It is also useful to outside parties who may need to assess the organisation's creditworthiness before providing a loan, credit or extended credit, or before investing in the company. Similarly, an organisation which relies on another organisation as a supplier or a customer will want to assess its ability to survive and grow. Ratio analysis enables a manager to do this.

While the information to carry out the calculations will be contained in financial statements – laws and regulations govern what must be disclosed – managers within an organisation normally have access to more relevant and detailed data than that which is made public in financial statements.

Some important points about financial ratios are:

- They are particularly useful when assessing performance, helping the manager to pinpoint good and bad aspects.

- They should never be considered in isolation, but should contribute to the broad profile of an organisation.

- To understand the meaning of ratios, those interpreting them should have a feel for the organisation they relate to, and for the averages for its industry type.

- Other performance indicators are essential in assessing the performance of an organisation.

Return on capital employed

The return on the capital employed in the organisation (ROCE) gives an overall measure of the success of the organisation in the market.

This ratio compares the operating profit that an organisation made from its trading activities with the material assets (the capital) that the organisation devoted to these activities. The ratio can be described in the following way:

$$\text{ROCE} = \frac{\text{Operating profit}}{\text{Capital employed in business}}$$

The return is usually shown as a percentage. Suppose that an organisation made an operating profit of £10,000 and employed material assets (capital) of £50,000 to make that profit. Then the return on the capital employed would be 10,000 ÷ 50,000, that is, 20 per cent. So a manager would say: 'The organisation earned a 20 per cent return on the assets it employed in the business'.

Using the ratio

The ROCE ratio can be used to compare the return on capital employed in one period with the return in a previous period. When the returns for a number of periods are set out, general features or trends may be evident. The ratio can also be used to compare the return (or returns) that the organisation has achieved with the return (or returns) that a competing organisation has achieved.

When making these comparisons, ensure that the terms 'operating profit' and 'average capital employed' are defined in a consistent way. Usually, the operating profit is taken to be the net reported profit, plus any interest that has been paid to lenders. The capital employed is usually taken to be the shareholders' capital, plus the amount that is due to long-term creditors. But remember that these terms can have different meanings.

Asset utilisation ratio and return on sales

See Return on capital employed, p. 263.

The overall return on the capital employed (ROCE) can be calculated by multiplying together the asset utilisation ratio (AUR) and the return on sales (ROS).

Asset utilisation ratio

The AUR compares the value of the sales (the turnover) with the material assets (the capital) employed in the business. The ratio can be described in the following way:

$$AUR = \frac{\text{Value of sales}}{\text{Capital employed in the business}}$$

Suppose, for instance, that an organisation's sales in a recent period were £100,000. Suppose too, that the value of the material assets (the capital) that were used (employed) in the business was £50,000. Then the AUR would be 2, that is, the value of the sales would be twice that of the assets that were used in the business.

Return on sales

The ROS ratio compares the operating profit with the total value of the sales (the turnover). The ratio can be described in the following way:

$$ROS = \frac{\text{Operating profit}}{\text{Value of sales}}$$

Suppose that the operating profit in the recent period was £10,000, and that the sales were £1,000,000. The ROS, in this case, would be 0.1 (that is, 100,000 ÷ 1,000,000). Usually, the ROS is shown as a percentage, so instead of saying that the ROS was 0.1, it would be customary to say: 'The return on sales ratio was 10 per cent'. The ratio gives the manager a broad measure of the profit that was made from the typical or the average sale. In this instance, the manager could say something like: 'We made one unit of profit from the sale of every ten units of our products or services'.

Two drivers of overall return

The ROCE reflects both the volume of sales that the organisation achieved and also the profit that the organisation made from each sale. That is, the

ROCE reflects both the AUR and the ROS. The relationship between the three ratios is as follows:

ROCE = AUR × ROS

Suppose that the AUR was 2 and the ROS was 10 per cent, then the ROCE would be 20 per cent. As the AUR and the ROS are the two drivers of the overall return, a manager who wants to increase the overall return can do one of the following:

- increase the AUR

- increase the ROS

- increase both the AUR and the ROS.

Margins and mark-ups

'Margin' is the term used to describe the profit earned as a percentage of the sales value. For example, a retailer has sold goods for £1,000,000 that originally cost her £750,000. She has made a gross profit of £250,000 (£1,000,000 − £750,000). Her *gross margin* is 25 per cent (£250,000 ÷ £1,000,000 × 100). After expenses, she is left with a net profit of £80,000. Her *net margin* is 8 per cent (£80,000 ÷ £1,000,000 × 100). It can be helpful to compare margins from one period to the next and between similar organisations.

'Mark-up' is the term used to express the amount added on to cost to arrive at the selling price as a percentage of cost. In the example above, the retailer has added £250,000 on to the cost price of £750,000 to arrive at a selling price of £1,000,000. Her mark-up is therefore 33.3 per cent (£250,000 ÷ £750,000 × 100).

If you are told the selling price and the mark-up, you can calculate the cost of the goods by working backwards. This can be useful if selling prices are more readily available than cost prices. Consider the following example of conducting a stock take (assessing the amount of stock) in a sweet shop:

All the sweets are marked with the selling price.

The total value of the sweets in the shop at their selling price is £5,000.

The shopkeeper applies a mark-up of 60 per cent to all goods.

What did the stock in the sweet shop originally cost?

Selling price represents 160 per cent of the cost price:

= Original cost (100% × Cost price) + Mark-up (60% × Cost price).

Original cost of the goods is therefore:

= Selling price ÷ 160% = £5,000 ÷ 160 × 100 = £3,125.

GLOSSARY OF FINANCIAL TERMS

The term organisation has been used in the glossary. It refers to commercial companies and firms of all kinds, public sector organisations and other non-profit, social and voluntary enterprises. However, non-commercial organisations may refer to 'surplus' rather than profit and are unlikely to have shareholders.

Absorption costing	The procedure that charges fixed as well as variable overheads to cost units. The term may be applied where production costs only, or all functions, are so allotted. Also known as recovery costing, full costing.
Accounting concepts	The four fundamental concepts, or principles, on which accounts in the UK and in many other countries are prepared. The principles are *prudence* (also known as conservatism), *consistency, going concern* and *accruals* (also known as *matching principle*).
Accounting entity	The subject, such as a firm, company or enterprise, for which accounting is undertaken.
Accounting period	The period to which a set of accounts refers, usually a year.
Account	A record of an individual financial item or activity.
Accounts	See *financial statements.*
Accounts receivable	See *debtors.*
Accruals concept	See *matching principle.*
Activity-based costing (ABC)	A costing system that attempts to charge overheads into costs on the basis of activity relationships.
Aggregation	The totalling of figures.
Amortisation	Gradually writing off an asset, in the same way as *depreciation*; usually associated with intangible assets such as leases and goodwill.
Assets	The resources of an organisation. They are normally divided into *current assets* (cash, stock, debtors), *fixed assets* (buildings, equipment), and *intangible assets* (knowledge, skills, brands). These assets are one part of the information needed to construct a balance sheet. See also *balance sheet, liabilities.*
Asset turnover ratio	See *asset utilisation ratio.*
Asset utilisation ratio (AUR)	The ratio that reflects the intensity with which assets are employed. The ratio is obtained by dividing sales by operating assets. Also known as asset turnover ratio, capital turnover ratio.
Auditors	People who are professionally qualified to conduct an official inspection of an organisation's accounts.
Bad debts	Debts that are known, assumed or expected not to be settled. They are usually written off as a charge to the profit and loss account. Also known as delinquent receivables.

Balance sheet	A statement of the financial position of an organisation at a given date. The statement discloses the value of the assets, liabilities and accumulated funds such as shareholders' contributions and reserves, to give a true and fair view of the state of the organisation at that date. See also *financial position statement*.
Bottom line	A colloquial expression derived from the last line in a profit statement, which shows the overall profit or loss.
Break-even analysis	A tool identifying the points at which sales income equals total costs for various levels of output, prices, etc., i.e. where there is no profit or loss. See also *break-even point*.
Break-even chart	A chart that represents the relationships between costs and income. The lines plotted on such a graph are the sales line, the variable costs line, the fixed costs line and the total costs line.
Break-even point	The point at which an activity generates neither profit nor loss, nor surplus or deficit.
Budget	A financial plan in the form of a quantitative statement for a defined period of time that may include planned revenues, expenses, assets, liabilities and cash flows. A budget provides a focus for the organisation, aids the co-ordination of activities and facilitates control.
Budget controls	The application of the broader principles of the planning and control process in an organisation to the budgets of all its departments and activities.
Budget planning cycle	The four stages of budgeting: preparation; collation and iteration; authorisation; and implementation.
Burden	See *indirect costs*.
Capital	The funds provided to an organisation by its owners and lenders.
Capital budget	The budget prepared for anticipated capital expenditure.
Capital employed	The funds used by an organisation for its operations.
Capital expenditure	Expenditure on assets that will be used by the organisation over a number of years. It is the opposite of *revenue expenditure*.
Capital turnover ratio	See *asset utilisation ratio*.
Cash	Banknotes, cash and cheques.
Cash flow statement	A statement listing the inflows and outflows of cash. It normally details such flows in relation to day-to-day items and capital items and may be a forecast (projection) or historical.
Conservatism	See *prudence concept*.
Consistency concept	The concept that requires the method of recording similar items to be consistent with previous years. This enables fair comparison of accounting information.
Constraints	See *limiting factors*.

Continuous budgets   See *rolling budgets*.

Contribution   The difference between sales value and the variable cost of those sales, expressed either in absolute terms or as a contribution per unit or a percentage of sales.

Contribution costing   See *marginal costing*.

Cost centre   One of the four *responsibility centres*. The budget holder is responsible for minimising costs for the required outputs.

Cost-effective   An acceptable financial return for an outlay.

Cost of sales (COS)   The sum of direct costs or variable costs of sales plus overheads attributable to the turnover. In management accounts, this may be referred to as production cost of sales. COS is often referred to as COGS, Cost of Goods Sold or Cost of Generating Services.

Cost-plus pricing   A method of pricing in which the cost of one unit is computed (using *absorption costing* or *marginal costing*) and then a percentage mark-up is added. See also *rate of return pricing*.

Creditors   The people and organisations to whom or to which money is owned.

Creditors' turnover ratio   A ratio that relates the total money owed to creditors (usually suppliers) at a particular date to the current rate of purchase of the goods and services supplied. This is normally expressed in calendar days, indicating the average time taken to pay for goods and services bought on credit.

Current assets   Cash or other assets (including stocks, debtors, and short-term investments) that are likely to be converted into cash in the normal course of trading.

Current liabilities   The liabilities that an organisation would normally expect to settle within a relatively short period (normally one year). It includes creditors, dividends and tax due for payment and that part of a long-term loan due for repayment within one year.

Current ratio   The relationship between current assets and current liabilities, reflecting the working capital situation.

Debtors   Those who owe money to an organisation, also known as accounts receivable or receivables.

Debtors' turnover ratio   A ratio that relates the total money owed by debtors (usually customers) at a particular date to the current rate of sale of the goods or services purchased. Normally expressed in calendar days, indicating the average time taken for debtors to pay for goods and services bought on account.

Declining balance method   A method of depreciation applying a constant percentage (determined by management) to the period-end net book value of a fixed asset over its useful life. Also known as the reducing balance method. See also *depreciation*, *net book value*, *straight line method*.

Delinquent receivables   See *bad debts*.

Depreciation	The charge made by an organisation against its revenue to provide for the use and/or progressive deterioration or obsolescence of its fixed assets within operations.
Direct costs	Costs that can be traced directly to units of production (or other activity of the organisation). In a production environment, these would typically include materials used, production labour and certain production expenses.
Dividends	Distributions made to shareholders of a limited company in proportion to the number of shares they hold, generally from post-tax profits. An 'interim' dividend is usually declared half-yearly whereas the 'final' dividend is declared at the year-end.
Earnings	See *profit*
EBIT	Earnings before interest and tax. Also known as *operating profit*.
Entity	See *accounting entity*
Financial accounts	See *financial statements*
Financial position statement	See *balance sheet*. The use of the word 'position' arises from the financial position recorded in the accounting records. It is used particularly in the USA, Australia and New Zealand.
Financial statements	Also known as '*accounts*' or '*financial accounts*', these are the summarised reports produced, mainly, for the benefit of external users of accounting information. They show a summary of the revenue, expenses, assets and liabilities of a business over a period of time; and they include the Balance Sheet, Profit and Loss Account, and Cash Flow Statement.
First in, first out (FIFO)	The assumption that the items of stock (inventory) that were purchased or made first are sold first and, consequently, the items remaining in stock at the end of the period are those most recently-purchased or produced.
Fixed assets	Assets that will be used as resources over a number of accounting periods, such as plant, equipment, furniture and fittings and motor vehicles.
Fixed budget	A budget that is designed to remain unchanged irrespective of the level of output or turnover attained.
Fixed costs	Costs that do not vary as the level of activity varies.
Flexible budget	A budget that, by recognising the differences in behaviour between fixed costs and variable costs in relation to fluctuations in output, turnover or other variable factors (such as number of employees), is designed to change appropriately with such fluctuations.
Four Es	Economy, the right consumption of resources; Efficiency, how well activities are undertaken; Effectiveness, the degree to which targets are achieved; and Equity, fair and equal treatment of all service users.

Full costing	See *absorption costing.*
Going concern	The concept that makes the assumption for accounting purposes that an organisation will continue to operate. This enables assets to be valued at their worth to the organisation, assuming their continued use, which is higher than would be the case if the organisation ceased trading.
Goodwill	An intangible asset that appears on some balance sheets under fixed assets. It is sometimes expressed as the difference between the value of an organisation as a whole and the aggregate of the fair value of its separable identifiable assets.
Gross profit	The difference between sales and the cost of goods or services sold.
Gross profit margin	Gross profit divided by sales expressed as a percentage. Also known as *margin.*
Historical cost (accounting)	A method of accounting that does not make allowance for the effects of inflation and in which all values (in revenue and capital accounts) are based on the costs actually incurred.
Hockey stick effect	Colloquial term given to the situation that arises when a manager spends or releases hitherto accrued expenditure just before the year-end. If expressed as a graph, it would look like a horizontal hockey stick, facing up or down, as the case may be.
Income and expenditure (account)	See *profit and loss account.*
Income statement	See *profit and loss account.*
Incremental budgeting	An approach to budgeting that bases a new budget on the previous year's actual or budgeted figures, plus an allowance for, say, inflation and perhaps a percentage deduction to encourage cost reductions.
Indirect costs	Costs that cannot be directly traced to units of production (or other activity of the organisation). Typically these may include property costs, administration costs and selling costs. Also known as overheads or burden.
Intangible assets	The resources you cannot see or touch, e.g. brands. See also *goodwill.*
Internal controls	The controls and procedures that managers are expected to comply with and administer.
Inventory	See *stock.*
Investment centre	One of the four *responsibility centres.* The budget holder is responsible for costs, revenues, profits, cash flows and finding funding/investment.
Irrelevant costs	See *non-relevant costs, sunk costs.*
Joint venture	A contractual arrangement whereby two or more parties undertake an economic activity that is subject to joint control.

Liabilities	The term for amounts owed to those financing an organisation – the sources of funding.
Limiting factors	Also known as constraints. For example, a manufacturer could be constrained by the amount of material available and the amount of machine time available.
Linearity	The assumption that costs and revenues are proportional to output, and that unit variable costs and the selling price are constant.
Liquidity	The speed with which or manner in which an organisation manages its short-term cash flow, meeting debts as they fall due.
Long-term liabilities	Liabilities that fall due for payment after more than one year.
Management accounts	Accounts issued entirely for internal use, including budget, cost and project statements. They may look forward to future events as well as look back to past events.
Margin	See *gross profit margin.*
Margin of safety	The difference between the break-even point and the assumed level of activity.
Marginal costing	The approach to costing in which only the variable costs are charged to cost units. The fixed costs attributable to the relevant period are not apportioned to individual units or activities but are met out of the total contribution generated. Also known as contribution costing, variable costing.
Marginal costs	The costs of producing one extra unit.
Mark-up	Gross profit divided by the cost of sales expressed as a percentage.
Master budget	The overall budget of an organisation, built up from a range of individual budgets and comprising the cash budget, the forecast profit and loss account, and the forecast balance sheet.
Matching principle	Recognition of income generated and resources consumed in a period irrespective of the cash flow during that period. Also known as the accruals concept.
Materiality	The principle that financial statements should separately disclose items which are significant enough to affect evaluation or decisions.
Money measurement	The convention that financial accounting information relates only to those activities which can be expressed in money terms.
Net book value	The cost of an asset less its accumulated depreciation to date. It is also known as written-down cost.
Net current assets	Equal to current assets less current liabilities. Also known as *working capital.*

Net profit	See *net reported profit*.
Net reported profit	The profit remaining after deducting all expenses, including interest and taxation, from sales. It is also known as net profit or PAT (profit after tax.)
Net worth	The book value of an organisation as reflected by the value of shareholders' funds on the balance sheet.
Non-relevant costs	Those costs that have already been incurred and costs that have yet to occur but will remain the same no matter what course of action is undertaken. See also *sunk costs*.
Non-traded	Outputs that are not sold for cash, but the cost of which needs to be known.
Not for profit organisation	An organisation which is organised for public benefit rather than for private benefit. Also known as a *social enterprise organisation*.
Operating profit	The profit remaining after deducting all operating expenses (not cost of capital expenses) from sales. It can also be arrived at by adding the cost of capital interest to net reported profit. It is also known as *trading profit*, *PBIT* (profit before interest and tax) or *EBIT* (earnings before interest and tax).
Operational gearing	The ratio, usually expressed as a percentage, that seeks to measure the proportion of total costs that are fixed costs. It is also known as operating leverage.
Opportunity cost	The cost incurred by not doing something. For example, the opportunity cost of using a property for a project could be the rental income forgone.
Overdraft	Money borrowed, nominally for a short period; the amount borrowed may fluctuate from day to day.
Overheads	See *indirect costs*.
P&L account	See *profit and loss account*.
PAT	Profit after tax. Also known as *net reported profit* or *net profit*.
PBIT	Profit before interest and tax. Also known as *operating profit*.
Performance indicators	A measurement system to help an organisation assess how well a process (for example, the number of items sold per staff member) is managed. Also known as performance measures.
Primary ratio	See *return on capital employed (ROCE)*.
Priority-base budgeting	See *zero-base budgeting*.
Profit	A positive financial return.

Profit and loss account	A summary of an organisation's transactions over a stated period (usually one year), which shows revenue(s) generated, the related costs and thus the profit or loss for the period. It may also show the appropriation of profit before tax into taxation, dividends and reserves. In a not-for-profit organisation, income and expenditure account is the preferred term. It is also known as income statement, P&L account, revenue account or, for not for profit organisations, statement of financial activities (SOFA).
Profit centre	One of the four *responsibility centres*. The budget holder is responsible for costs and revenues and hence profit.
Prudence concept	The concept that requires that no profit or surplus will be anticipated although provision should be made for all known costs or losses. The concept is also known as conservatism. See also *accounting concepts*.
Pyramid of ratios	The ratios used to analyse the profitability of an organisation. These include the primary ratio, return on capital employed (ROCE), the two secondary ratios, asset utilisation ratio (AUR) and return on sales ratio (ROS) and all further ratios based on subdividing the secondary ratios. When the hierarchy of ratios is set out diagrammatically, the diagram is pyramid-shaped, hence the term 'pyramid of ratios'.
Quarterly budgeting	The move, by some organisations, away from annual budgets to quarterly budgets, which are revisited, revised and updated quarterly.
Quick ratio	The comparison of liquid current assets (normally cash and debtors) with current liabilities.
Ratio analysis	The study of the financial value and performance of an organisation through ratios derived from items in the financial statements.
Rate of return pricing	This refers to the use of the desired rate of return (see *return on capital employed*) on an investment to calculate how much to add to the cost of product or service in order to arrive at the selling price.
Receivables	See *debtors*.
Recovery costing	See *absorption costing*.
Reducing balance method	See *declining balance method*.
Relevant costs	Costs that occur only if the course of action in question is undertaken.
Responsibility accounting	A reporting procedure which recognises that managers should be held responsible only for the costs and revenue they are able to influence.
Responsibility centres	Aspects of an organisation for which managers can be held responsible, a consequence of responsibility accounting. See *cost centre, investment centre, profit centre* and *revenue centre*.
Retained profit	The part of *net reported profit* that is not paid out in dividends but is retained by the company.

Return on capital employed (ROCE)	A ratio that relates operating profit (the profit generated from core day-to-day activities) to all the capital sums invested in an organisation. It is derived from profit before interest and tax (operating profit) divided by total capital employed, and is expressed as a percentage. It is also known as the primary ratio.
Return on investment (ROI)	The overall profit (or loss) of an investment expressed as a percentage of the total invested.
Return on sales ratio (ROS)	A ratio that measures the return of operating profit from sales. It is derived from profit before interest and tax (operating profit) divided by sales and is expressed as a percentage.
Revenue centre	One of the four *responsibility centres*. The budget holder's responsibility is for generating revenue.
Revenue expenditure	Expenditure on items that will be used by an organisation in the short term. It is the opposite of *capital expenditure*.
Rolling budget	A continuously-updated budget in which, as one period passes, another is added (e.g. a one-year budget would have a new month or quarter added as each month or quarter passes). It is beneficial when future costs and/or activities cannot be forecast reliably. It is also known as a continuous budget.
Share capital	The part of a limited company's capital that represents funds raised from investors in the company. It is divided into equal proportions (or shares) and an investor can hold any number of these shares. In some countries (mostly in the USA) the word 'stock' is used instead of share capital.
Shareholders' funds	Issued share capital plus reserves, i.e. that part of the capital in the organisation owned by the shareholders. They are also known as capital and reserves.
Social enterprise organisation	See *not for profit organisation*.
Solvency	The state in which an organisation is able to pay its debts when they are due and is generating enough cash to continue its operations in the longer term.
Stakeholder(s)	Individuals, groups or organisations with a stake or interest in an organisation, such as managers, employees, customers, clients, lenders, owners, shareholders, etc.
Statement of financial activities	See *profit and loss account*.
Stepped costs	Those fixed costs that are unchanged within certain limits of activity level, but which step up or down to a new level when these limits are exceeded.
Stewardship	The responsibility of managers to protect an organisation's assets from theft or fraud, thereby safeguarding the interests of the owners or trustees.

Stock turnover ratio	A ratio that measures the speed at which raw materials or stocks for resale are consumed or sold.
Stock(s)	That portion of an organisation's assets held for further production and/or sale. Stock(s) are also known as inventory.
Straight line method	The method of depreciating an asset in such a way that its value is used up in approximately equal proportions each period. See also *declining balance method*, *depreciation*.
Sunk costs	Those costs that have already been incurred, cannot be retrieved and, thus, play no part in a particular decision. They are also known as irrelevant costs. See also *non-relevant costs*.
Tangible assets	The resources you can see and touch, e.g. property and stock.
Trading profit	See *operating profit*.
True and fair	In broad terms, 'true and fair' implies that accounts, and the accounting information on which they are based, are adequate in quality and quantity for the users of those accounts.
Useful life	The life of an asset: how long it will last until the organisation deems its use to be no longer economic.
Value for money	Economy, efficiency and effectiveness in the use of resources.
Variable costs	Costs that vary in proportion to the level of activity (sales level or production level). For example, raw material costs would generally double if production or sales doubled and thus would be regarded as variable. Variable costs are also known as marginal costs.
Variance	The difference between planned, budgeted or standard costs and actual costs (or revenues). Variance is generally referred to as favourable or adverse, depending on whether it increases or decreases profit.
VAT	Value-added tax. A tax levied on outputs, against which relief is given for VAT paid on inputs. Thus the net tax is on the value added by an organisation to those inputs.
Working capital	See *net current assets*.
Working capital cycle	The cycle associated with the flow of cash through the purchase of stocks, receipt of money owed and payments of money owing.
Written-down cost	See *net book value*.
Zero-base budgeting	An approach to budgeting that requires managers to start from scratch when estimating future targets, inputs, outputs and activities. It is also known as priority-base budgeting.

CHAPTER 13 LEADERSHIP, MANAGEMENT AND MOTIVATION

Leading for results

Management involves far more than planning, implementation and the exercise of co-ordination and control. If an organisation is to operate successfully in the wider environment, effective leadership and management of people, informed by an understanding of what motivates people to work, will be vital to an organisation's ability to meet externally-imposed competitive demands and pressures. Leadership – the ability to communicate a vision, influence others and gain their trust – will be crucial to achieving your objectives as a manager, and in turn, those of the organisation. You will need to exert influence in many directions in order to secure the resources and support that you and your team need to do your job, while also ensuring that you lead and manage your team well. Your ability to influence others will depend on your sources of power and authority, your leadership skills and how effectively you use them. It will also involve understanding the sometimes puzzling behaviour of others, for example, individuals who remain committed to their work despite being under great stress, and others who seem demotivated despite being very well paid. You will need to be familiar with the idea of culture, including organisational culture, because aspects of leadership, management and motivation – the subject of this chapter – are shaped by culture.

See Culture, p. 215.

What makes a good leader?

What is leadership? Common to most definitions of leadership is the ability to influence others. Leadership can be described as the way a person guides, shows the way or holds a group together. Approaches to understanding leadership have sought to explain it in different ways. These approaches can be ordered chronologically from the earliest to the most recent:

- **The trait approach** – in which attempts were made to identify sets of individual traits that characterised effective leaders.

- **Situation theories** – which sought to identify the leadership traits and behaviours that might be most effective in particular situations.

■ **Social process accounts** – which have sought to understand leadership as a social process rather than an attribute of an individual or an interaction between an individual and a situation.

Neither the trait approach nor situation theories have been found to possess much explanatory power. Within the third approach, the social process perspective, two kinds of leadership have been distinguished: *transactional* leadership in which a manager manages a series of exchanges or transactions, and *transformational* leadership which involves the 'management of meaning'.

Transactional leadership

The transactional leader influences others by appealing to their self-interest, primarily through the exchange of valued rewards for services or other desired behaviours. The relationship between leader and follower is seen as a series of rational exchanges or transactions that enable each to reach their own goals. Transactional leaders supply all the ideas and use rewards as their primary source of power. Followers comply with the leader when the exchange – the reward – advances their own interests. The relationship continues as long as the reward is desirable to the follower, and both the leader and the follower see the exchange as a way of achieving their own ends.

Transformational leadership

The transactional leader motivates followers to perform as expected. The transformational leader – sometimes described as the charismatic, or visionary, leader – inspires followers to do more than originally expected. Transformational leaders motivate followers to work towards goals that transcend immediate self-interests – to strive for higher-order outcomes. These leaders transform the needs, values, preferences and aspirations of followers, so that followers become less motivated by self-interest and more motivated to serve the interests of the wider group. The danger of transformational leadership is that followers may become emotionally and intellectually deskilled through abandoning their own sense of ability, direction and meaning. Equally, leaders can become seduced by their followers' investment in them, and cease to be mindful of uncertainties or to be adaptive. Leaders of dangerous cults are often transformational leaders.

Table 13.1 summarises the key differences between transactional and transformational leadership.

Table 13.1 Characteristics of transactional and transformational leaders	
Transactional leader	**Transformational leader**
Contingent reward – contracts exchange of rewards for efforts, promises rewards for good performance, recognises accomplishments.	**Charisma** – provides vision and sense of mission, instils pride, gains respect and trust.
Management by exception (active) – watches and searches for deviations from rules and standards, takes corrective action.	**Inspiration** – communicates high expectations, uses symbols to focus efforts, expresses important purposes in simple ways.
Management by exception (passive) –intervenes only if standards are not met.	**Intellectual stimulation** – promotes intelligence, rationality and careful problem solving.
Laissez-faire – abdicates responsibility, avoids making decisions.	**Individualised consideration** – gives personal attention, treats each employee individually, coaches and advises.

(Source: based on Bass, 1990)

Competencies of transformational leaders

As described in Table 13.2, four major competencies have been found to be common to transformational leaders: the management of attention, meaning, trust and of self.

Leadership as negotiation

People in positions of leadership normally have formal authority – a top-down approach. But leadership is engaged in by different people at different times, without such formal authority. Without formal authority, it is not enough for a person to offer direction: the direction needs to be accepted by others, and negotiation is a way of reconciling the different needs of people and influencing them to work to common goals. Such leadership – sometimes described as a bottom-up approach – can influence:

■ **Strategic issues** These are the ends or results that a group seeks. Strategic issues concern the direction in which a group should go in a changing environment, correctly identifying opportunities and avoiding threats.

■ **Task issues** These are the means of achieving the desired results of a group or an organisation. Task issues include how best the necessary tasks can be performed and whether there is tension between the ends and the means.

Table 13.2 Competencies of transformational leaders	
Competency	**Explanation**
Management of attention	One of the competencies most apparent in transformational leaders is their ability to draw others to them, not because they have a vision, a dream, a set of intentions, an agenda, or a frame of reference, but because they communicate an extraordinary focus of commitment which attracts people to them.
Management of meaning	To make dreams apparent to others, and to align people with them, leaders must communicate their vision. Communication and alignment work together. Transformational leaders make ideas tangible and real to others, so they can support them. No matter how marvellous the vision, an effective leader must use metaphors, words, or models, to make that vision clear to others.
Management of trust	Trust is essential to all organisations. The main determinants of trust are reliability and consistency. People prefer to follow individuals they can count on, even when they disagree with their viewpoint, rather than people they agree with but who shift positions frequently.
Management of self	The fourth transformational leadership competency is management of self: knowing one's skills, and deploying them effectively. Management of self is critical; without it, leaders and managers can do more harm than good. Like incompetent doctors, incompetent managers can make life worse, make people sicker and less vital.

(Source: based on Bennis, 1998)

■ **People or maintenance issues** Leadership is largely about the relationship between leaders and followers, thus leaders will build and maintain a solid relationship with others. A leader will also maintain the morale, cohesion and commitment of individuals while pursuing the aims of the group or organisation.

A group can have more than one leader. Different people may exercise leadership in different areas. For example, one person may take the lead in group strategy, and another in maintaining group morale and commitment.

Providing an external perspective

A group usually requires some knowledge of the wider environment and how it is likely to affect the group. A leader will be prepared to keep in touch with, and understand, this wider environment. This will involve effective networking and being a good ambassador, so that the leader understands the threats and opportunities that may face a group and can mobilise resources and support as necessary.

Contingency, leadership and management

The relevance both of circumstances and people's expectations are emphasised in many explanatory models of behaviour. They emphasise that appropriate behaviour or leadership styles are contingent on local circumstances. This implies that there is no invariably 'right way' of behaving, irrespective of local circumstances. A leader or manager must know the local circumstances in order to understand what motivates a person and what outcomes they want from work, rather than assuming that all staff have the same needs.

A contingent approach to leadership and management

A contingent approach to leadership and management is one in which the appropriate leadership style will depend on local circumstances. The leader's or manager's own preferred style will be but one factor in this. Other relevant factors will be:

- the style that the staff expect
- the job that has to be done
- the organisational culture.

For example, the staff in an organisation have a current preference for a style of leadership that is directive, their task is one that calls for direction, and the surrounding organisational culture endorses a directive style.

Suppose that a new manager is appointed. The local circumstances – the staff's expectations, the task, and the culture – point towards a directive style as the appropriate one. If the manager is able to adopt a directive style, then that style will be consistent with the local circumstances. Different circumstances, however, might point towards a consultative style.

The contingent approach emphasises the importance of local circumstances and the idea that appropriate behaviour is that which takes account of them.

Management style

It is possible to analyse your own management style, and that of others, on the basis of concern for output and for people. The management grid is used to identify a person's favoured management style. Suppose a manager's dominant concern was to achieve the targeted output with little consideration for the staff. That manager would be placed at Position A in Figure 13.1. In contrast, suppose a second manager's dominant concern seemed to be the wellbeing of the staff rather than the achievement of targeted output. That manager would be placed at Position B. By numbering each of the axes from 1–9, it is possible to describe the first manager as a '9,1 manager' and the second one as a '1,9 manager'.

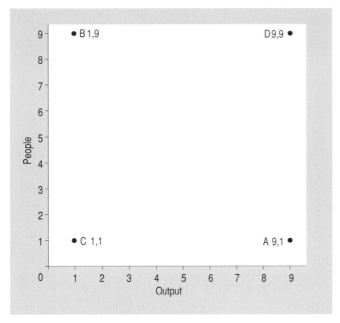

Figure 13.1 **The management grid**

(Source: Blake *et al.*, 1962)

Using the idea

The grid immediately presents a manager with two crucial questions:

■ Am I (or is the person I am assessing) sufficiently concerned to achieve the targeted outputs of the organisation?

■ Am I (or is the person I am assessing) sufficiently concerned for the wellbeing of the staff?

A well-rounded manager needs to aim for a rating that is high on both criteria, rather than low on one and high on the other, or low on both.

Extending the idea

You can extend the idea by changing the label on the horizontal axis to 'Hard' and the label on the vertical axis to 'Soft'. The horizontal axis now prompts you to think about the extent to which you or other people are concerned for, or comfortable with:

■ hard outcomes – what is measurable, concrete and down-to-earth.

The vertical axis prompts you to think about the extent to which a person is concerned for, or comfortable with:

■ soft outcomes rather than hard ones

■ qualitative matters rather than quantitative

■ ideas and images rather than actual courses of action.

It can be useful to think about people's attributes in this way when you are forming or managing a team.

BOX 13.1   ELEMENTS OF FAVOURABLENESS

The appropriate management style is likely to depend on the extent to which the manager's situation is favourable. Views vary, however, about the extent to which leaders can change their style to suit the circumstances.

■ Task-orientated leaders perform better in situations which are either very favourable or very unfavourable.

■ Relationship-orientated leaders perform better in situations of moderate favourableness.

■ The performance of the leader depends as much on the situation as on the style of the leader.

(Source: Fiedler, 1976)

See Contingency, leadership and management, p. 280.

Fayol's management processes

According to one of the early management thinkers, Henri Fayol (1949), management comprises five processes:

1   **Forecasting and planning** The manager must look ahead, assess the future and make provision for it.

2   **Organising** There must be an appropriate organisational structure, one that will allow the organisation's activities and plans to be carried out.

3   **Leading** Once the plan has been agreed and the appropriate structure is in place, the staff must get to work. The manager is there to inspire the staff, to secure their commitment to the organisation and to the job.

4   **Co-ordinating** One department's activities, or job, must fit or harmonise with those of other departments. The activities in all departments must be directed towards the overall organisational goals. As a result, the manager of a department must be in constant touch with other managers to secure this co-ordination.

5   **Controlling** Lastly, there must be a system of control, a system to
    discover what is happening (or has happened) so that it can be
    compared with what should have happened.

(Source: based on Fayol, 1949)

A circular process

Fayol's view is a useful way of thinking about management as a general
process or, in a more concrete way, about a manager's job. The five
processes can be set out in a circular fashion as shown in Figure 13.2. This
emphasises the continuous nature of the whole process. In a well-managed
organisation, large or small, the activities derive from a plan, which may be
simple or complex. The structure is an appropriate one, the staff are
committed to the plan, and what is done in one part of the organisation
harmonises with what is done elsewhere. The actual outcomes are measured
and compared with the plan; the manager takes the appropriate action, and
the cycle continues or a fresh cycle begins.

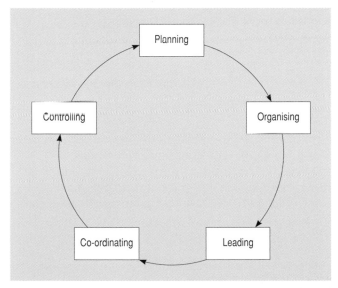

Figure 13.2 **Fayol's process account of management (1949)**

Mintzberg's management roles

Henry Mintzberg (1991), a well-known management thinker, recorded what
some managers did during their working days and came to the conclusion
that there was a gap between theory and practice. He found that the
manager's work was characterised by pace, interruptions, brevity and a
fragmentation of activities. The managers liked talking to people and they
spent much of their time in contact with others, in meetings and in
networks.

Managerial roles

Mintzberg identified ten roles that describe the variety of the manager's work. He grouped those ten roles into three clusters. These are shown in Table 13.3.

Table 13.3 Mintzberg's ten managerial roles	
Interpersonal	The manager:
	1 acts as a figurehead, the person who represents the organisation
	2 leads the staff
	3 liaises between the organisation and the people outside it.
Informational	The manager:
	4 monitors the information flows within and outside the organisation
	5 disseminates relevant information to those who need it
	6 acts as spokesperson for the organisation.
Decision making	The manager:
	7 sometimes acts as an entrepreneur, initiating a course of action intended to change something within the organisation
	8 sometimes reacts to events, acting as a disturbance-handler
	9 allocates resources, such as the matching of people and jobs, the allocation of money, equipment, and so on
	10 negotiates with others, that is, trades resources with them.

(Source: Mintzberg, 1991)

Fulfilling all the roles

While different managers will have different skills and preferences, Mintzberg's account of managerial roles prompts a manager to attend to the development of interpersonal skills, to recognise the importance of managing information, and to recognise the different kinds of decision that the manager will face.

Scientific management

Scientific management or 'Taylorism' (so called after its developer, Frederick Taylor) is a way of managing operations within an organisation that focuses on reducing each job to a narrowly defined set of tasks and activities, with very little discretion over how they are performed.

The background to scientific management

After the First World War, the work of Taylor had great influence on ideas about the role of the manager. Taylor was trying to address the problems of companies seeking to implement mass production. He believed the role of the manager was to find 'the one best way' of carrying out a piece of work. The manager should specify precisely how that work was to be carried out, removing all elements of discretion and, by providing an appropriate rate for the work, link pay directly to output to motivate high productivity. Taylor's ideas became highly influential both in the USA and Europe. Despite the resistance of a few large employers (such as Cadbury, the UK chocolate manufacturer), Taylorist ideas took root on both sides of the Atlantic.

The assumption

Scientific management is based on the assumption that the best results will come as people behave more and more like parts in a machine. The classic example of this kind of job design is the mass production factory such as the automotive assembly line. But a similar approach can be found in service operations such as call centres, fast-food outlets and theme parks, where every aspect of each worker's job is narrowly prescribed. This approach has been criticised by some on ethical grounds and because, it is argued, designing jobs in this way fails to capitalise on each individual's talents and energies, and so fails to maximise their potential. This can create boredom, alienation and even hostility towards the organisation.

See Approaches to job design, p. 294.

The socio-technical systems approach

In some countries, especially in Scandinavia, a different school of thought known as the 'socio-technical systems approach' attempts to balance the needs of the operation with the needs of those that work in it. Practices associated with this approach to job design include:

- the use of autonomous work groups or teams

- making staff directly responsible for monitoring the quality of their own work, rather than using a separate quality control function

- cross-training workers to perform different jobs (job enrichment) or to include more skills in their present jobs (job enlargement)

- employee involvement and teamwork

- using technology to increase the skills and content of jobs.

Management by objectives

Management by objectives (MBO) provides a framework for supervision in pursuit of agreed goals. It can also provide the basis for an organisation's way of working. The essence of MBO is that instead of telling people exactly how to do their work, managers provide staff with tasks and assignments which have targets or objectives to be reached.

Setting targets and objectives

These objectives provide a clear set of standards against which to measure an employee's progress – the employee's accomplishments are measured by what he or she achieves. MBO relies on objectives or targets being:

- challenging – they should be something to aim for

- attainable – they should be realistic

- subject to measurement – so that the employee and manager will know whether something has been achieved or not

- relevant – there is a clear and direct relationship to the employee's job.

MBO is a way of controlling activities while involving both manager and employee in the process. Although it can be difficult to quantify or measure an objective or target, MBO is useful for negotiating with staff regarding what will be achieved and for placing an agreement within an explicit framework. Objectives should be discussed and agreed, and action plans formulated so that it is clear how they are to be carried out. Periodic progress reviews are important and will help staff to exercise self-regulation and to correct mistakes by showing if they are on target or not.

BOX 13.2   POTENTIAL PROBLEMS WITH MBO

- The objectives may be too high or low, with consequent effects on morale.

- Employees may feel guilty or suffer adverse career outcomes if they fail to reach targets, even if there are valid reasons for the failure that lie beyond the control of the employee or manager.

- In a team or across the organisation, objectives may conflict unless care is taken to communicate and to train managers in the principles of MBO.

- The focus may be on what is measurable, at the expense of more qualitative aspects.

Using the SMART framework to set objectives

When we set objectives, it is in the interests of all that they are clear and unambiguous. Clear and unambiguous objectives have particular characteristics. There is an easy way to remember these characteristics: the widely-used SMART acronym. To be SMART, objectives must be: **S**pecific, **M**easurable, **A**greed, **R**ealistic and **T**imed.

- **Specific** They must state clearly what is to be achieved.

- **Measurable** They must state how success will be measured.

- **Agreed** They must be agreed with the person who will carry out the objective and ideally with anyone who will be affected by the result.

- **Realistic** They must be achievable within the constraints of the situation and in alignment with other objectives.

- **Timed** There must be a target time set for achieving the objective.

Motivation

Why do people work? There are some self-evident reasons such as the need for an income, as a source of stimulation, for activity and social contact, as a means of structuring time and as a source of self-fulfilment. The power of money as a key motivator comes rather low on the list, except perhaps when pay is almost wholly performance related, as it sometimes is for salespeople. Investigators have sought to explain motivation using quite different approaches. Two of these are *needs* theories and *expectancy* theories.

- **Needs theories** These are based on the idea that people behave in particular ways to satisfy particular needs. Needs theories do not necessarily focus on the same kinds of need. Examples are Maslow's hierarchy of needs and Hertzberg's two-factor theory of job satisfaction.

- **Expectancy theories** These theories attempt to explain motivation as the result of people's expectation that they will receive the rewards they want from their work.

Maslow's hierarchy of needs

Probably the best-known theory of motivation is Abraham Maslow's hierarchy of needs. It describes human behaviour in terms of innate needs ranging from primary physiological needs (food and shelter) to the need for self-expression. According to Maslow, five kinds of need are common to everyone. These needs can be represented in a pyramid as shown in Figure 13.3.

At the base of the pyramid is the primary physiological need, the need for food and shelter. Once that need is satisfied, the need for safety against arbitrary events becomes the active one. When stability is in place, the safety need gives way to the social need for society and for belonging. That need, when satisfied, is replaced by the need for esteem, self-respect and recognition by one's peers. At the top of the pyramid is the need for self-actualisation, the need to realise one's own potential and find self-fulfillment.

The problem with the model is there is very little evidence that needs are activated in this hierarchical way. Consider, for example, situations in which

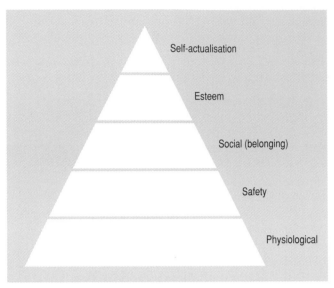

Figure 13.3 **The hierarchy of needs**

(Source: Maslow, 1954)

persecution, deprivation and danger may conversely promote self-actualising behaviour.

Implications for managers of the hierarchy of needs

The model provides a rule of thumb for managers. Maslow's first four needs are known as deficiency needs which must be met, while the fifth is regarded as a growth need. This suggests that pay, security, companionable work and recognition are likely to be necessary, but not sufficient for growth. People also need opportunities for personal growth and professional development. Self-actualised people are said to be characterised by being problem-focussed, have an appreciation of life that is always fresh, and have a concern for personal growth.

Hertzberg's two-factor theory

Hertzberg's two-factor theory of motivation focuses on job satisfaction, attempting to distinguish between events or changes that are likely to lead to an increase in job satisfaction (motivation factors) and events or changes likely to reduce job dissatisfaction (hygiene factors). The factors are separate, so a reduction in dissatisfaction may not affect a person's job satisfaction. Figure 13.4 shows this distinction.

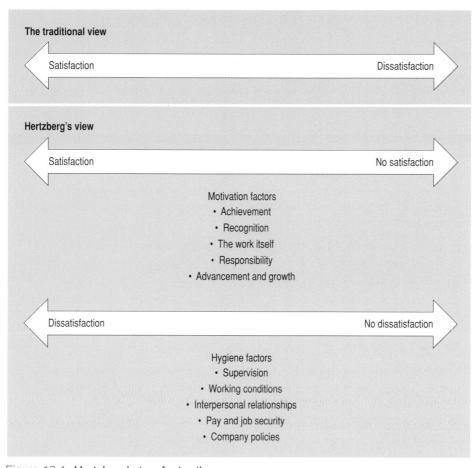

The traditional view

Satisfaction   Dissatisfaction

Hertzberg's view

Satisfaction   No satisfaction

Motivation factors
- Achievement
- Recognition
- The work itself
- Responsibility
- Advancement and growth

Dissatisfaction   No dissatisfaction

Hygiene factors
- Supervision
- Working conditions
- Interpersonal relationships
- Pay and job security
- Company policies

Figure 13.4 **Hertzberg's two-factor theory**

(Source: Hertzberg, 1959)

The satisfaction features (motivation factors) concern the person's relationship with the job itself, whilst the dissatisfaction-reducing features (hygiene factors) concern the context or environment in which the job is done.

The stronger the person's feeling about any one of the motivation factors, the more satisfied the person is likely to be. For example, if the person began to feel an increased sense of achievement from work, then, without any other change, that change in the person's perception or experience of the job could be expected to result in an increased satisfaction with the job.

The position is the same for the hygiene factors. There is a positive correlation between the strength of a person's feelings about any one of these features and the strength of the person's potential dissatisfaction with the job. For example, in the absence of any other changes, a worsening of the working conditions could be expected to lead to an increase in dissatisfaction. Conversely, an improvement in working conditions could be expected to lead to a decrease in dissatisfaction.

Implications for managers of the two-factor theory

The theory has little empirical support, but it is useful to managers when thinking about job satisfaction: changing one factor may not have the desired effect. Hertzberg's theory implies that only some needs are motivating and that financial reward is not a major motivator.

Expectancy theory

Expectancy theory refers to the understanding of human behaviour which concentrates on the link between the effort that a person is willing to expend and the person's expectation that the effort will lead to an outcome that the person will value.

The core of the theory can be represented as shown in Figure 13.5.

Figure 13.5   **Expectancy theory**

The theory describes the general condition that a person's effort is expressed in performance, and that performance will result in a set of outcomes. Another way of describing this is that outcomes are the result of a person's willingness to do the job (the effort) and their ability to do it (the performance).

Using the theory

The theory provides a relatively sound explanation of motivation and performance, although its ability to predict is limited in the sense that many employees have constraints on what they do, particularly in lower-level jobs. The theory is helpful because it reminds the manager that willingness alone is not enough: the requisite ability, including the necessary tools, must also be in place. A person's willingness to make the effort depends on their expectation that the effort will lead to outcomes that they will value. A person who does not expect to be able to do the job will be reluctant to begin. It will be up to the manager to persuade the person to put in the effort to ensure that the person develops the required ability (and is properly equipped).

Even so, a person may expect to be able to do the job, and yet be unwilling to do it, because the person does not expect the outcomes will be sufficiently valuable. In this case the manager can improve the outcomes, or prompt the person to take a different view of the original outcomes. Remember that the outcomes may be intrinsic as well as extrinsic. A manager, for instance, may convince a person that the intrinsic outcomes –

the feelings that the person will experience on completion – when added to any extrinsic ones, will be sufficient reward.

This approach requires managers to take account of the individual employee's calculation of the costs and benefits – the effort and the outcomes – of a task.

The psychological contract

The psychological contract is the private, unwritten set of expectations that an employee has of the organisation – in the person of the responsible manager – and that the organisation has with the employee.

Beyond the formal contract

Both the employee and the organisation have expectations of each other. Some of these expectations, such as pay, working hours, and so on, will be dealt with in the written contract of employment. But other expectations, such as the extent of the employee's commitment to the organisation, will be more difficult to deal with. As a result, there may be a mismatch between the expectations. For example, a manager may expect an employee to work late to complete a task that the manager regards as important; the employee, however, may feel no obligation to work beyond the normal time, no matter how important the task may be to the manager. Or, an employee may have an expectation that the organisation will provide opportunities for personal growth and development. If these opportunities are not forthcoming, then the employee will be disappointed, the degree of the disappointment depending on the degree of the desire.

Using the concept

A manager should recognise that every employee has expectations of the organisation. Some of these will be explicit, but some will remain private. The manager's expectations of the employee may not coincide with the employee's expectations of the manager – the manager being the representative of the organisation.

The existence of a mismatch between expectations will lead to conflict or disappointment. The organisation may expect more than the employee is willing to give, and there may be a feeling that the employee is insufficiently committed to the organisation. On the other hand, the employee may expect more than the organisation seems willing to provide and so may feel exploited.

A manager needs to remember that employees' expectations may change. What employees may be willing to do for an organisation when they are young is likely to differ from what they will be willing to do in later years.

Employee empowerment

Empowerment can be seen as the giving of increased responsibility and control to employees over their working lives. Figure 13.6 shows the various methods of employee involvement as a series of steps in a progression.

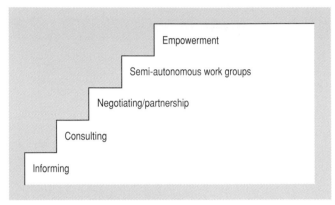

Figure 13.6 **The staircase of employee involvement and empowerment**

As the staircase ascends, the methods are likely to have more profound implications for the way organisations are managed. At the most basic level, employees are simply kept informed. At the top level, all employees have considerable influence across many areas of the business. The model is best used as a general guide to the stages employees and organisations go through on the way to employee involvement and empowerment.

Reasons for involvement and empowerment

Research shows that employee involvement initiatives enhance the commitment and motivation of staff and can lead to improved product and service quality.

Some reasons for promoting employee involvement and empowerment are:

- They can bring about enhanced commitment from employees.

- They can encourage all workers to pull in the same direction.

- Increased competition, instability, uncertainty and complexity in the global economy mean that managers realise they no longer have the capacity to issue commands and directives which simply require unquestioned implementation.

- The costs of maintaining traditional managerial hierarchies are increasing.

Managing the process of empowerment

Moving an organisation, or part of an organisation, towards an empowerment model does not mean abdicating responsibility. On the contrary, the process needs skilful management as shown in Figure 13.7.

See Employee empowerment, p. 292.

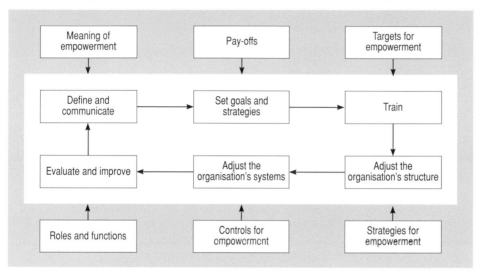

Figure 13.7 **Empowerment process management model**

(Source: based on Kinlaw, 1995)

The model identifies six steps that you might follow in planning, implementing and evaluating an empowerment initiative. Taken together, they constitute a closed-loop system which should result in continuous organisational improvement.

The six steps towards empowerment

The steps are summarised below.

1 **Define and communicate** the meaning of empowerment to everyone at all levels of the organisation.

2 **Set goals and strategies** that provide a framework for people at every organisational level as they make their own efforts to extend and strengthen empowerment.

3 **Train** people to fulfil their new roles and perform their functions in ways that are consistent with the company's goals for extending and strengthening empowerment.

4 **Adjust the organisation's structure** to achieve leaner management, reduced bureaucracy and greater autonomy.

5   **Adjust the organisation's systems** for example, planning, rewarding, promoting, training and hiring, to support empowerment.

6   **Evaluate and improve** the process of empowerment by measuring the progress being made and the perceptions of the organisation's members.

(Source: Kinlaw, 1995)

All six steps in the empowerment process management model are shown as interrelated in the inner box of Figure 13.7. Around this is a series of smaller boxes which represent the necessary supporting mechanisms and information inputs. From this you will realise that empowerment is far more than a bolt-on to existing practices. It changes the fundamental nature of an organisation.

Approaches to job design

It is a truism that people are better motivated and more productive when they are doing a job they enjoy. For this reason, job design is of interest to managers. The idea of job design has a long history during which it has been influenced by a variety of approaches, not all of them focused on human principles or factors. Scientific management (or Taylorism) and, in particular, ergonomic and method studies, emphasise productivity benefits as a result of the division of labour. In contrast, behavioural models argue that jobs designed to fulfil people's self-esteem and personal development are more likely to result in satisfactory work performance. Empowerment principles concentrate on increasing the autonomy of individual workers in shaping the nature of their jobs.

See Scientific management, p. 284.

At one extreme are work systems that are based on close control: employees are closely monitored and tasks are tightly specified. At the other extreme are work systems based on developing employee commitment to clearly understood goals; these depend on the exercise of discretion by employees. The socio-technical approach to work design is that, in designing work, both the social and technical aspects must be given equal emphasis.

Issues in job design

A well designed job will be interesting, safe, give reasonable satisfaction, and lead to high productivity, quality and flexibility. But how should jobs be designed? Design will depend on the quantity and mix of skills and tasks to be accomplished, and the degree of technology (or automation) involved. In some cases (depending on the approach taken) there will also be an attempt to balance the need of the operation to be undertaken with the needs of those who will carry it out.

Job design involves making decisions regarding:

- what tasks to give to each person in the organisation
- in what sequence they should be performed
- where to locate each job
- who else should be involved in it
- how people should interact with their workplace and their immediate work environment
- how much autonomy to give staff
- what skills to develop in staff.

CHAPTER 14 MANAGING PEOPLE

Managing individuals

Human resource (HR) management is of direct relevance to anyone who has to achieve results through the efforts of other people. It concerns all management decisions and actions that affect the relationship between an organisation and its members. Managers with a wide range of responsibilities will be involved in such decisions. For example, an IT manager may make decisions about information systems design which have important consequences for the way work is organised. Or a marketing manager may make decisions about customer service strategies with consequences for the way employee performance is judged and their efforts rewarded. Line managers make HR decisions every day in the course of managing those who report to them.

The flow of people

HR policy concerns the flow of people into, through and out of an organisation. This includes:

- planning for staffing needs
- selecting and recruiting the right people
- their induction into the organisation
- internal staffing and promotion decisions

- the management of employees – including contract staff or, in the not-for-profit sector, volunteers

- exit from the organisation, whether voluntary or involuntary.

Managers need to make such choices as:

- the extent to which they rely on temporary or permanent staff

- the flexibility they require from employees in terms of patterns of working hours

- the extent to which they invest in employee development and training, or recruit for the skills they need

- the extent to which they will meet changes in demand by varying the numbers employed or hours worked.

Factors affecting choices

These choices can be affected by a wide range of factors, including but not restricted to:

- legal restrictions – for example restrictions on dismissal, requirements for compensation for redundancy, restrictions on working hours

- the level of expertise needed to do the work

- the availability of skilled labour outside the organisation

- the time taken to train staff internally

- variability and predictability of work flow.

The strategic fit of human resource policies

To be effective, HR policies need to fit the strategic goals and environment of the organisation. Table 14.1 gives an example of some possible relationships between HR practice and strategy.

Some possible orientations and consequences

Table 14.1 describes three generic strategic orientations and some likely consequences for desired employee behaviours and hence for HR management.

Table 14.1   The strategic fit of HR practices

Strategic orientation	Desired employee behaviours	Consequences for HR management
Seek advantage through innovation.	A high degree of creative behaviour. Longer-term focus. A relatively high level of co-operative, interdependent behaviour. A moderate concern for quantity of output. Concern both for process and results. A greater degree of risk taking. A high tolerance of ambiguity and unpredictability.	Jobs that require close interaction and co-ordination among groups of individuals. Performance appraisals that are more likely to reflect longer-term and group-based achievements. Jobs that allow employees to develop skills that can be used in other positions in the firm. Compensation systems that emphasise internal equity rather than external or market-based equity.
Seek advantage through supplying at low cost.	Relatively repetitive and predictable behaviour. A rather short-term view. Moderate concern for quality. High concern for quantity of output. Primary concern for results. Low risk-taking activity. Relatively high degree of comfort with stability.	Relatively fixed and explicit job descriptions that allow little room for ambiguity. Narrowly designed jobs and narrowly defined career paths that encourage specialisation, expertise and efficiency. Short-term, results-orientated performance appraisals. Close monitoring of industry pay levels for use in making compensation decisions. Minimal levels of employee training and development.
Seek advantage through high quality of goods or services.	Relatively repetitive and predictable behaviours. A more long-term or intermediate focus. A moderate amount of co-operative, interdependent behaviour. A high concern for quality. A modest concern for quantity of output. High concern for process. Low risk-taking activity. Commitment to the goals of the organisation.	Relatively fixed and explicit job descriptions. High levels of employee participation in decisions relevant to immediate work conditions and the job itself. A mix of individual and group criteria for performance appraisal that is mostly short-term and results-orientated. A relatively egalitarian treatment of employees and some guarantees of employment security. Extensive and continuous training and development of employees.

Recruitment and selection

The process of recruitment and selection is the first means by which an organisation seeks to engage employees with the right set of skills, motivation and potential to meet its needs. It is also the first stage in forming a relationship with employees.

Validity and fairness

Selection processes with high validity for predicting job performance may be seen as unfair by applicants. Conversely, processes that seem fair can be poor predictors of job performance. For example, past performance is a very good indicator of future performance but applicants regard interviews as a fairer method of assessment even though interviews have been shown to be a poor indicator of performance. Table 14.2 gives a summary of typical predictive validity and typical applicant perceptions of fairness for a range of selection processes.

Table 14.2 Selection processes – predictive validity and fairness of a range		
Selection process	**Typical predictive validity**	**Typical applicant perception of fairness**
Interview	Low	High
Personality test	Moderate	Low
Detailed collection of personal biographical information	High	Low
Cognitive ability test	High	Moderate
Assessment centres	High	High

(Source: Folger and Cropanzano, 1998)

Assessment centres, where applicants are observed performing a range of job-related tasks, have high predictive validity. The use of them is also seen as fair by applicants. But while assessment centres are undoubtedly a highly effective method of selection, they are costly. When using other selection processes managers will have to make trade-offs between validity of selection methods and perceived fairness.

What makes a process seem fair?

Applicants are more likely to believe selection processes are fair when particular practices are followed. Box 14.1 provides a checklist for selection processes.

BOX 14.1   CHECKLIST FOR SELECTION PROCESSES

- The selection process has an obvious relationship to the job.

- Applicants are not asked invasive or improper questions.

- Applicants have an opportunity to demonstrate job-related competencies.

- The selection is carried out in a consistent manner between candidates.

- The selectors have good interpersonal skills – they are courteous, open, good listeners and willing to provide information.

- There are opportunities for two-way communication.

- Applicants are given information about the organisation as part of the selection process.

- Applicants are given clear and detailed feedback on reasons for the selection decision.

- The nature of the selection process is clearly explained.

- Selectors are honest about the organisation and about reasons for selection decisions.

(Source: Gilliland, 1993)

The selection interview

The aim of the selection interview is to ascertain whether the candidate is interested in the job and competent to do it. It also has other functions:

- to explain the work of the organisation, the job and any features such as induction and probation

- to set expectations on both sides, including a realistic discussion of any potential difficulties (if appropriate)

- to enable the candidate to assess whether they want the job being offered.

Preparing for the interview

There are a number of issues to consider when preparing for an interview, as shown in Box 14.2.

BOX 14.2   CONSIDERATIONS IN INTERVIEW PREPARATION

Needs of the interviewer(s)

- job description and person specification
- individual's application form, curriculum vitae (CV), and any other supporting material supplied
- details of the terms and conditions of employment including hours of work, benefits and any perks (perquisites)
- information on the general prospects, training and induction offered by the organisation.

Needs of the candidate

- job description and person specification
- details of where the interview will be held
- to be met on arrival
- access to facilities such as toilets
- access to any facilities needed by candidates with special needs
- a comfortable waiting area.

Location requirements

- a suitable interview room and layout – consider what type of setting is most appropriate, formal or informal
- freedom from interruptions and other discomforts and distractions such as extraneous noise, uncomfortable furniture or extremes of temperature
- appropriate access for people with special needs.

Interview requirements: a structured plan

A structured interview plan enables the interviewer(s) to assess whether a candidate:

- could do the job – job assessment against person specification
- would do the job – judgements about motivation and commitment
- would fit in – evaluation of the 'person-organisation' fit.

A structured plan should include the following:

- areas of questioning for candidates to check that they fulfil the criteria
- agreement on the roles of those involved in the interview if there is a panel
- a schedule for interviews and timing management – enough time for each candidate and not too many candidates in one day.

Performance management

Managing employee performance involves setting standards in relation to terms and conditions, quality of work, quantity of work and interpersonal behaviour.

Quantitative aspects

Some aspects of performance lend themselves to the setting of clear objectives and quantitative targets such as:

- timescales
- deadlines
- amounts produced
- costs
- resource usage.

Qualitative aspects

Other aspects of performance may be more subjective and require a qualitative judgement. Subjective measures are associated with a variety of problems. When assessing people subjectively, social influences and personal preferences can come into play. Judgements may reflect ethnicity, gender, appearance or personal biases rather than pure performance.

Assessing performance will be easier if, at the outset, performance criteria and standards have been communicated to people and they agree and understand them.

Performance appraisal

A performance appraisal process is designed to formalise the feedback and performance assessment that has taken place throughout the year. It looks back to review performance, and forward to plan future objectives and opportunities.

The appraisal framework

Employees are often understandably concerned about the way in which judgements about them may be made in a performance appraisal. Box 14.3 provides a framework aimed at ensuring appraisals are seen to be fair.

> ### BOX 14.3 A FRAMEWORK FOR FAIRNESS
>
> - If you promise to do a performance appraisal, then do it.
> - Appraise people on appropriate criteria.
> - Have knowledgeable appraisers.
> - Use a fair rating format.
> - Include goal setting as part of the format.
> - Rate behaviours – not personal characteristics.
> - Keep good records on which to base the appraisal.
> - Consider the source of the ratings – are they biased in any way?
> - Ensure appraisers are supportive, invite the involvement of the appraisee, and offer only constructive criticism.
> - Train and encourage employees to play an active role in their own appraisal.
>
> (Source: based on Folger and Cropanzano, 1998)

The performance appraisal is part of an ongoing process of review and communication and, as such, should include nothing that comes as a surprise to the manager or employee.

An effective performance appraisal meeting

For an effective performance appraisal meeting, the following practice should be followed:

- Assess performance outcomes against agreed targets and standards.
- Provide useful and constructive feedback supported by relevant and accurate information.
- Use positive reinforcement by emphasising and celebrating the things that have been done well.
- Arrive at joint agreement on what needs to be done, including areas to be improved, key targets, and how to overcome any work-related problems.

Benefits of appraisal

Table 14.3 sets out the benefits of the appraisal process for the various parties.

Table 14.3 Benefits of appraisal		
For the individual	**For the manager**	**For the organisation**
Opportunity to encourage staff to review their recent performance and development.	Opportunity to motivate staff by recognising achievements.	Assistance with succession planning – identifying employees who might be promoted in the future and any development training they might need.
Recognition of the aspects of work they find difficult or irksome, and of contributions that have been appreciated.	Chance to clarify and reinforce important goals and priorities so that employees can see precisely where their contribution fits in.	Help with workforce planning: identifying areas of strengths and weaknesses in terms of existing skills and development requirements across the organisation.
Review and confirmation of agreed goals and standards to be worked to in the future.	Opportunity to learn about employees' concerns and hopes regarding their current and future roles.	Ensure that objectives agreed for groups and individuals harmonise with corporate objectives.
Identification of any specific measures to improve current performance – for example training or coaching.	Basis for discussing and agreeing courses of action with employees.	Improved communications throughout the organisation.
Chance to discuss career aspirations or possible development moves.	Clarification of areas of overlap between jobs, improving overall efficiency of team.	Above all, improved performance.
Improvement of working relationship by increasing communication and understanding.		

(Source: based on Evenden and Anderson, 1992)

Measuring performance

When talking about standards of performance it is useful to break performance down into different components. For each component it is possible to set appropriate standards to guide the work of employees as shown in Box 14.4.

BOX 14.4   DIFFERENT COMPONENTS OF PERFORMANCE AND STANDARDS

Terms and conditions and meeting contractual obligations

- hours of attendance

- procedures – for example notification of absence through sickness

- adherence to the rules of the organisation as set out in the formal contract of employment.

Quality of work

- standard of written work

- appearance of finished items of work

- acceptable error rates.

Work output and timing

- quantity of finished items of work

- production norms

- deadlines and timescales for completion of work.

Interpersonal behaviour and dealing with others

- standards of behaviour in relating to customers and clients

- appropriate behaviour in relation to colleagues and management.

Methods of assessment

The most common methods of assessing individual performance are similar to those used for monitoring the performance of projects, programmes or organisations. They are:

- observation and involvement

- questioning and discussion

- routine statistics and reporting

- your own statistics

- other reports.

Dealing with underperformance

If underperformance is identified it will need to be addressed in a way that produces an improvement. This is best done by agreeing on the problem, the cause and the solution with the person involved, as described in Box 14.5

BOX 14.5   FIVE STEPS TO ADDRESS UNDERPERFORMANCE

1 Identify and agree on the problem.

2 Establish the reason(s) for the shortfall – is the problem one of support, understanding, ability, skill or attitude?

3 Decide and agree on the action required – for example develop skills, provide more guidance.

4 Resource the action – for example provide coaching or training.

5 Monitor the situation and provide feedback.

360-degree feedback

In the 360-degree feedback system, assessments are sought from a variety of people with whom the individual interacts – most notably from the line manager, the individual's own direct reports, their co-workers and colleagues, and their internal and external customers. This scheme of assessment is shown in Figure 14.1.

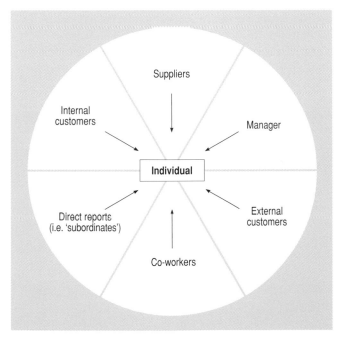

Figure 14.1 360-degree feedback

The 360-degree feedback method (also known as the multi-rater and multi-source feedback method) has increased rapidly in recent years. The underlying rationale has two elements. First, it corrects for the bias and the imperfect and incomplete information associated with single-rater feedback. Second, it encourages self-awareness and personal development by allowing individuals to identify and reflect on the gap between their own perceptions of their performance and those of others with whom they work.

One of the criticisms of traditional performance appraisal is that it involves the judgement of a single line manager. In the light of changes to work and organisational design, when key internal customers can be many and varied and when devolved responsibility has given wider responsibilities to individuals, it is perhaps unsurprising that the idea of 360-degree feedback has aroused such interest. The core principle for many organisations which use 360-degree feedback is that it is for the purpose of individual development only, and separate from the performance-review system used for promotion and reward.

Variations in approach

There are variations in the use of the 360-degree feedback method. For example, a line manager may consult an individual's peers, direct reports and co-workers before conducting a conventional appraisal meeting. Alternatively, an appraiser who is not the line manager may contact a range of stakeholders for information. In some cases written questionnaires might be distributed for completion and returned anonymously. This information is usually confidential to the individual concerned, although in some instances it may also be given to the line manager or provided in summary form. Depending on the type of data and the collection method, when processed the information may be supplied directly to the target individual graphically, showing levels of perceived achievement against a given set of criteria.

Developing people

One of the major outcomes of an appraisal interview should be agreement on any development needs for the person concerned.

Ideally the three discs shown in Figure 14.2 should stack neatly on top of each other, ensuring that the work being done fits well with the individual's aspirations and abilities and the organisation's priorities. Of course this will not always be so. In some cases there will be a need for coaching and mentoring as ways of developing people in line with the organisation's needs.

Coaching and coaching styles

Coaching involves a systematic and deliberate approach to helping staff to develop their knowledge and skills. It is a way of transferring knowledge and skill from a more experienced person to a less experienced person. It is important to recognise that people learn in different ways. Different coaching styles are shown in Table 14.4. Each coaching style has different effects. These are summarised in Table 14.5.

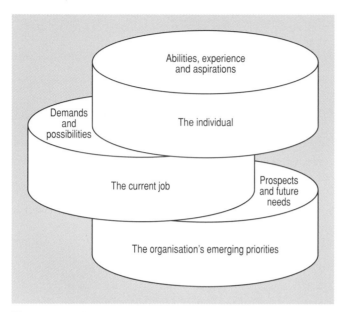

Figure 14.2 Aligning the individual, the job and the organisation

Table 14.4	Types of coaching style	
Interpersonal role	**Coaching style**	**Some characteristics**
Judge	Tough	Pushes hard, challenges, makes demands, is critical.
Helper	Protective	Takes care not to hurt, kindly, reassuring.
Thinker	Calculated	Calm, dispassionate, logical, questioning.
Fun lover	Whoopee	Everything is 'a ball', creative, exciting.
Defendant	Manipulative	'Winds you up', provokes, teases, cajoles, humours.

Table 14.5	Positive and negative effects of coaching styles	
Positive	**Coaching style**	**Negative**
Can push through difficulties when the going is hard.	Tough	Can produce rebellion. May lead to bad feelings.
Can lift up a person when they are low.	Protective	Can stunt development by being over-protective.
Can help a person find solutions and help them to work things out.	Calculated	Can be seen as impersonal and distant. All head and no heart.
Can motivate by energy and enthusiasm.	Whoopee	Can be seen as frivolous. May avoid tough issues.
Can energise and influence.	Manipulative	May produce anger and feelings of betrayal.

Mentoring and how to organise it

See Being
mentored, p. 30,
and Peer
relationships, p. 31.

Mentoring is a similar activity to coaching, although a fundamental difference is that a mentor should not be an employee's line manager. Mentors are people with responsibility for overseeing the development of others outside the normal manager–employee relationship. The line manager, however, has one of the four roles to play in the overall mentoring programme shown in Figure 14.3.

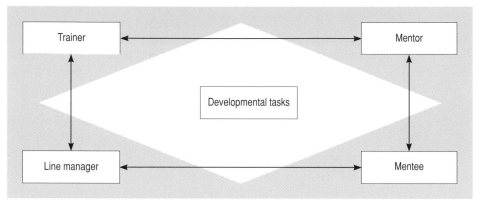

Figure 14.3 Clutterbuck *et al.*'s mentoring model (1991)

The preparations for a mentoring programme should include the following:

- ensuring that there is commitment from senior management

- locating mentoring within the organisation's other human resource development programmes

- ensuring that there is commitment to participation by all parties

- ensuring effective mentor–mentee–manager–trainer relationships

- ensuring that support systems are in place – in particular a tracking and monitoring process for mentors and mentees

- making time and money available for the effective involvement for all four participants in the mentoring model

- matching mentors and mentees carefully

- clearly explaining what is involved to all participants

- ensuring confidentiality – in classic mentoring, the mentor should have no reporting relationship with the mentee's line manager.

Managing groups, teams and committees

See Chapter 4
Working with
others.

Groups, teams and committees all involve two or more people who interact together, and all are similar in important ways. First, all seem to be carrying out some kind of work. Second, to state the obvious, each is made up of people. In consequence, and regardless of the explicit purpose of the group, there will be an important social dimension. People are social beings with social needs. Our emotional reactions to each other are an important part of our interactions. So, in all groups, teams and committees, social interaction will play an important role.

Some differences between groups, teams and committees

There are also some important differences between groups, teams and committees. The members of a work group are not necessarily working on a common task. They may all be doing similar work in parallel, or carrying out discrete components of a larger task; but they may be only working together in a very limited sense – sometimes only in the sense of being located together. Generally we can say that members of a work group are engaged in creating individual work products. By contrast, members of a team are engaged in creating collective work products.

Team members also need to interact with one another to achieve a task, whereas a group of people may work on a common task with common goals without interacting: this could, for example, describe the activity of a group of workers on an assembly line.

Members of a committee or a team can be said to be working on a common task. However, there is an important difference between the two. Committees often exist to allow conflicts of interest between different parties to be expressed and resolved. Each member of a committee may be representing a different constituency – for example finance versus marketing, or one division versus another. They may be working on a common task or decision, but each committee member may seek to achieve different goals. In contrast, a team not only has a shared task but also common goals.

Table 14.6 summarises some of these points.

Table 14.6 Characteristics of groups, teams and committees			
Characteristics	**Group**	**Team**	**Committee**
Social interaction between individuals is important	Yes	Yes	Yes
Common task	Not necessarily	Yes	Yes
Common goals	Possibly	Yes	No
Work products	Individual	Collective	Collective
Need to work interdependently to achieve tasks	No	Yes	Sometimes

Formal and informal groups

A group may be defined as two or more people who interact together and share some common attitudes and behaviours. A team is a particular form of group.

Types of group

Figure 14.4 shows a framework that can be used to categorise groups.

	Formal	Informal
Primary	e.g. a department, a project team	e.g. a group of friends
Secondary	e.g. a large committee	e.g. a network of black managers

Figure 14.4 **Different types of groups**

(Source: based on Kakabadse *et al.*, 1988)

■ **Formal groups** have some formal recognition and authority within the organisation and usually have a defined purpose related to the organisation's broad aims. The groups may be departments, work groups or project teams. An organisation can be regarded as an interlocking set of such groups.

■ **Informal groups** do not have formal authority. Individuals within organisations interact with a wide range of people who may not be part of their formal groups. They may form relationships with those people to pursue work-related and other common interests, or to make various exchanges. Informal groups may form to fulfil special needs and attain special goals: for example, to provide friendship, a sense of identity and a feeling of belonging, or to pursue a common interest, such as a sport.

■ **Primary groups** are those whose members have regular and frequent interactions with each other, in the pursuit of some common interest or task. A small work group, a project team and a family are all primary groups. They usually have an important influence on their members' values, attitudes and beliefs.

- **Secondary groups** are those whose members interact less frequently. They are often larger than primary groups. Large committees, professional bodies and associations are examples. Their members do not have the opportunity to get to know each other well. As a result they are usually less cohesive than primary groups.

Formal groups

In an organisation formal groups can be used for:

- distributing and managing work

- problem solving and decision making

- passing on information

- co-ordinating and liaising

- enabling people to participate in decision making

- negotiation or conflict resolution

- inquest or inquiry into the past.

Different factors will affect how groups operate and how they affect the manager and the organisation.

The development of a group

There are recognisable stages in the development of a group – or a team – from the first meeting to the time when the group is ready to tackle its task. A manager who knows about these stages will be better able to support the group.

Stages of development

There is an intuitive appeal to the idea that a group – like any organism – has to grow to maturity. The development of a group from its first meeting, to the point where it is ready to tackle its tasks, can be set out as a four-stage process shown in Figure 14.5.

Forming Members go through the forming process. They introduce themselves, they listen to each other, perhaps they test each other in some way. There is a sense of finding out about each other and about the task.

Storming In this stage group members discuss, in a non-informed way, methods of achieving the task and how the group will conduct itself. In the normal course of events, there will be differences, and the members will discuss them. This second stage is likely to be characterised by the expression and management of differences.

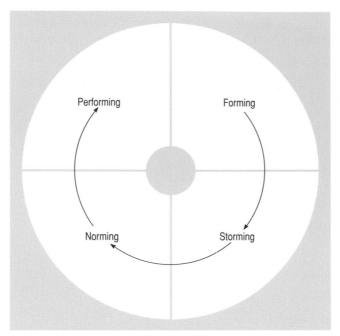

Figure 14.5 **The stages in the development of a group**

(Source: based on Tuckman and Jenson, 1977)

Norming Having worked its way through the arguments, the group can now establish agreements about the task, about the preferred way of achieving it, and about the way that the group will conduct itself. The group establishes its norms: its procedures, its purposes, and so on.

Performing The group now regards itself as being ready to get on with the agreed task – it is performing.

Using the developmental model

The idea of stages is a helpful one, both to those who work in groups and to those who manage them. The progression recognises and thus validates the expression of differences. This seeming conflict can be recognised as part of the journey from first meetings to maturity.

Factors that affect groups

A number of factors affect the workings and management of groups. Understanding them will help you to identify problems and solutions when working with groups.

Group size

The larger the group, the greater the diversity of skills and knowledge available to it.

However, in larger groups there are fewer opportunities for each individual to participate and influence proceedings. Between five and seven people is best for effective participation by all. However, to achieve the range of expertise and skills required, the group may need to be larger. As a group increases beyond ten to twelve people it may become less effective and may split into smaller subgroups.

The nature of the task

A group with a clear and unambiguous task can perform more quickly than one that is given an open-ended ambiguous task. Groups given ill-defined tasks will probably need more support and should consist of people who can tolerate greater stress. They will also take more time to become an effective group. When a group is expected to perform two different functions simultaneously, problems can be avoided by separating each function by time, place or title and/or by a change of style.

Resources and support

To function effectively, the group should have access to appropriate equipment, finance and support services, otherwise group morale and effectiveness can diminish.

External recognition

Groups are more likely to be motivated if members feel their work is accepted as being important to the organisation.

Group composition

Group members should possess the range of competencies necessary to tackle the task. Homogeneous groups tend to produce higher member satisfaction and less conflict, but they may be less creative and produce greater pressures for conformity. Heterogeneous groups are likely to experience greater conflict but have the potential for greater creativity and innovation.

Teams and innovation

A team is a group of people with common goals, working together on a common task, who need to work interdependently to achieve a collective outcome.

Teams can be useful in the *innovation* process. However, that does not mean they are necessarily good at coming up with original ideas. How many artistic masterpieces have been created by a team? Teams can sometimes act as a damper on the creative process by being too quick to start critically evaluating ideas. However, they do play an important role in evaluating and developing ideas that have been generated by individuals.

Two other main benefits of teams are *synergy* and *commitment*. Teams are good at bringing together diverse skills and viewpoints to produce more effective solutions than any individual could have managed alone. The process of working together on a task tends to bind the members of a team into mutual commitment to the task and its consequences.

However, these outcomes are by no means automatic. Much depends on how teams are constructed and managed, and on the quality of interaction within them. Generating synergy requires a high quality of interaction between team members. Clarity about goals, active listening, attention to social processes and willingness to engage in constructive disagreement are all necessary ingredients for generating synergy. Generating commitment requires the active inclusion of all team members. Commitment arises only as team members feel valued and included.

Self-managing teams

There are times when teams need to be self-managing. A number of factors need to be considered if such teams are to be effective. These are shown in Figure 14.6.

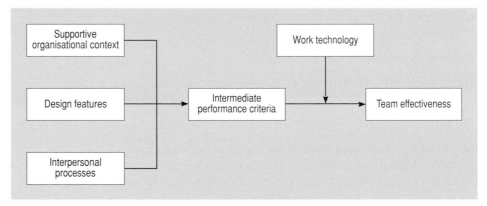

Figure 14.6 The effectiveness of self-managing teams

(Source: based on Hackman and Oldham, 1980)

BOX 14.6 FACTORS IN THE EFFECTIVENESS OF SELF-MANAGING TEAMS

A supportive organisational context includes:

- rewards and objectives for good performance
- task-relevant training and technical advice
- clear task requirements and constraints.

Team design features embrace motivational factors such as:

- the use of a range of different skills – skill variety
- a complete and meaningful piece of work – task identity

- a task which makes a difference to people inside or outside the organisation – task significance

- significant scope for team members to make decisions about how the work is carried out – autonomy

- reliable information about team performance – feedback.

Interpersonal processes embrace the need for team members to:

- co-ordinate efforts and foster commitment

- weight the inputs of team members appropriately – according to skill, knowledge or experience rather than status or seniority

- put effort into generating and implementing appropriate strategies for task performance.

Work technology

The factors listed in Box 14.6 (a supportive organisational context, team design features and interpersonal processes) contribute to what are called 'intermediate performance criteria' – the level of effort team members bring to the work, the amount of knowledge and skill applied to the work and the appropriateness of the task performance strategies. In turn, these will be important to overall team effectiveness. However, the extent to which these intermediate performance criteria lead to team effectiveness depends on the work technology. For example, for a team engaged in simple low-skill tasks such as filling envelopes or packing boxes, levels of effort are likely to be more important to performance than knowledge and skill or task performance strategies. In contrast, all three intermediate performance criteria may be important to a team working on a new product development.

Assessing the climate for creativity

Innovation, whether by teams, groups or individuals, is essential for an organisation to thrive. For there to be innovation there needs to be a climate that encourages creativity. In Table 14.7 criteria are described that are either stimulants or barriers to creativity. By rating your organisation (or the part of it you work in) using the 1–5 scale you can assess how favourable your organisation's climate is for creativity. You may also find it useful to ask the opinion of others you work with.

Table 14.7 Stimulants and barriers to creativity		
Criterion	**Description**	**Rating**
Stimulants to creativity		
Organisational encouragement	An organisational culture that encourages creativity through the fair, constructive judgement of ideas, and reward and recognition for creative work.	1 2 3 4 5
Supervisory encouragement	A supervisor who serves as a good work model, sets goals appropriately, supports the work group, values individual contributions, and shows confidence in the work group.	1 2 3 4 5
Supportive work group	A diversely skilled work group in which people communicate well, are open to new ideas, constructively challenge each other's work, trust and help each other, and feel committed to the work they are doing.	1 2 3 4 5
Sufficient resources	Access to appropriate resources including funds, materials, facilities and information.	1 2 3 4 5
Challenging work	A sense of having to work hard on challenging tasks and important projects.	1 2 3 4 5
Freedom	Freedom in deciding what work to do or how to do it; a sense of control over one's work.	1 2 3 4 5
Barriers to creativity		
Organisational impediments	An organisational culture that impedes creativity through internal political problems, harsh criticism of new ideas, destructive internal competition, an avoidance of risk and an overemphasis on the status quo.	1 2 3 4 5
Workload pressure	Extreme time pressures, unrealistic expectations for productivity and distraction from creative work.	1 2 3 4 5

Rating scheme: 1 = Highly unfavourable, 2 = Unfavourable, 3 = Neutral, 4 = Favourable, 5 = Highly favourable.

(Source: based on Amabile *et al.*, 1996)

CHAPTER 15 MONITORING AND EVALUATION

Learning from the exercise of control

Effective organisations require effective management control and co-ordination – arguably the most central functions of management. Until recently, management control has been viewed primarily in the narrow context of management accounting. However, it is now considered to extend far wider than a set of routine activities that translates strategic goals into accounting-based controls. It embraces how organisations can improve their performance by more effective control over people, operations and processes. Necessarily this involves monitoring and evaluation of performance – the systematic collection, analysis and reporting of information – at various levels. These levels range from the simple management control loop to more holistic approaches, such as the balanced scorecard, that involve understanding performance from multiple perspectives. Comparison is sometimes necessary to assess and improve performance, thus internal and external benchmarking techniques are also relevant to the topic of monitoring and evaluation. The key to performance improvement, however, rests in what a manager does with the results of any assessment, including the adjustment of fixed goals as they become inappropriate in a changing environment.

See The balanced scorecard, p. 331.

Results can be used in single feedback loop – a simple model of learning in which performance is compared with a goal and then actions are adjusted accordingly. This is known as single-loop learning. In double-loop learning, the original goals are questioned along with other parts of the management control loop:

- Do we have the right performance measures in place?

- Do we have the right repertoire of possible responses to performance feedback?

Single-loop learning is concerned with learning how to cope and how to respond; in double-loop learning new ways of looking and thinking are generated.

The four Es

There are many ways in which we can think about organisational performance and these vary according to whose concerns we are considering. One way of organising our views of performance is through the four Es – **E**ffectiveness, **E**fficiency, **E**conomy and **E**thics. These are shown in Figure 15.1.

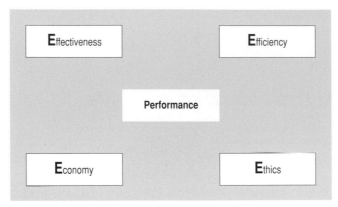

Figure 15.1 **The four Es**

Exploring the four Es

Effectiveness is the extent to which an organisation achieves its goals. Before we can judge effectiveness we first have to be clear about the goals.

Efficiency describes how well an organisation transforms inputs into outputs. An organisation becomes more efficient as it produces more or better outputs for the same inputs, or the same outputs from fewer inputs.

Economy describes how cheaply the inputs can be purchased. Economy is rarely a dominant criterion. It is simply a measure on the input side and takes no account of outputs. However, economy becomes more important in public-sector organisations and in the middle and lower levels of large private-sector organisations where managers are constrained by fixed budgets.

Ethical acceptability is the extent to which the behaviour of an organisation and its members is acceptable in terms of the moral standards of the wider society in which it operates. Organisations that behave in ways that stray too far from accepted moral standards can face a wide range of social sanctions from adverse media attention to customer boycotts and legal action.

You can summarise the four Es with the phrase: *do the right thing, do the thing right, do it cheaply and do right.*

Management control

The management control process is normally concerned with the link between the activities of people in an organisation and the organisation's goals. It begins when a line manager meets with a direct report to review past performance and to negotiate goals, objectives and targets for key variables for the next year. Once goals are negotiated, the subordinate records actual performance at periodic intervals during the period for which the variables are to be measured. The line manager meets with the direct report periodically to review performance. In traditional approaches to management control, the line manager ensures that the goals are met.

BOX 15.1   PRINCIPAL FEATURES OF TRADITIONAL MANAGEMENT CONTROL

The principal features of the traditional management control process are to:

- set goals and performance measures

- measure achievement

- compare achievement with goals

- compute the variances as a result of the preceding comparison

- report the variances

- determine cause(s) of the variances

- take action to eliminate the variances

- follow up to ensure that goals are met

(Source: Maciarello, 1984)

These eight principle features form a control loop to ensure that goals are achieved (and are not changed). The control loop is an example of single loop learning.

See Learning from the exercise of control, p. 317.

Traditional management control and the organisational context

Traditional management control frameworks such as the one described above rest on particular ways of viewing organisations. Organisations can be seen as machines or as information processing systems.

Organisations as machines

Classical management theory views organisations as having machine-like properties. Workers are seen as interchangeable and expected to have little discretion. Rather, they carry out work precisely as instructed. Managers are responsible for devising the one best way for work to be carried out. Tasks and responsibilities are precisely specified and divided into areas of specialism.

See Scientific management, p. 284.

The activities of the organisation are made to operate as precisely as possible through attention to patterns of authority, to the general process of direction and discipline, and to the subordination of individuals to general interest. Commands issued from the top of the organisation travel down in a precisely determined way, to create a precisely determined effect.

In many organisations, this machine metaphor has been an effective foundation for management. For example, fast food chains are able to deliver a consistent product in any of their restaurants, by precisely specifying how each task will be done.

Organisations as information processing systems

Another approach to understanding organisations rests on seeing them as information processing systems. The central idea here is of systems that can respond to their environment. As an example of this, Figure 15.2 shows a simple mechanical control loop, such as you might have in a central heating system. Essentially, the eight-step management control process described above is a similar simple control loop.

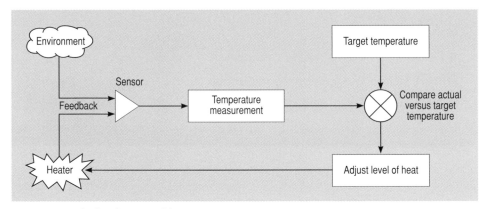

Figure 15.2 **A simple control loop**

The traditional control process in action

The traditional control process is usually described in standard management textbooks as comprising four *stages*. Typically, the stages involve:

- setting objectives and establishing standards of performance

- planning tasks, identifying performance measures, carrying out tasks and measuring performance

- monitoring progress by comparing performance against objectives and standards

- acting on results of monitoring and taking corrective action.

The process is shown in Figure 15.3.

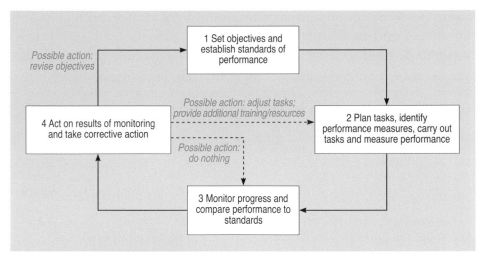

Figure 15.3 **Stages in the control process**

The four stages are described below.

Stage 1 – Set objectives and establish standards of performance

At this stage an *overall aim*, for example, opening a new redistribution warehouse on time and within budget, needs to be refined into a more specific set of objectives. Some of these objectives will specify *what* needs to be done (output objectives) and some will specify *how* these objectives need to be met (process objectives). Standards of performance will be derived from these objectives and actual performance will be measured against these standards or criteria.

Stage 2 – Plan tasks, identify performance measures, carry out tasks and measure performance

The planning process involves identifying the tasks that need to be done, linking tasks to people and resources, identifying performance measures and drawing up a working plan (a Gantt chart or network analysis, also referred to as critical path analysis). As the plan is implemented, control aspects are involved as progress and performance are measured. Plans are revised accordingly.

See Network analysis, p. 139

Performance criteria may relate to quality, quantity, timeliness or customer service – or all of these as a package of quantitative measures of this kind. However, it may not be possible to 'manage through the numbers' cheaply and easily. Decisions will need to be made about *what* precisely to measure and *how* to measure. For example, in a hospital ward quality of care may be equally or more important than the number of patients treated. Possible sources of information include personal observation, computer counts and written and oral reports.

Stage 3 – Monitor progress and compare performance to objectives and standards

At this stage progress needs to be monitored. Monitoring techniques can be formal or informal. They include: observation; the provision of regular reports; exception reporting (when deviation from the plan is reported); questioning and discussion; keeping records and routine statistics.

Actual performance is then compared with targets, although this sounds more straightforward than it often is. Most managers will prioritise the measures and will focus on those which are regarded as most important.

Stage 4 – Act on results of monitoring and take corrective action

If there is a discrepancy between performance and standards, corrective action may need to be taken. But first there will be an interpretive stage. Does an employee need training? Has the standard been set too high? Have circumstances changed? What will be the effect on morale and motivation of any criticism or disciplinary action? Is attention overly focused on shortfalls, so that a team which constantly meets or exceeds targets is ignored? What if the person or team exceeding key targets is also the one failing to meet other targets?

Corrective action can involve:

- Revising the objectives
- Adjusting the tasks still to be completed (the most common course of action)
- Providing additional resources/training
- Doing nothing.

Vicious circle of control

A system of formal controls, feedback loops and sanctions may turn out to be ineffectual, and even counterproductive. Managers may get drawn into a vicious circle in which tighter and tighter attempts at control provoke more and more resistance, leading to weaker rather than stronger control of the organisation. This paradoxical cycle is depicted in Figure 15.4.

A downward spiral

In this vicious circle, analysis by the management concludes that a failure to meet expectations requires the imposition of stronger controls. Employees perceive the introduction of more controls as an expression of mistrust and blame. Morale is likely to suffer, and discretionary effort and goodwill may be withheld. As a result, productivity and quality standards may decline further. Management then decides that even tighter controls are required – in part to counter the recalcitrance that has been engendered. These tighter controls are

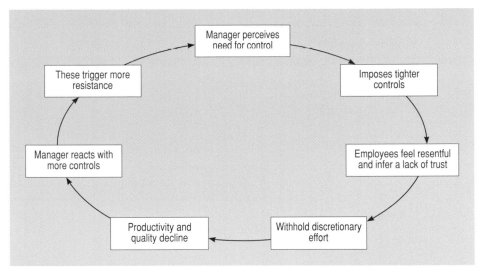

Figure 15.4 **Vicious circle of control**

perceived by the workforce as unfair and oppressive, and higher degrees of resistance are provoked. The vicious circle thus takes a further turn.

Even where this vicious circle is avoided, the imposition of management controls may still have an adverse and unplanned effect. For example, even simply measuring output or work speed is likely to affect behaviour.

Performance improvement using double loop learning

Traditional management control frameworks are based on what is called 'single loop' learning: how to cope and how to respond to ensure that goals are met. They are useful in particular circumstances. The classical control framework based on the metaphor – the view – of the organisation as a machine may be appropriate when firms are carrying out straightforward tasks in a stable environment or when standard products or services are required. The control framework based on the metaphor of the organisation as an information processing system is useful in placing emphasis on feedback. However, these frameworks can quickly become inappropriate in a changing environment in which previously fixed goals need to change. Paradoxically, highly efficient traditional control processes can be an impediment to change.

One way of dealing with this is to introduce 'double loop' learning into the management of performance. This allows not only the goals to be questioned, but also the performance measures used and the repertoire of responses to feedback on performance. Figure 15.5 shows the main elements of double loop learning in terms of performance management.

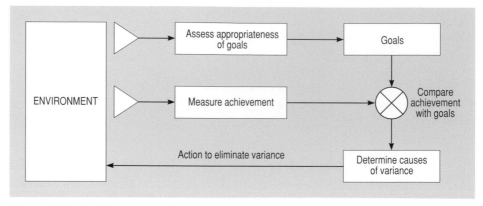

Figure 15.5 **Double loop learning.**

(Source: adapted from Argyris and Schon, 1978)

Barriers to double loop learning

Applied to managing in a changing environment, double loop learning seems a sensible approach to adopt. In practice, however, is not easy to put into place because:

■ bureaucratic structures often do not encourage managers to think for themselves

■ bureaucratic accountability may encourage managers to find ways of obscuring issues and problems

■ when accountability systems foster defensiveness, an organisation is rarely able to tolerate high levels of uncertainty – managers want to 'tie things down' and be 'on top of the facts.'

(Source: based on Morgan, 1986)

How can organisations overcome these barriers? Some suggested approaches are:

Encourage and value an open and reflective approach Error and uncertainty need to be seen as normal features of complex and changing environments. Avoid a blame culture in which people are fearful of making mistakes rather than seeing them as occasions for reflection and improved understanding.

Encourage the use of multiple viewpoints Many issues faced by organisations in complex and turbulent environments are multi-dimensional and unclear. Probing the different dimensions of a problem and allowing constructive conflict and debate helps to define the nature of the problem and generate possible solutions.

Do not impose overly specific goals, objectives and targets Tight, predetermined goals and objectives tend to provide a framework for single-loop learning but can discourage double loop learning.

(Source; based on Morgan, 1986)

Traditional approaches to management control are founded on the idea of hierarchal arranged co-ordination, on communication up and down a chain of demand, and on the idea of an organisation as an arrangement of tightly-coupled components. Moving beyond these forms of management control allows for mutual co-ordination laterally, across functions or departments, and recognises that organisations carry out tasks that may be complex, changeable and not clearly specified.

Operations management

An understanding of the principles of operations management is important for all managers because the principles provide a systematic way of looking at an organisation's processes.

The transformation model of operations management

Operations management involves the systematic direction and control of the processes that transform resources (inputs) into finished goods or services for customers or clients (outputs). This basic transformation model applies equally in manufacturing and service organisations and in both the private and not-for-profit sectors. This is shown in Figure 15.6.

Figure 15.6 The transformation model

Inputs

Many people think of operations as being mainly about the transformation of inputs – materials or components – into finished products, as when an automobile is assembled from its various parts. But all organisations that produce goods or services transform resources. Many are concerned with the transformation of information (for example, consultancy firms or accountants) or the transformation of customers (for example, hairdressers or hospitals). Some inputs are used up in the process of creating goods or services; others play a part in the creation process but are not used up. The two types of transforming resource that are not used up are:

1   staff (or labour) – the people who are involved directly in the transformation process or who support it

2   facilities (or capital) – land, buildings, machines and equipment.

Operations vary greatly in the mix of labour and capital that make up their inputs. Highly automated operations depend largely on capital; others rely mainly on labour.

Outputs

The principal outputs of a doctor's surgery are cured patients; the outputs of a nuclear reprocessing plant include reprocessed fuel and nuclear waste. Many transformation processes produce both goods and services. Transformation processes may result in some undesirable outputs as well as the goods and services they are designed to deliver. Important aspects of operations management in some organisations are:

- minimising the environmental impact of waste over the entire life-cycle of their products

- protecting the health and safety of employees and of the local community

- taking ethical responsibility for the social impact of transformation processes, both locally and globally.

Transformation processes

A transformation process is any activity or group of activities that takes one or more inputs, transforms and adds value to them, and provides outputs for customers or clients. There are three types of input that can be transformed – materials, information and customers.

Transformation processes include:

- changes in the physical characteristics of materials or customers

- changes in the location of materials, information or customers

- changes in the ownership of materials or information

- storage or accommodation of materials, information or customers

- changes in the purpose or form of information

- changes in the physiological or psychological state of customers.

Often all three types of input are transformed by the same organisation. For example, withdrawing money from a bank account involves information about the customer's account, materials such as cheques and currency, and the customer. Treating a patient in hospital involves not only the 'customer's' state of health, but also any materials used in treatment and information about the patient.

Feedback

Feedback information is used to control the operations system, by adjusting the inputs and transformation processes that are used to achieve desired outputs. It can come from both internal and external sources. Internal sources include testing and evaluation, external sources include those who supply products or services to customers as well as feedback from customers themselves. Feedback can result in a change to the inputs or a change to the transformation process. For example, a restaurant could buy better potatoes or change the cooking method used on the basis of feedback from customers.

New forms of control

In the post-industrial economy a premium is often placed on commitment, responsiveness and flexibility, rather than obedience and conformity.

More flexible structures

The classical model of scientific management, famously espoused by the car manufacturer, Henry Ford, was rigid, conformist and mechanistic. New forms of competition and new market characteristics may need more flexible modes of production, and an enterprise culture. The characteristics of each form of control are summarised in Table 15.1.

Table 15.1 Features of classical and post-industrial forms of control	
Classical	**Post-industrial**
Mass production of standardised products, assembly lines.	Flexible production systems, multi-batch production for niche markets.
Hierarchical organisation structures, bureaucratic, vertically-integrated.	Flat, flexible structures; decentralised.
Administrative controls – rules, timetables.	Normative controls – through cultures, values, manipulation of meanings and attitudes.
Institutional controls – collective bargaining.	Identity control – through programmes such as service excellence and total quality management.
Insecurity experienced as a collective sense of social and economic injustice.	Insecurity based on individual self-doubt, weakness or absence of alternative allegiances.

Understanding quality

In a quality organisational culture, there will be a commitment to satisfying or even delighting the customer. There will also be recognition throughout the organisation that achieving high-quality final outputs depends on the quality of earlier outputs right through the supplier–customer chain.

See Figure 15.10 The EFQM business excellence model, p. 333.

What is meant by quality?

In debates about quality, the emphasis is less on the absolute qualities of the product or service than on the extent to which the final product sufficiently meets the customer's requirements. From this perspective, the distinction is not between high-quality and low-quality outputs but between outputs of sufficient quality and insufficient quality.

Ideally, an organisation should also be driving towards supplying more than the customer wanted. A delighted customer is more likely to resist the offers from competing suppliers and instead may provide the organisation with repeat orders.

The drive towards exceeding customers' expectations is also consistent with the commitment towards the continuous improvement of the product itself.

Internal quality

A culture of quality is likely to be one where training will be timely and sufficient, where there will be a general recognition that everyone takes personal responsibility for their own outputs and where there will be opportunities for the staff to contribute to the programme. A quality culture will be vibrant and customer focused.

Assessing service quality

If you expect to have to serve yourself at a petrol station then you will not be surprised or disappointed with the service. But if you visited a restaurant where you expected to be served and to discuss menu choices, but then had to serve yourself, you would be disappointed and complain of poor service. Customer perception of quality is dependent on their expectations.

A model for service quality

The service quality inventory – or SERVQUAL as it is sometimes called – is a set of criteria customers may use in judging the quality of their service experience. Ten dimensions are used to assess service quality:

1 **Tangibles** – the appearance of the physical facilities associated with the service.

2 **Reliability** – the ability to reproduce the same level of service every time.

3 **Responsiveness** – the speed with which the service provider responds to customer requirements, including dealing with queries, complaints, etc.

4 **Communication** – the clarity and comprehensibility of the information given to the customer.

5 **Credibility** – the trustworthiness of the service provider.

6 **Security** – the physical safety of the customer, or privacy of customer-related information.

7   **Competence** – the technical expertise of the provider in delivering the service.

8   **Courtesy** – the attitude of the service provider and the manner adopted by the server.

9   **Understanding** – how well the provider of the service understands the customer's needs.

10 **Access** – the ease of reaching the service provider, physically or electronically.

(Source: Parasuraman *et al.*, 1988)

Gaps in quality

The service quality inventory requires customers to rate their expectations of these ten dimensions on an 'excellence' scale and again on an 'experience' scale. The results help organisations to understand what their customers want and to identify the gaps between customer expectations and their experience of provision. From this a quality-gaps model can be drawn up, highlighting where these gaps are likely to occur. This is illustrated in Figure 15.7.

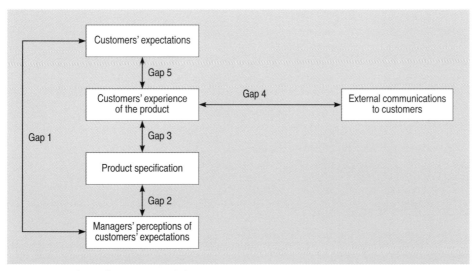

Figure 15.7 **A quality-gaps model**

(Source: Parasuraman *et al.*, 1985)

Benchmarking

Benchmarking is the process of identifying the best practice in relation to products and processes, both within an industry and outside it. The benchmarks are then used as reference points for comparing and improving practices in your own organisation.

Best practice benchmarking involves the examination of processes, rather than merely results, in order to identify gaps where performance needs to be improved and to provide information on how to improve performance. Benchmarking is continuous and requires considerable investment of time and resources if it is to be successful.

The route to improving performance by continuous benchmarking is illustrated in Figure 15.8.

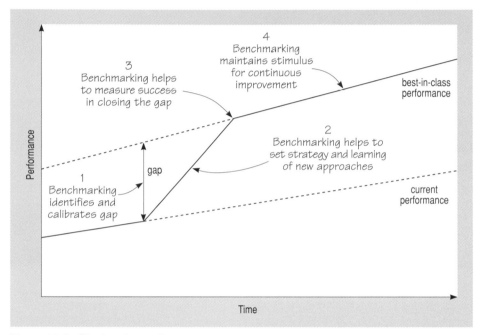

Figure 15.8 **Closing the performance gap**

(Source: Coopers and Lybrand, 1994)

Types of benchmarking

Table 15.2 sets out the four main types of benchmarking.

Table 15.2	A benchmarking classification
Type	**Description**
Internal	A comparison against similar operations within an organisation.
Competitive	A comparison against the best of the direct competitors.
Functional	A comparison of processes against companies with similar processes in the same function.
Generic	A comparison of work processes against others who have innovative exemplar work processes.

(Source: Camp, 1995)

Internal benchmarking

In the case of internal benchmarking, the organisation benchmarks one area of the organisation against another area. For example, an organisation that runs holiday parks could benchmark its different sites against one another on criteria such as occupancy rates. However, many of the advantages of benchmarking that arise from seeking out and striving to emulate best practice within a sector or particular type of activity are lost.

Competitive benchmarking

In competitive benchmarking, activities and processes are benchmarked against competitors in the same sector. This is easier for large organisations where information on competitors may be available in the public domain through trade reports and surveys. If such information is not available then this type of benchmarking is dependent on competitors being willing to share information, which may potentially damage their competitive advantage.

Functional benchmarking

In functional benchmarking, comparison is made against the processes of organisations with similar functional processes but in other sectors. Administrative functions such as human resource departments are classic examples. Comparing your own organisation's processes against processes used outside your own industry sector removes the problem of sharing information with competitors. It can also lead to innovative solutions to old problems, by enabling you to see how they have been resolved in different industries.

Generic benchmarking

With generic benchmarking, there is no attempt to find direct comparability, but instead an attempt is made to learn from others who have innovative exemplar work processes. For example, a postal service has benchmarked a chemical company as an exemplar of safety. The heath and safety contexts are very different yet the postal service has been able to adopt the processes used by the chemical company to inculcate safety awareness in all staff. The chemical company was not chosen for ease of comparison but because it had an excellent safety reputation.

The balanced scorecard

A relatively new model for operational control is the balanced scorecard shown in Figure 15.9 overleaf.

The scorecard provides answers to four basic questions by assessing four perspectives:

1   How do our customers see us? (The customer perspective.)

2   What must we excel at? (The operational or internal business perspective.)

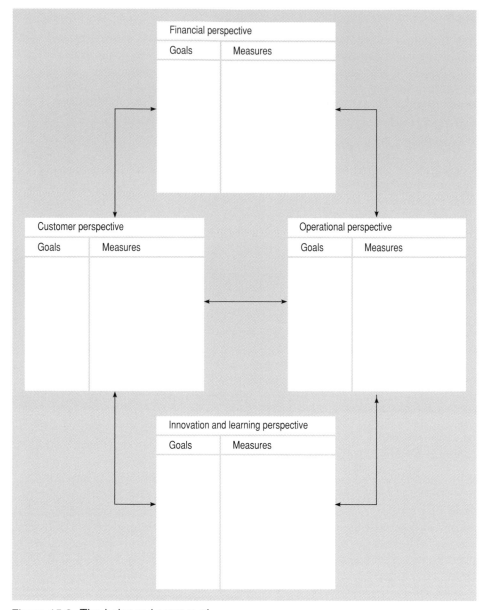

Figure 15.9 **The balanced scorecard**

(Source: based on Kaplan and Norton, 1996)

3   Can we continue to improve and create value? (The innovation and learning perspective.)

4   How do we look to shareholders? (The financial perspective.)

The need for wider measures

The rationale for the balanced scorecard is the need for wider performance measures than those traditionally used. For example, senior executives understand that their organisation's measurement system strongly affects the behaviour of managers and employees. Executives also understand that traditional financial accounting measures such as return on investment and earnings per share can give misleading signals for the continuous improvement and innovation that today's competitive environment demands. These traditional measures are out of step with the skills and competencies companies are trying to master today.

The balanced scorecard is one way of bringing together the perspectives of different functions and different stakeholders. Some users of the balanced scorecard have developed it to emphasise enablers – those factors that underlie successful outcomes. A leading UK company describes the balanced scorecard to its staff as follows:

> If we have the right staff and they are well trained and motivated [*innovation and learning perspective*] and we are doing the right things efficiently [*operational perspective*] then customers will be delighted and customer loyalty will improve [*customer perspective*] hence we will keep/get more business [*financial perspective*].

The business excellence model

The business excellence model, shown in Figure 15.10, is the basis for the European Quality Award and is also referred to as the European Foundation for Quality Management (EFQM) model. Organisations can use it as a tool for self-assessment and to help them to quantify quality practices and performance. From self-assessment, organisations can identify areas of underperformance and so target improvement efforts where they will have the greatest impact.

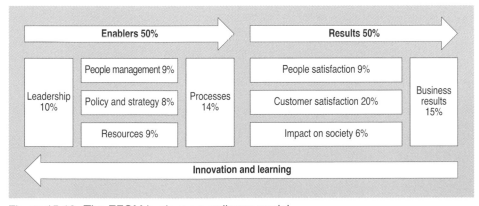

Figure 15.10 The EFQM business excellence model

(Source: based on the European Foundation for Quality Management, 2000)

The elements of the model

The model has nine elements, weighted according to their contribution to the excellence of an organisation:

1 **Leadership** – how senior people inspire and drive an organisation in the pursuit of long-term success through total quality management.

2 **People management** – how the organisation realises the full potential of its employees to support its policy and strategy, and the effective operation of its processes.

3 **Policy and strategy** – how the organisation implements its mission and vision through a clear stakeholder-focused strategy, supported by relevant policies, plans, objectives, targets and processes.

4 **Resources** – how the organisation plans and manages its external partnerships and internal resources to support its policy and strategy and the effective operation of its processes.

5 **Processes** – how the organisation designs, manages and improves its processes to support its policy and strategy and generate increasing value for its customers and other stakeholders.

6 **People satisfaction** – what the organisation is achieving for its employees.

7 **Customer satisfaction** – what the organisation is achieving for its external customers.

8 **Impact on society** – what the organisation is achieving for local, national or international society, as appropriate.

9 **Business results** – what the organisation is achieving with regard to its planned performance.

Using the model

An organisation can appraise its own performance by awarding itself a score out of 100 for each of the model's nine elements. The model can also be used in the following ways:

■ As a framework to help organisations develop their vision and goals for the future, in a tangible, measurable way.

■ As a framework to help organisations identify and understand the systemic nature of their business, its key linkages and cause-and-effect relationships.

■ As the basis for the European Quality Award, which enables Europe to recognise its most successful organisations and promote them as role models of excellence for others to learn from.

■ As a diagnostic tool for assessing the current health of the organisation, so helping it to better balance its priorities, allocate resources and generate realistic business plans.

(Source: European Foundation for Quality Management, 2000)

Conclusion

This compendium contains a wealth of the most well-known and well-used management concepts and models. We have grouped them into the main functional areas of management: organisations, finance, marketing and managing people. What the compendium does not do is teach you how to use the concepts and models or about the interdependence of the management functions, that is, how a change in one will have an impact on another. For this, you may need to follow a formal course of study or support your informal study with appropriate learning materials. For managers who are following (or have followed) formal courses, we hope that the compendium will provide a valuable reference work.

See Appendix 3, p. 354.

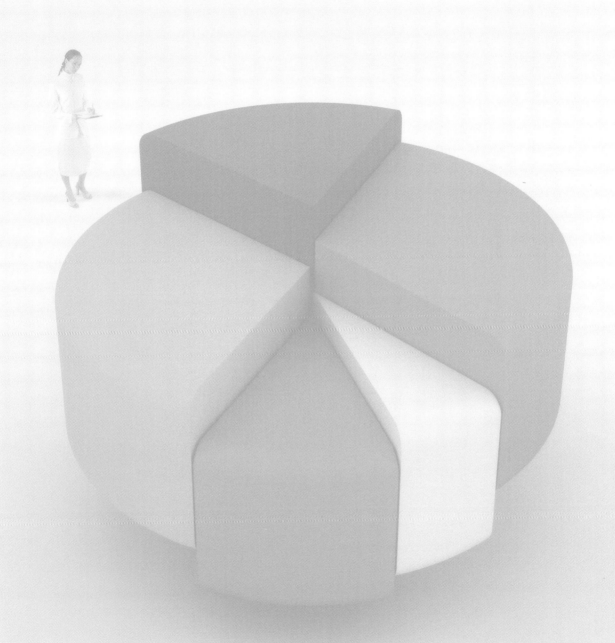

APPENDICES

APPENDIX 1 APPROACHES TO LEARNING AND STUDYING INVENTORY: SELF-SCORE VERSION

Copyright © Tyler, S. and Entwistle, N.J.

This inventory has been designed to allow you to describe, in a systematic way, how you go about learning and studying. The technique involves asking you to respond to 36 statements which overlap to some extent to provide good overall coverage of different ways of studying. Most items are based on comments made previously by other learners. Please give your **immediate** reaction to **every** comment, indicating how you **generally** go about your studying and learning even if you are not currently following a formal programme. If you have not encountered a particular situation, try to imagine how you would react.

Approaches to Learning and Studying Inventory: Self-score Version					
Put a tick in the appropriate box to indicate how strongly you agree with each of the following statements.					
Try not to use the UNSURE box unless you really have to, or unless the item cannot apply to you.	Agree	Agree somewhat	Unsure	Disagree somewhat	Disagree
1. I usually set out to understand for myself the meaning of what we have to learn.					
2. When I'm communicating ideas, I think over how well I've got my points across.					
3. I'm pretty good at getting down to work whenever I need to.					
4. Topics are presented in such complicated ways I often can't see what is meant.					
5. When I've finished a piece of work, I check to see it really meets the requirements.					
6. I try to make sense of things by linking them to what I know already.					
7. I try really hard to do just as well as I possibly can.					
8. On the whole, I'm quite systematic and organised in my studying.					
9. Often I have to learn over and over things that don't really make much sense to me.					
10. I'm quite good at preparing for classes in advance.					
11. I tend to take what we are taught at face value without questioning it much.					
12. For an essay or report, I don't just focus on the topic, I try to improve my writing skill.					

Put a tick in the appropriate box to indicate how strongly you agree with each of the following statements.

Try not to use the UNSURE box unless you really have to, or unless the item cannot apply to you.

	Agree	Agree somewhat	Unsure	Disagree somewhat	Disagree
13. Ideas I come across in my academic reading often set me off on long chains of thought.					
14. If I'm not understanding things well enough when I'm studying, I try a different approach.					
15. I try to relate ideas I come across to other topics or other courses whenever possible.					
16. I carefully prioritise my time to make sure I can fit everything in.					
17. I often have trouble in making sense of the things I have to remember.					
18. I generally keep working hard even when things aren't going all that well.					
19. I'm just going through the motions of studying without seeing where I'm going.					
20. Concentration is not usually a problem for me, unless I'm really tired.					
21. Much of what I've learned seems no more than lots of unrelated bits and pieces in my mind.					
22. I generally put a lot of effort into my studying.					
23. I think about what I want to get out of my studies so as to keep my work well focused.					
24. It's important for me to follow the argument, or to see the reason behind things.					
25. I organise my study time carefully to make the best use of it.					
26. I go over the work I've done to check my reasoning and see that it makes sense.					
27. In making sense of new ideas, I often relate them to practical or real-life contexts.					
28. Whatever I'm working on, I generally push myself to make a good job of it.					
29. I don't think through topics for myself, I just rely on what we're taught.					
30. When I find something boring, I can usually force myself to keep focused.					
31. I tend to just learn things without thinking about the best way to work.					
32. I work steadily during the course, rather than just leaving things until the last minute.					
33. When I'm reading for a course, I try to find out for myself exactly what the author means.					
34. I try to find better ways of tracking down relevant information in my subject.					
35. I look at evidence carefully to reach my own conclusion about what I'm studying.					
36. I pay careful attention to any advice or feedback I'm given, and try to improve my understanding.					

Have you responded to every statement? Please check before continuing.

Now score your responses and work out your learning profile.

How to work out your learning profile and interpret it

Step 1 Score the inventory

Score your ticks in the following way:

Agree	5
Agree somewhat	4
Unsure	3
Disagree somewhat	2
Disagree	1

Step 2 Add the scores

In Table 1 below, write your score for EACH STATEMENT in the blank box next to that statement. Then follow the instruction in the table.

Table 1 Your scores									
Aspect 1		**Aspect 2**		**Aspect 3**		**Aspect 4**		**Aspect 5**	
Statement	Your score	Statement	Your score	Statement	Your score	Statement	Your score	Statement	Your score
1		2		3		7		4	
6		5		8		18		9	
13		12		10		20		11	
15		14		16		22		17	
24		23		25		28		19	
27		26		32		30		21	
33		34						29	
35		36						31	
Write down your score total for EACH COLUMN in the corresponding box below.									

Step 3 Convert the scores

Now turn your score for each aspect into a percentage. To do this, multiply your score for each column by the number in the corresponding box in Table 2 below. For example, if you scored a total of 20 for *Aspect 2*, multiply your score of 20 by 2.5, using a calculator if necessary: 20 x 2.5 = 50%. Note that for Aspects 3 and 4, the multiplier is a different number.

Table 2 Score conversion				
Aspect 1	**Aspect 2**	**Aspect 3**	**Aspect 4**	**Aspect 5**
2.5	2.5	3.33	3.33	2.5
Write your percentage for each column in the boxes below.				

Step 4 Create a bar chart

Now transfer your percentages on to Bar chart 1 below. Look at the scale on the left of the chart and the labels on each column. Draw a line corresponding to your percentage for each aspect on the appropriate column.

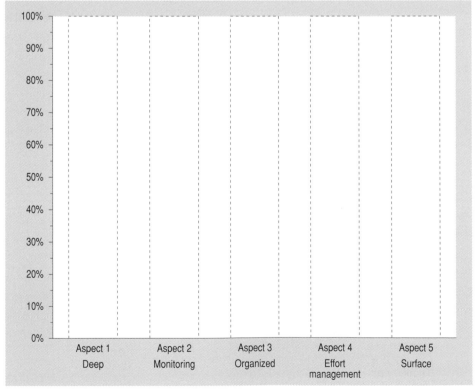

Bar chart 1 **Blank chart**

When you have constructed your bar chart, the height of each bar will correspond to your percentage score for each aspect of learning and studying. This is the PROFILE of your overall approach to learning at the moment. Now you need to know what your profile means.

Step 5   Understand that your profile is not a perfect fit and can change

It is important to realise that standardised questionnaires like the one you have just completed will not reflect perfectly your individual perspectives and experiences. Your profile will be like an off-the-peg suit rather than one that has been made to fit *you* (and no one else). Your profile is a *guide* to your approach to learning and while it may not fit exactly, it will help you identify what you need to work on to improve your approach to good effect. It is important to realise too, that this profile describes how you see yourself learning *just now*. How you learn can change: it is up to you.

Step 6   Identify the five aspects of learning and studying

Within the *Approaches to Learning and Studying Inventory* there are sets of statements which cover **FIVE** different aspects of learning and studying. The bar chart you produced indicates your relative position on each of these aspects. These five aspects are explained in Table 3. Read this now to see what each bar on your chart is referring to. You will need to refer to the table again later.

Table 3   Five aspects of learning and studying
Aspect 1: Deep approach
This aspect of learning is called the *deep approach*, although it is one aspect of an overall approach to learning and studying of the same name. It covers:
■ Intention to understand for yourself: Working out for yourself the meaning of what you have to learn Finding out for yourself exactly what an author means.
■ Relating ideas: Trying to make sense of things by linking them to knowledge you already have Coming across ideas when reading that set you off on long chains of thought Trying to relate ideas you come across to other topics or other courses whenever possible In making sense of new ideas, relating them to practical or real-life contexts.
■ Use of evidence: Attaching importance to following an argument, or seeing the reason behind things Looking at evidence carefully to reach your own conclusions.
Aspect 2: Monitoring study
This aspect of learning – *monitoring study* – covers:
■ Monitoring study effectiveness: Checking a finished piece of work to see it meets requirements Thinking about what you want to get out of your studies so as to keep your work well focused.

- Monitoring understanding:
  Trying a different approach if you find you're not understanding things well enough
  Going over assignments to check your reasoning and see that it makes sense
  Paying careful attention to any advice or feedback in order to improve your understanding.

- Monitoring generic skills:
  When communicating ideas, thinking over how well you've got your points across
  Not just focusing on the topic of an essay or report, but also on trying to improve your writing skill
  Trying to find better ways of tracking down relevant information in your subject.

Aspect 3: Organised studying

This aspect of learning – *organised study* – covers:

- Study organisation:
  Being quite systematic and organised when you are studying
  Preparing for classes in advance.

- Time management:
  Getting down to work when you need to
  Prioritising your time to make sure you can fit everything in
  Organising your study time carefully to make the best use of it
  Working steadily during the course, rather than just leaving things until the last minute.

Aspect 4: Effort management

This aspect of learning – *effort management* – covers:

- Effort:
  Trying hard to do as well as possible
  Working hard even when things aren't going very well
  Putting a lot of effort into studying
  Pushing yourself to do a good job.

- Concentration:
  Finding no difficulty in concentrating on the work you are doing
  Keeping yourself focused even when something is boring.

Aspect 5: Surface approach

This aspect of learning and studying is called the *surface approach*, although it is one aspect of an overall approach to learning and studying of the same name. It covers:

- Memorising without understanding:
  Learning over and over things that don't really make much sense
  Having trouble in making sense of the things you have to remember.

- Unreflective studying:
  Going through the motions of studying without really seeing where you're going
  Learning things without thinking about the best way to work.

- Fragmented knowledge:
  Not seeing how the parts of a topic combine into a meaningful whole
  Feeling that you've learned lots of unrelated bits and pieces.

- Unthinking acceptance:
  Tending to take what's taught at face value without questioning it much
  Not thinking through topics for yourself and instead, relying on what's taught.

An *ideal* pattern of scores would show high scores on the first four aspects of learning – *deep, monitoring study, organised studying* and *effort management.* Conversely, a high score on the *surface approach* alone indicates a pattern that requires serious attention. However, most people have rather mixed patterns, and some of the most common are discussed below. Bear in mind that the aspects of learning that make up an overall approach have much more to do with *attitudes* than anything else. If you believe that learning is simply the intake of information, then this will be reflected in the way you go about your studies. If you are studying because of personal interest in the subject and want to apply new concepts and ideas at work, this will be reflected in the way you approach learning tasks. Modifying your approach, then, will involve placing your attitudes under scrutiny and, if necessary, adopting and practising new skills that are consistent with your new ways of thinking about learning. Skills and techniques need to be underpinned by attitudes that drive you to truly embrace them and use them because *that's the way you think now.* It is a self-sustaining system.

Step 7 Identifying your current profile

Study carefully Bar charts 2–7. They are idealised to make each one easily distinguishable from the others. In most cases the chart you created will be less well-defined than these. Decide which of the charts shown is *most like*

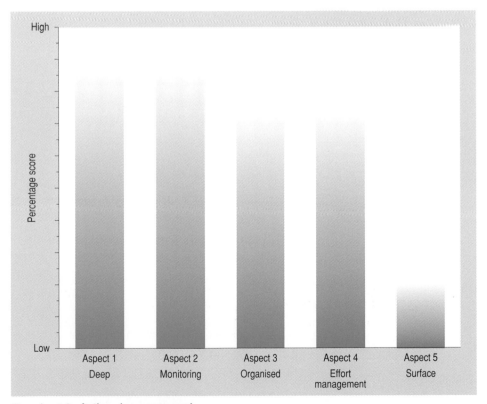

Bar chart 2 **Active deep approach**

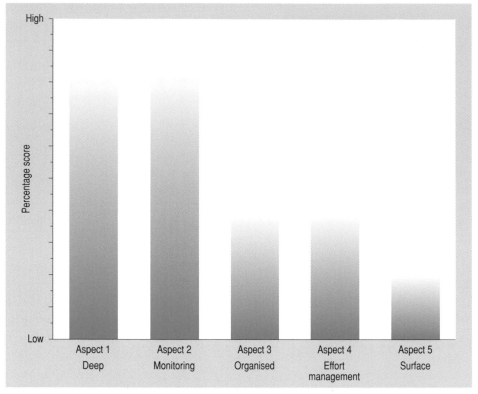

Bar chart 3 **Deep approach without much effort**

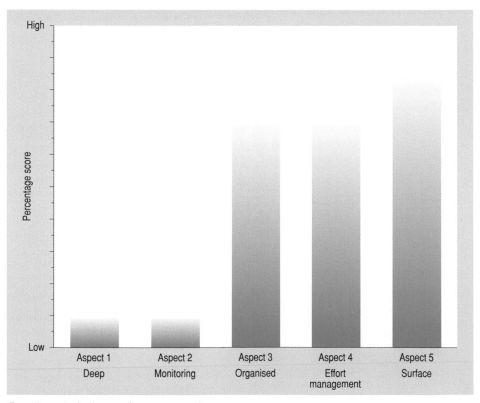

Bar chart 4 **Active surface approach**

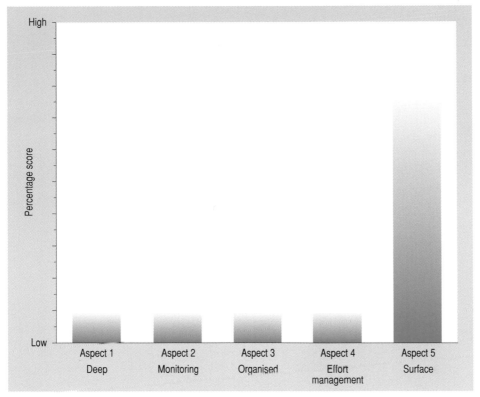

Bar chart 5 Surface approach without much effort

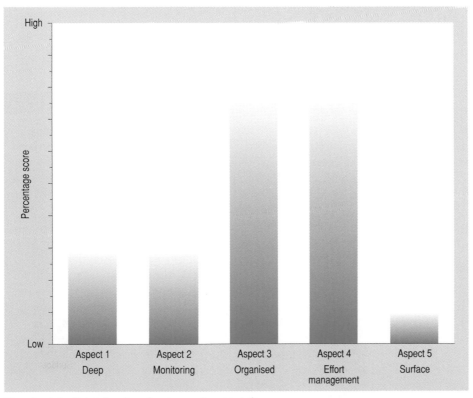

Bar chart 6 Organised and managed approach

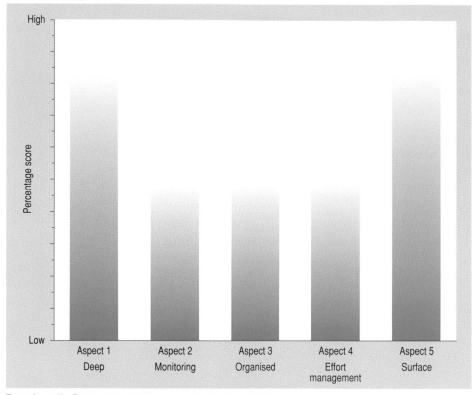

Bar chart 7   Deep and surface approaches combined

the one you created from your own scores on the inventory. Then look up the interpretation for that approach to studying and learning.

Active deep approach

If the lines on your graph are like those in Bar chart 2 – high in the **deep approach** and **monitoring** columns, with average levels in the **organised study** and/or **effort management** columns – you have a 'good' approach to learning, that is, an *active deep approach*. You learn with the intention of understanding. You are interested in the content of a course and in learning for yourself just as much as you are in grades or level of academic performance. You are actively interested in what you are studying and engage personally with learning materials and resources. You use your prior knowledge when learning to help you understand new knowledge but you examine both the prior knowledge and the new knowledge with which you are being presented. You question and use evidence critically; you seek out the main points and aim to gain an overview; you draw conclusions. You see the purpose of a task or its use in a wider context than the study situation. You also monitor the effectiveness of your studies to ensure that your work meets your own requirements as well as assessment demands. You monitor the understanding of the material you are studying, check your own reasoning, and pay attention to feedback. You also monitor general skills such as communication and finding learning resources.

Strength in the **organised study** column shows that you are systematic, prepare for study sessions, organise your time, prioritise, and work steadily through a course. Strength in the **effort management** column shows that you are able to direct your efforts and to concentrate. You push yourself and keep going even when things aren't going too well. You don't seem to find concentration a problem and can force yourself to keep focused even when you are bored by what you are studying. There is usually room for improvement, however! Is your 'surface approach' column too high? Could you improve on study organisation? Look again at Table 3 to identify specific areas in which you could be stronger and then follow the action plan for *Deep approach without much effort.*

Deep approach without much effort

If you showed strength in the **deep approach** and **monitoring** columns, but little in the **organised study** or **effort management** columns, your profile is similar to that of a learner who has adopted a deep approach but who is less well-organised and does not manage their efforts as effectively as they could. You have a *deep approach without much effort.*

Suggested action plan

1   If your profile lacks strength in the area of **organised study** you are likely to improve your learning by working on this. Disorganised study wastes time, and deep learning takes longer. You may need to adopt techniques to produce efficiencies to avoid overload. If you lack strength in **effort management**, getting down to work may be easier if you are more disciplined *and* more flexible. Setting aside study time is important. If you are finding it hard to 'get into' the study session, however, then be flexible and re-order your tasks so that you can start with a short or relatively easy one.

2   Look at the grouped statements in Table 3 and identify areas where you know you can make improvements. Use the relevant study skills advice in this book to develop good learning practices.

3   If the height of your **surface approach** column is too high, follow the suggested action plan for *Surface approach without much effort.*

Active surface approach

If your graph shows a high level in the **surface approach** column, with moderate or high levels in the **organised study** and **effort management** columns, you have the characteristics of a learner who has adopted an *active surface approach.* You may approach study without much sense of purpose. You may be concerned less with understanding learning material than with memorising information with a view to reproducing it when required, for example, in assignments and tests. Your learning appears to be unreflective (you may accept information rather unthinkingly) and you may feel that your knowledge of a topic is fragmented. You are not one to stray beyond the syllabus of a course. However, the moderate levels of study organisation and effort management mean that you are fairly organised and may manage your efforts quite well. Learners with an active surface approach may not succeed in the way that they would like to, and wonder why. Your study organisation and effort management are strengths to build on, placing you in an excellent position to spend time digging deeper into ideas, linking them to your own experience and applying them at work. To improve how you go about your learning and to achieve more from it, follow the suggested action plan for *Surface approach without much effort*.

Surface approach without much effort

If your graph shows a high level in the **surface approach** column and rather low levels in all the others, you have adopted a *surface approach without much effort*. Your profile is similar to that of a learner who has adopted an active surface approach, but it differs in that you are less well organised and do not manage your efforts as effectively as you could.

Suggested action plan

1   Conduct an 'attitude check'. What are your beliefs and attitudes towards learning and studying? Are they consistent with the kind of learning that can change the way a person thinks and behaves? Seek support if necessary from teachers or peers.

2   Look at Table 3 and identify areas where you know you can make improvements. Pay particular attention to the characteristics of the deep approach. You will need to work on trying to gain a deeper understanding of the material you study, to learn to question. Read Chapter 3 'Learning skills' and concentrate in particular on the topic of critical thinking (p. 60).

3   Consider your motives for studying. These may be affecting your approach and your engagement. Did you enrol on your course because you wanted to develop knowledge and skills you can use in your career, to study management in depth, to develop yourself? Or did you enrol to prove yourself to others, because you want a management qualification (or were told you needed one), or because studying the course would look good on your CV? It will be hard to engage with learning if you are not very interested in the content of your course. Perhaps you can redefine your motives so that they are more constructive. For example, there is nothing wrong with wanting a management qualification, but you would probably not want to gain the qualification without also gaining real knowledge.

4   It may be that you find it easier to learn using a highly practical approach. If so, you are particularly likely to benefit a good deal from opportunities to apply your learning at work. Negotiate this, preferably in conjunction with a coach or mentor who will help you relate what you are learning to practical situations. When you 'see' how an idea can be used at work, you may find you engage more with course material and find it more interesting.

5   If you have not already enrolled on a course, consider the type of learning situation that might best help you. You might prefer a course which brings you into regular contact with your teachers or peers. This can help with motivation and will provide opportunities to discuss your work with others: conversations about learning material with other learners on the same course aid understanding. Also ensure that you have chosen a course which is at the appropriate level for you: the material you are studying needs to be sufficiently challenging to be engaging. Too little challenge can lead to boredom; too much challenge may result in the feeling that the effort needed to understand the learning material is not worth making.

Organised and managed approach

If the lines on your graph are high in the **organised study** and **effort management** columns, and are higher than those in the other three columns, your approach to learning is neither deep nor surface. Rather, you may be concerned to excel at your studies and be successful, but perhaps at the expense of thorough engagement with ideas, meaning and understanding. This can be thought of as an *organised and managed approach* to study and learning. Learners who are organised are systematic, prepare for study sessions, organise their time, prioritise, and work steadily through a course. Learners who direct and manage their efforts channel their endeavours and push themselves. They put effort into their studies and keep going even when things aren't going too well. They don't seem to find concentration a problem and can force themselves to keep focused even when they are bored by what they are studying. When the characteristics of organised studying and effort management *predominate*, however, the learner may be someone who is very keen to succeed in terms of course grades, but whose understanding may not be equal to that of a deep learner.

These two aspects of studying – being organised and working hard – are excellent characteristics. But if they are the main characteristics, that is, if your line in the deep approach column is lower, you may not be making the most of your study organisation and effort management in terms of knowledge gain. Consider the difference between 'efficient' and 'effective'. A driver can be a thoroughly efficient driver, negotiating a difficult road with skill and precision. But the efficient performance will not be very effective if the person is driving down a road that doesn't go to the appropriate destination. You may get high assessment grades, but will your understanding be sufficiently deep and comprehensive for you to be able to transfer your knowledge to the workplace – the place where it 'needs to go'?

Suggested action plan

See these items under *Surface approach without much effort.*

Deep and surface approaches combined

You have an unusual but rather problematic approach to learning with high levels in the **deep** and **surface** columns and moderate levels in the other three – **monitoring**, **organised study** and **effort management**. Your profile is that of *deep and surface approaches combined*. Learners possessing this approach seem to fare worse on courses. Because the profile seems contradictory and implausible, a good deal of research has been conducted into this pattern. The approach seems to be due to a misunderstanding of what is involved in learning and a lack of awareness of how to use the support and advice available, or that you sense a contradiction between the ways you want to learn and what you feel you have to do to get good marks.

Suggested action plan

1   See items 1 and 2 under the suggested action plan for *Surface approach without much effort*. Item 1 is of particular importance.

2   Explore what is involved in learning with the help of someone – your teacher or tutor, or even other learners. Read or re-read Chapter 1 'Working with your natural resources', concentrating particularly on the topic of how we learn, (p. 6). Explore, too, any personal conflicts or anxieties you may have about learning or the learning context.

3   Make a concerted effort to find out what study advice and support is available, and then use it. You have everything to gain from adopting new and different study habits and practices.

4   Remember that you have strengths to draw on. You can use them as you discover what is involved in learning.

Other profiles

We have outlined the most common learning profiles and one rather rare one, the combined approach. If your profile does not fit any of these, don't worry. Study Table 3 and try to identify your strengths and weaknesses. Discuss these with your teacher or tutor, and together work out some priorities for action. With good support you should be able to try out new strategies and tactics and abandon old ones. Read Chapter 3 'Learning skills' which describes a number of fundamental learning skills.

APPENDIX 2 USING AN APOSTROPHE: ANSWERS TO TEST

The answers to the test from Chapter 3, (p. 32), are shown below.

1   Its stark exterior looked forbidding.

Possessive pronouns such as *its* never have an apostrophe. Clearly, the word *its* is being used as a possessive pronoun because the writer of the sentence did not use an apostrophe to indicate the shortened form of *It is* or *It has*. That would not have made sense (It is stark exterior looked forbidding).

2   The women's cloakroom is over there.

The word *women* is already plural, but does not end with an *s*, therefore an apostrophe and then an *s* must be added.

3   The red coat is hers.

Hers is a possessive pronoun and possessive pronouns never have an apostrophe.

4   I work for a not-for-profit organisation. My organisation's logo is a black and white shield.

A single organisation is being referred to, so the apostrophe goes before the *s* when the logo belonging to the organisation is being described.

5   The managers were furious about the changes.

No possession is involved in either *managers* or *changes*. They are simply plurals and should have no apostrophe.

6   There was a long queue for the ladies' changing rooms in the fashion store.

This example is the same as Example 3. The changing rooms are not for a single lady – they are for ladies (a plural that already ends in an *s*) and the apostrophe comes after the *s*.

7   I always think of accountancy primarily as a men's profession.

The word *men* is already plural but does not end with an *s* so an apostrophe and then an *s* must be added.

8   This building was designed in the 1820s.

There is no reason for 1820s to have an apostrophe (it is just a plural form and no possession or omission is involved). However, it would have required an apostrophe if the sentence had read: 'The 1820s' building was designed to...' (i.e. the building belonging to the 1820s). A quick test of whether dates and numbers should have an apostrophe (and, in the case of possession, where) is to write them out in words: e.g. the eighteen twenties (a simple plural). It is clear then whether or not an apostrophe is needed and where it should be positioned if one is required.

9   I have lots of CDs at home.

Like the last example, there is no need for an apostrophe because no letters have been omitted and no possession is involved. *CDs* is short for compact disks – a simple plural. The *incorrect* use of the apostrophe in plural forms of words (for example ripe banana's, 100's of bargains) can be found everywhere in the UK from greengrocers' stores to national newspaper advertisements by companies who should know better!

10   The management consultancy company Joop Coopes has relocated to a larger site. Coopes' (or Coopes's) old office block is for sale.

The final *s* is part of the name Coopes and is treated like any plural that ends in an *s:* we do not add another one. The apostrophe goes after the existing *s.* The reason for the alternative form *Coopes's* is that it acknowledges that (a) names can end in an *s* but be singular, and (b) names can be plural but apply to single subjects and thus be treated like any singular word that just happens to end in *s,* such as *bus.* A person called Coopes belongs to the Coopes family – The Coopeses or the Coopes – and one might want to distinguish between one Coopes family member and all the members. We could refer to *Coopes's desk* or *the bus's livery* when dealing with a single family member or bus, and *The Coopeses'* (or Coopes') *desks* or *the buses' livery* when referring to more than one.

APPENDIX 3 THE OPEN UNIVERSITY BUSINESS SCHOOL

The Open University Business School is the largest business school in Europe, the world's biggest provider of MBAs (Master of Business Administration) and a faculty of The Open University.

We are an 'open access' university Whatever your background, we can offer you an opportunity to develop your management skills. We provide management development at all levels right through to Master's degree.

Our courses and programmes are designed for working people We are the premier provider of part-time education. Our professional management courses are designed for working managers so that you can earn while you learn *and* put your new knowledge and skills into practice right away.

We teach across the globe Wherever you live, we can probably reach you. We teach students across the UK, Europe and many other parts of the world. Our supported distance learning courses use a blend of printed texts, CD-ROMs, computer conferencing and on-line and face-to-face tuition. Many of our students are sponsored by their employers.

We aren't just big – we're good! Our teaching ratings in the British Government's higher education quality assurance system place The Open University among the top ten universities in the UK[1]. The Open University Business School is accredited by EQUIS (the European Foundation for Management Development) and AMBA (the UK Association of MBAs).

What we offer

We offer a range of programmes for you to choose from, including:

- Master of Business Administration (MBA) (for experienced managers)
- Professional Diploma in Management
- Professional Certificate in Management
- Certificate in Accounting
- Bachelor of Arts in Business Studies
- Batchelor of Law.

You can pace your study programme to suit your circumstances and you can also study single courses from our Continuing Professional Development portfolio.

Find out more

Visit our website at *oubs.open.ac.uk* or contact:

The Open University Business School

Michael Young Building

Walton Hall,

Milton Keynes

MK7 6AA

United Kingdom.

[1] Times Higher Education Supplement league table August 2002

REFERENCES

Allan, J. and Lawless, N. (2003) *Stress caused by on-line collaboration in e-learning: a scoping study,* Paper presented to the Fourth International Conference on Human-System Learning, July.

Amabile, T.M., Conti, R., Coon, H., Lazenby, J. and Herron, M. (1996) 'Assessing the work environment for creativity', *Academy of Management Journal,* Vol. 39, No. 5, pp. 1154–8.

Ansoff, H.I. (1988) *The New Corporate Strategy,* John Wiley & Sons Inc., p. 83.

Anthony, R.N. and Herzlinger, R.E. (1980) *Management Control in Non-profit Organizations* (revised edition), Irwin.

Argyris, C. and Schon, D.A. (1978) *Organisational Learning: A theory of action perspective,* Addison-Wesley.

Argyris, C. (1999) 'Teaching smart people how to learn', *Harvard Business Review,* Vol. 69, No. 3, pp. 99–110.

Bass, B.M. (1990) 'From transactional to transformational leadership: learning to share the vision', *Organizational Dynamics,* Vol. 18, No. 3, pp. 19–31.

Bennett, M. (1987) 'Towards ethnorelativism: A developmental model of intercultural sensitivity' in Paige, M. (ed.) *Cross Cultural Orientation: New conceptualizations and applications,* University Press of America, pp. 27–69.

Bennis, W. (1998) *On Becoming a Leader,* Arrow.

Blake, R.R., Mouton, J.S. and Bidwell, A.C. (1962) 'The managerial grid', *Advanced Management Office Excecutive,* Vol. 1, No. 1, pp. 32–5.

Bransford, J.D. and Stein, B.S. (1993) *The IDEAL problem solver,* W.H. Freeman

Bronfenbrenner, U. (1979) *The Ecology of Human Development: Experiment by Nature and Design,* Harvard University Press.

Buzan, T. (1982) *Use Your Head,* Ariel Books.

Camp, R.C. (1995) *Business Process Benchmarking: Finding and implementing best practices,* ASQC Quality Press.

Clutterbuck, D., Devine, M. and Beech, H. (1991) *Everyone Needs a Mentor; Fostering talent at work,* Institute of Personnel Management.

Coopers and Lybrand (1994) *Survey of Benchmarking in the UK,* Coopers and Lybrand and CBI National Manufacturing Council.

Data Protection Act 1998 (UK), HMSO http://www.hmso.gov.uk/ acts/ acts1998/19980029.htm [accessed 25 October 2003].

Davidson, H. (1997) *Even More Offensive Marketing,* Penguin Books.

Easterby-Smith, M., Thorpe, R. and Lowe, A. (1991) *Management Research: An introduction*, Sage.

Einon, G. (1997) *Creating and Collaborating* (T293, Block 5, Chapter 3) from *Issues in Computer-Supported Collaboration*, The Open University.

Elder, L. (2000) 'Critical thinking: nine strategies for everyday life', *Journal of Developmental Education*, Vol. 24, No. 2, pp. 39–40.

Entwistle, N. (2000) *Promoting deep learning through teaching and assessment: conceptual frameworks and educational context*, Paper presented at the Economic and Social Research Council's Teaching and Learning Research Programme Conference.

Entwistle, N. and McCune, V. (2004) 'The conceptual basis of study strategy inventories', *Educational Psychology Review*, Vol. 16, No. 4, pp. 325–345.

European Foundation for Quality Management, http://www.efqm.org/ [accessed 20 September 2000].

Evenden, R. and Anderson, G. (1992) *Making the Most of People*, Cambridge University Press.

Fayol, H. (1949) *General and Industrial Management*, Pitman.

Fiedler, F.E. (1976) 'Situational control and a dynamic theory of leadership' in King, B., Streufert, S. and Fiedler, F.E. (eds) *Managerial Control and Organizational Democracy*, Winston and Sons

Folger, R. and Cropanzano, R. (1998) *Organizational Justice and Human Resource Management*, Sage.

Gilliland, S.W. (1993) 'The perceived fairness of selection systems: an organisational justice perspective', *Academy of Management Review*, pp. 694–734.

Gilovich, T. (1993) *How we know what isn't so*, Free Press.

Hackman, J.R. and Oldham, G.R. (1980) *Work Redesign*, Addison-Wesley.

Hatch, M.J. (1997) *Organisation Theory*, Oxford University Press.

Hertzberg, F., Mausner, B. and Snydeman, B.B. (1959) *The Motivation at Work*, Wiley.

Hussey, J. and Hussey, R. (1997) *Business Research: A practical guide for undergraduate and postgraduate students*, Macmillan.

Johnson-Lenz, P. and Johnson-Lenz, T. (1991) 'Post-mechanistic groupware primatives: rhythms, boundaries and containers', *International Journal of Man-Machine Studies*, Vol. 34, pp. 395–417.

Kakabadse, A., Ludlow, R. and Vinnicombe, S. (1988) *Working in Organizations*, Penguin.

Kaplan, R.S. and Norton, D.P. (1996) *The Balanced Scorecard*, Harvard Business Press.

Kinlaw, D. (1995) *The Practice of Empowerment*, Gower.

Knowles, M.S. (1978) *The Adult Learner: A neglected species,* Gulf.

Kolb, D.A. and Fry, R. (1975) 'Towards an applied theory of experiential learning' in Cooper, C.L. (ed.) *Theories of Group Processes*, John Wiley, pp. 33–57.

Kram, K.E. (1985) *Mentoring at Work: Developmental relationships in organizational life*, Scott, Foresman and Company.

Kram, K.E. and Isabella, L.A. (1985) 'Mentoring alternatives: the role of peer relationships in career development', *Academy of Management Journal*, Vol. 28, No. 1, pp. 110–32.

Krathwohl, D.R. (2002) 'A revision of Bloom's taxonomy: an overview', *Theory into Practice*, Vol. 41, No. 4, pp. 212–18.

Lewin, K. (1951) *Field Theory in Social Science*, Harper & Row.

Maciarello, J.A. (1984) *Management Control Systems*, Prentice-Hall.

Marton, F., Dall'Alba, G. and Beaty, E. (1993) 'Conceptions of learning', *International Journal of Educational Research,* Vol. 19, No. 3, pp. 277–300.

Maslow, A.H. (1954) *Motivation and Personality*, Harper & Row.

Mingers, J. (2000) 'What is it to be critical? Teaching a critical approach to management undergraduates', *Management Learning*, Vol. 31, No. 2, pp. 219–37.

Mintzberg, H. (1991) 'The effective organization: forces and forms', *Sloan Management Review*, Vol. 33, No. 2, pp. 54–67.

Morgan, G. (1986) *Images of Organisation*, Sage.

Murray, J. and O'Driscoll, A. (1996) *Strategy and Process in Marketing*, Prentice Hall.

Pascal, B. (1657) 'Lettres Provinciales', www.pinkmonkey.com/dl/library1/letter.pdf [accessed 23 October 2003].

Parasuraman, A., Zeithaml, V.A. and Berry, L.L. (1988) 'SERVQUAL: a multiple item scale for measuring consumer perceptions of service quality', *Journal of Retailing*, Vol. 64, No. 1, pp. 14–40.

Paul, R. (2000) 'Critical thinking: nine strategies for everyday life', *Journal of Developmental Education*, Vol. 24, No. 1, pp. 40–2.

Perry, W.G. (1970) *Forms of Intellectual and Ethical Development in the College Years: A scheme,* Holt, Rinehart and Winston.

Piccinin, S.J. and Mason, G. (1991) *Enhancing Teaching and Learning through the Effective Use of Feedback and Criticism,* Paper presented at 17th International Conference on Improving University Teaching.

Piercy, N. (1997) *Market-led Strategic Change*, Butterworth-Heinemann.

Plummer, K. (1983) *Documents of Life*, George Allen & Unwin.

Porter, M.E. (1980) *Competitive Strategy: Techniques for analysing industries and competitors*, Free Press.

Porter, M.E. (1985) *Competitive Advantage: Creating and sustaining superior performance*, Free Press.

Säljö, R. (1979) 'Learning about learning', *Higher Education,* Vol. 8, pp. 443–51.

Salmon, G. (2002) *Etivities: The key to active online learning,* Kogan Page.

Sargeant, A. (1999) *Marketing Management for Nonprofit Organisations,* Oxford University Press.

Scheung, E.E. and Johnson, M.E. (1989) 'New product development and management in financial institutions', *International Journal of Bank Marketing*, Vol. 7, No. 2, pp. 17–21.

Shannon, C. and Weaver, W. (1949) *The Mathematical Theory of Communication*, University of Illinois Press.

Targett, D. (1983) *Coping With Numbers: A management guide*, Blackwell.

Taylor, F.W. (1911) *The Principles of Scientific Management,* Harper & Bros.

The Columbia World of Quotations (1996) Andrews *et al.* (eds.) Columbia University Press. www.bartleby.com/66/ [accessed 6 March 2003].

Tuckman, B. and Jenson, M. (1977) 'Stages of small group development revisited', *Groups and Organisation Studies*, Vol. 2, pp. 419–27.

Tyler, S., Green, M. and Simpson, S. (2001) 'Experimenting in Lotus LearningSpace' in Lockwood, F. and Gooley, A. (eds.) *Innovation in Open and Distance Learning: Successful development of online and web-based learning*, Kogan Page, pp. 63–75.

Tyler, S. (2002) *Communication*, Book 2, B823 Managing Knowledge (3rd edn), The Open University.

Acknowledgements

Grateful acknowledgement is made to the following sources for permission to reproduce material in this book:

Text

Appendix 1: © Tyler, S. and Entwistle N.J., 2003.

Tables

Table 1.1 and 1.2: based on Krathwohl, D.R. (2002) 'A revision of Bloom's taxonomy: an overview', *Theory into Practice*, Vol. 41, No. 4, pp.212–18; Table 2.1: Kram, K.E. and Isabella, L.A. (1985) 'Mentoring alternatives: the role of peer relationships in career development', *Academy of Management Journal*, Vol. 28, No. 1, pp.110–32; Table 3.1: Paul, R. (2000) 'Critical thinking: nine strategies for everyday life', *Journal of Developmental Education*, Vol. 24, No. 1, pp.40–2; Table 3.2: based on Paul, R. (2000) 'Critical thinking: nine strategies for everyday life', *Journal of Developmental Education*, Vol. 24, No. 1, pp.40–2 and Elder, L. (2000) 'Critical thinking: nine strategies for everyday life', *Journal of Developmental Education*, Vol. 24, No. 1, pp.39–40; Table 13.1: based on Bass, B.M. (1990) 'From transactional to transformational leadership: learning to share the vision', *Organizational Dynamics*, Vol. 18, No. 3, pp.19-31; Table 13.2: based on Bennis, W. (1998) *On Becoming a Leader*, Arrow; Table 13.3: Mintzberg, H. (1991) 'The effective organization: forces and forms', *Sloan Management Review*, Vol. 33, No. 2, pp.54–67; Table 14.2: Folger, R. and Cropanzano, R. (1998) *Organizational Justice and Human Resource Management*, Sage; Table 14.3: based on Evenden, R. and Anderson, G. (1992) *Management Skills: Making the most of people*, © 1992 Addison-Wesley Publishers Ltd, reprinted by permission of Pearson Education Ltd; Table 14.7: based on Amabile, T.M. *et al* (1996) 'Assessing the work environment for creativity', *Academy of Management Journal*, Vol. 39, No. 5, pp.1154–8; Table 15.2: Camp, R.C. (1995) *Business Process Benchmarking: Finding and implementing best practices*, ASQC Quality Press.

Figures

Figure 1.1: Kolb, D.A. and Fry, R. (1975) 'Towards an applied theory of experiential learning' in Cooper, C.L. (ed) *Theories of Group Processes*, John Wiley & Sons Ltd; Figure 1.2: Entwistle, N. (2000) *Promoting Deep Learning Through Teaching and Assessment: Conceptual frameworks and educational context*, paper presented at the Economic and Social Research Council's Teaching and Learning Research Programme Conference; Figure 10.1: based on Bronfenbrenner, U. (1979) *The Ecology of Human Development: Experiment by nature and design*, Harvard University Press; Figure 10.3: Porter, M.E. (1980) *Competitive Strategy: Techniques for analysing industries and competitors*, Free Press, Inc. Reprinted by permission of Simon & Schuster International Group, Inc; Figures 10.5 and 10.8: Porter, M.E. (1985)

INDEX